P9-CAN-536

TREASURY
OF
BASEBALL DRILLS

TREASURY

OF

BASEBALL DRILLS

Danny Litwhiler

PARKER PUBLISHING COMPANY, INC.

WEST NYACK, NEW YORK

© 1979 *by*

Parker Publishing Company, Inc.
West Nyack, New York

*All rights reserved. No part of this
book may be reproduced in any form
or by any means, without permission
in writing from the publisher.*

Library of Congress Cataloging in Publication Data

Litwhiler, Danny.
  Treasury of baseball drills.

  Includes index.
  1. Baseball coaching--Addresses, essays, lectures.
I. Title.
GV875.5.L57   796.357'077   78-27909
ISBN 0-13-930495-9

Printed in the United States of America

Dedication

To all baseball coaches and their families. Without the love, interest and understanding of our families, coaching would not be fun or interesting. Without the interest, work, understanding and dedication of the coaches of pre-teen players and teenage players, college and professional baseball would soon die.

As a college coach, I am deeply indebted to all pre-college coaches and their families. It is, therefore, with great pride and respect that I dedicate this book to them.

CONTRIBUTORS TO "TREASURY OF BASEBALL DRILLS"

Dr. Robert "Bob" Bauman	Trainer	St. Louis Cardinals and Professor at St. Louis University, St. Louis, MO —Drills No. 1, 2, 6, 16
Milbrey "Moby" Benedict	Head Coach	University of Michigan, Ann Arbor, MI—Drill No. 55
Chuck "Bobo" Brayton	Head Coach	Washington State University, Pullman, WA—Drill No. 138
Jim Brock	Head Coach	Arizona State University, Tempe, AZ —Drill No. 116
Ray Borowicz	Head Coach	Huntington High School, Huntington, NY—Drills No. 44A, 52
Pat Daugherty	Head Coach	Indian Hills Community College, Centerville, IA—Drills No. 61, 103, 109
Rod Dedeaux	Head Coach	University of Southern California, Los Angeles, CA—Drill No. 102A
Ken Dugan	Head Coach	David Lipscomb College, Nashville, TN—Drill No. 62
Sam Esposito	Head Coach	North Carolina State University, Raleigh, N.C.—Drill No. 156
Don Fauls	Trainer	Florida State University, Tallahassee, FL—Drill No. 15
Ron Fraser	Head Coach	University of Miami, Coral Gables, FL—Drills No. 137, 229
Russ Frazier	Head Coach	Louisburg College, Louisburg, N.C. —Drills No. 152, 239B
Jim Frye	Head Coach	Mesa Community College, Mesa, AZ —Drill No. 65
Jim Gibbard	Head Coach	(Cross Country) Michigan State University, East Lansing, MI—Drill No. 10
Dick Groch	Head Coach	St. Clair County Community College, Port Huron, MI—Drill No. 121

Cliff Gustafson	Head Coach	University of Texas, Austin, TX —Drill No. 44B
Larry Hamm	Former Head Coach	North Hennepin State Junior College, Minneapolis, MN—Drill No. 14
Richard "Itchy" Jones	Head Coach	University of Southern Illinois, Carbondale, IL—Drill No. 54
Jack Kaiser	Athletic Director	(Former Head Coach) St. John's University, Jamaica, NY —Drill No. 228
Dave Keilitz	Head Coach	Central Michigan University, Mt. Pleasant, MI—Drill No. 234
Jerry Kindall	Head Coach	University of Arizona, Tucson, AZ —Drill No. 235
Ric Lessman	Head Coach	Meramec Community College, Kirkwood, MO—Drill No. 93
Demie Mainieri	Head Coach	Miami-Dade Community College (North Campus), Miami, FL —Drill No. 81
Mike Marshall	Major League Pitcher	—Drill No. 13
Ernie Myers	Head Coach	Charles Stewart Mott Community College, Flint, MI—Drill No. 157F
Ron Oestrike	Head Coach	Eastern Michigan University, Ypsilanti, MI—Drill No. 213
Al Ogletree	Head Coach	Pan American University, Edinburg, TX—Drill No. 94
Loyal Park	Former Head Coach	Harvard University, Cambridge, MA —Drills No. 102B, 122
Frank Pellerin	Asst. Coach	Michigan State University, East Lansing, MI—Drill No. 56
Ken Perrone	Head Coach	Salem High School, Salem, MA —Drill No. 57
Tom Petroff	Head Coach	Northern Colorado University, Greeley, CO—Drill No. 146

Jim Phipps	Former Head Coach	Niles-West High School, Skokie, IL —Drill No. 221
Walter Rabb	Assistant Athletic Director	(Former Head Coach) University of North Carolina, Chapel Hill, N.C. —Drills No. 19C, 147
Ken Schreiber	Head Coach	LaPorte High School, LaPorte, IN —Drill No. 87
Gene Shell	Head Coach	University of Tulsa, Tulsa, OK —Drill No. 231
Dick Siebert	The late Head Coach	University of Minnesota, Minneapolis, MN— Drills No. 30, 67, 233
Hal Smeltzly	Athletic Director	(Former Head Coach) Florida Southern College, Lakeland, FL—Drill No. 58
Tom Smith	Asst. Coach	Michigan State University, East Lansing, MI —Drills No. 130, 131
Paul Tungate	Former Head Coach	Clarkston High School, Clarkston, MI —Drills No. 59, 60, 150
Bill Wilhelm	Head Coach	Clemson University, Clemson, S.C. —Drill No. 53
Woody Woodward	Former Head Coach	Florida State University, Tallahassee, FL —Drills No. 180, 181, 192, 193

How This Treasury Will Help You

Have you often wondered what the top coaches do during their practice sessions? *Treasury of Baseball Drills* gives you that answer. It is a collection of the favorite defensive and offensive drills from many top coaches in high schools, junior and senior colleges throughout the United States. Many of these coaches have conducted clinics in foreign countries using many of these drills. They are drills that these successful coaches believe help them the most in their game plans, and that might give their team that little edge in close games. In addition, they are drills that their players enjoy.

The old adage "Practice, practice, practice makes perfect," is not true unless the practice sessions are instructive, done with enthusiasm and done correctly. One half hour of organized practice done in game-like fashion, using specific drills for specific purposes, is worth more than two hours of unorganized practice. Most unorganized practice sessions accentuate faults and improper methods of execution instead of correcting them.

I have long been looking for that magical key to success that goes along with hard work. I now believe that key to be the command and use of many drills that are game-like in execution, designed for a specific purpose and perhaps different from, or better than, those used by my opponents. Loyal Park, the former coach of Harvard, who has given us a variety of drills, says, "You can't coach without good drills." The 1975 Division I NCAA "Coach of the Year," Ron Fraser, of the University of Miami, has helped me develop many of these drills as a player and assistant coach of mine at Florida State University.

Mike Marshall, one of the best relief pitchers in major league history and an outstanding student of Kinesiology, shows us how to use muscle growth and development to hit a ball harder and farther.

This treasury of drills will be a guide for your daily practice sessions. You will be better organized and never miss teaching any important fundamental if you use it for a guide. These fine coaches fully explain their use of the drills. For example, Rod Dedeaux of Southern California, who wrote history in the record books, winning 11 NCAA National Championships, gives us "Pitchers' Fielding Skills," one of the most overlooked defensive fielding positions. Four of his former players were regarded as the top fielding pitchers in baseball: Tom Seaver of the Reds, formerly with the Mets, Jim Barr of the Giants, Bill Lee of the Expos in the National League, and Steve Busby of the Royals in the American League. Woody Woodward, a former outstanding major league defensive shortstop and second baseman and Coach at Florida

State, instructs us in drills for the double play. Dr. Robert ''Bob'' Bauman, trainer for the St. Louis Cardinals for many years and Professor at St. Louis University, presents some important conditioning drills. His pitching conditioning drills have prevented his pitchers from having sore elbows, a very common ailment in spring training camps. Dick Siebert of Minnesota, whose teams have won three National Championships and ten Big Ten titles, gives us a base-running and fielding drill. Hal Smeltzly of Florida Southern, who has won six regional NCAA Division II titles and two National Championships, describes the perfect practice game to get your team ready for a tournament if you can't play another team or you don't have enough players for a good intra-squad game. Cliff Gustafson of Texas, who coached his team to the 1975 NCAA Division I Championship and put seven of his teams in the College World Series, presents his outfield throwing drill. Jerry Kindall, ex-major leaguer and Coach of Arizona, the 1976 NCAA Division I Championship team, gives us a dual-purpose drill for base runners and catchers.

''Itchy'' Jones, the outstanding coach of Southern Illinois and perennially top ranked, gives us a wonderful multi-purpose team drill. You will learn the proper way to field a ground ball from Coach Tom Petroff, the fine coach of Northern Colorado University who is one of the very few coaches ever to bring two different schools (Rider and Northern Colorado) to the College World Series.

Having ''Treasury of Baseball Drills'' at hand should give any coach the basis for adapting and creating drills to develop his players or team and correct any problem dealing with the playing fundamentals of baseball. The drills developed must be interesting to the players, giving them confidence that they are being conditioned toward an outstanding season. These self-developed drills often give the team the feeling that they have something different from, and better than, their opponents. You will discover that the drills in the book simulate game-like action and play. Remember that when you make adaptations from the book. Arizona State's Jim Brock, the outstanding coach who keeps his team on top, does this with his pitching drill.

Little League coaches, who often have never coached a team, or played on an organized team in high school or college, will find this book invaluable, easy to understand and to apply to their program. They will find the drills to be just as suitable and advantageous to them as major league managers have found many of the drills to be useful for their program.

No book previously printed has compiled a list of drills from the top coaches to be used by other coaches. I am deeply indebted to them for their unselfish friendship and devotion to baseball and their contribution to this book which gives us an insight of how the top coaches operate. I take pride in presenting the drills of these fine coaches and know you will have much fun and success in using them.

D.W.L.

Contents

Off-Season or Winter Conditioning:

A.—Stretching; (1) Raise Your Hands, (2) Simulated Hanging Stretch, (3) Shoulder-Loosening and Flexibility Drills, (4) Abdomen Reducer, (5) Isometric Rope Drill, (6) Light Bulb Turning Stretch, (7) Thigh Stretch, (8) Hamstring Stretch, (9) Groin Stretch

B.—Running and Leg Development; (10) Running, (11) Jump Rope

C.—Throwing; (12) Weekly Throwing

D.—Weight Work; (13) Overload: for the Quick Bat, (14) Overload: for the Fastball, (15) Wrist Curls with a Barbell, (16) Exercise with the Medi Ball (Metal Ball), (17) Use of Ankle Weights and Weighted Innersoles

E.—Bat Swinging; (18) Weighted Bat Swing, (19) Hanging Target Swing and Stuffed Stocking, (20) Baseball Bat Figure Eight, (21) Isometric Bat Drill, (22) Hitting a Tire, A) Suspended Tire, B) Tire Against Wall

Spring Training and Pre-Game Conditioning:

(23) Recommended Drills Prior to Workout, (24) Instant Arm and Back Stretch, (25) Football Pass Drill, (26) Rolling Semicircle (Pickups), (27) Fifty-Fifty, (28) Touch Grass Right and Left, (29) Shift and Toss, (30) Developing Soft Hands and Reaction Drill, (31) Diving Drill with Pitching Machine, (32) Step on Bench, (33) Rubber Ball Squeeze, (34) Arm Strengthener and Conditioner, (35) The Pepper Game

(36) Rhythm Warm-up-Catching and Throwing, (37) Pre-Warm-up-Quick Grip and Throw, (38) Control Development, (39) Crow Hop and Throw, (40) Pepper Games, (41) Multiple

2. TEAM DRILLS *(Continued)*

Ball Drill, (42) Pop-Flies with All Players in Position, (43) Hit-and-Run Base Running, (44) Cut-off Plays and Live Relay Throws; A) Three-Day Orientation Sessions, B) Fifteen-Minute Relay Practice, (45) Special Drills For Cut-off Play Procedure, (46) Bunt Defense, (47) General Pick-off Plays, (48) One Pitch—Six Outs, (49) Two Pitch—Six Outs, (50) Full Count— Six Outs, (51) Three Balls and Two Strikes, (52) Two Strikes and One Ball— Six Outs, (53) Twelve-Man Game, (54) Multi-Purpose Drills, (55) Short Hop, (56) Baseball Game in a Tunnel Batter Cage, (57) Getting the Most Out of a Day's Practice, (58) Keeping a Team Sharp for Tournament Play, (59) Circle Drill, (60) Utilizing Space and Time for Comprehensive Practice Drills for 18 Men, (61) Rundown Drill, (62) Pitcher-Infield Base Running-Fielding Drill.

(63) Checklist for Proper Execution—Bat Grip, (64) Ball Toss Fungo Batting, A) On One Knee, B) Use of Extra Heavy Bat, C) Use of Regular Bat, (65) Soft Toss From Side Drill; A) With Two Hands, B) With Top Hand Only, (66) Swing Strengthener, (67) Dry Swing Team Batting, (68) Mirror Swing, (69) Hanging Target Swing and Stuffed Stocking; A) Stuffed Stocking on String, B) Stuffed Stocking, C) Boxer's Heavy Punching Bag, (70) Baseball Bat Figure Eight, (71) Shadow Drill, (72) Isometric Bat Drill, (73) Hip Rotation Drill, (74) Bat Throwing Drill (75) Breaking From Home, (76) Batting Tee Drill, (77) Pepper Games, (78) Improving a Poor Hitter, (79) Place Hitting and Hit-and-Run Drill, (80) Team Batting Practice, A) Early Season, B) During Season, (81) Batting Practice Drills

(82) Checklist for Proper Execution, (83) Instructional Bunting Bat for All Bunting Drills, (84) Position of Feet and Body, (85) Angle of Bat, (86) Sacrifice Bunting to Proper Infield Area, (87) Strings to Denote Perfect Bunting Area, (88) Bunt for a Base Hit—First Base Area, (89) Bunt for a Base Hit—Third Base Area, (90) The Squeeze Bunt, (91) Fake Bunt and Hit, (92) Fake Bunt and Steal, (93) Wet Grounds Bunting Time

(94) Conditioning a Pitcher for Completing a Game, (95) Checklist for Proper Execution, (96) Spot Control Pitching Drill, (97) String Target, (98) Control Practice in Gym, (99)

5. PITCHING DRILLS *(Continued)*

Pitcher's Control Drill, (100) Eye Patch Drill for Control, (101) Prevention of Steal Drill, (102) Pitcher's Fielding Drills, A) Rod Dedeaux Method, B) Loyal Park Method, (103) Pitcher's Four Corners Drill, (104) Quick Reaction Drill, (105) Fielding Bunts, (106) Covering First Base, (107) Backing Up Bases, (108) Wild Pitch-Pass Ball—Covering Home, (109) Rundowns for Pitchers, (110) Pitcher's Rhythm Drill, (111) In-Stride, Snap Throw Drill, (112) Bare Hand Drill, (113) Snap Throw Wrist Developer, (114) Isometric Rope Drill, (115) Early Curve Ball Practice, (116) Progression for Teaching the Curve Ball, (117) Pitcher's Stride Drill, (118) Pitcher's Follow-through Drill, (119) Developing a Follow-through for Pitchers, (120) Fork Ball—Pitcher's Hand Drill, (121) Improving Left Hander's Move to First, (122) Pick-off Plays, (123) Pitcher's Sign Drill, (124) Batting Practice Throwing Schedule, (125) Alternate Batting Practice Pitchers, (126) Rotation of Pitchers, (127) Game Poise Drill for Pitchers, (128) Using Speed Gun for Pitchers A) Check Velocity, B) Correct Speed for all Pitches.

(129) Checklist for Proper Execution, (130) Catching Body Positions, A) Giving Signals, B) Catching Stance with Nobody on Base, C) Catching Stance with Runners on Base, D) Giving the Target, E) Position of Bare Hand and Glove, (131) Using a Chair for Proper Crouch Position, (132) Catcher's Signals, A) For Pick-offs, B) For Pitches, (133) Across-Seam of Ball Grip for Catchers, (134) Footwork Drill—Intentional Walk, (135) Steps for Throwing, (136) Boxing Glove and Football Forearm Guards—Ball-in-Dirt Drill, (137) Soft-Quick Hands for Catchers, (138) Passed Ball-Wild Pitch Drill, (139) Arm Strengthener to Develop Correct Throwing Form, (140) Catcher Making Tag Plays at Home, (141) Catcher Making Force-out Play at Home, (142) Double Steal Prevention, (143) Fielding Bunts, (144) Pop Fly Practice, (145) Catcher Covering First and Third Bases

(146) Proper Technique for Fielding Ground Balls, (147) Early Season Infield Fundamentals Drill, (148) Touch Grass Right and Left, (149) Orientation—Rapid Fire Drill, (150) Infield Circle Drill, (151) Equilibrium Drill, (152) Defensing the First and Third Steal, (153) Rundown Play Drills, A) Runner Between First and Second, B) Runner Between Second and Third, C) Runner Between Third and Home, D) Ball Hit to the Pitcher, E)

12. OUTFIELD DRILLS *(Continued)*

Fielder's Right, E) Balls to the Fielder's Left, F) Short Fly Balls in Front of Fielder, (216) Playing the Ball in the Sun, (A) Without Sun Glasses or if the Sun Is Directly Behind the Hitter, B) With Sun Glasses, (217) Catching Fly Balls at the Fence, (218) Fence Drills, A) Ball Lying Against the Fence, B) Ball Rebounding from a Fence, C) Crashing the Fence, (219) Throwing to Bases, (220) Faking a Throw to a Base for a Pick-off, A) Right Fielder, B) Center Fielder, C) Left Fielder, (221) Hitting the Cut-off and Relay Man, (222) Bunting Situations— Covering Bases, A) Right Fielder, B) Center Fielder, C) Left Fielder, (223) Back-up Plays, A) Backing Up Other Outfielder, B) Backing Up Bases, 1—Right Fielder, 2—Center Fielder, 3—Left Fielder, (224) Outfielder Teamwork Drill, (225) Duty Drill— Pre-Game, A) Opposing Team, B) Self-Orientation, (226) Game Situation Drill

(227) Checklist for Proper Execution, (228) Base Running with a Purpose, (229) Full Team Base-Running, (230) Rounding Bases, A) First Base, B) Second Base, C) Third Base, (231) What to Teach a Base Runner, A) Base Running from the Plate, B) Breaking from First Base, C) Breaking from Second Base, D) Breaking from Third Base, (232) Alternate Speed Base-Running Drill, (233) Timed Base-Running Practice, A) Short Distance, B) Base Running for Time, C) Clock the Base Running During Game, (234) Leads, Returns and Steals at First Base, (235) Base Running and Catching, (236) Lead-off Base Drill, A) Lead off First Base, B) Lead off Second Base, C) Lead off Third Base, (237) Sliding Drills—Indoors, (238) Sliding Drills—Outdoors, A) Straight-in-Slide, B) Hook Slide, C) Bent Leg Slide, D) Bent Leg-and-go Slide, (239) Delayed Steal Drills, A) Walk-off, B) Forced Balk, (240) Getting Out of a Rundown, (241) Base Coach Drill, (242) How to Give Signs A) By the Coach, B) By the Batter, 1—Hit-and-Run, 2—Suicide Squeeze, C) Signs to Give

(243) Pre-Game Batting Practice, (244) Infield-Outfield Practice, (245) Pitcher Warm-up, A) Home Team, B) Visiting Team

(246) Checklist for Proper Execution, (247) Running Performance—Time, (248) Throwing Performance, A) Outfielder and Infielder, 1—Accuracy, 2—Distance, B) Pitchers, C) Radar

NOTE TO THE READER: The symbols on this page are the same for each of the applicable drills, and the key below may be used as a single reference to determine functions and positions.

KEY

(R) BASE RUNNER

(X) COACH

(F) FUNGO HITTER

(H) HITTER

(P) PLAYER OR PICK UP MAN

(1)-(9) NUMERICAL POSITIONS

∿∿∿∿➤ GROUND BALL

⎯⎯⎯➤ PATH OF BASE RUNNER

⎯⎯⎯⊣ PATH OF DEFENSIVE PLAYER

- - - - -➤ THROWN BALL OR FLY BALL

CHAPTER **1**

HOW TO CONDITION YOUR
PLAYERS AND TEAM

It is very important to condition legs first and continue to keep them in condition throughout the entire year. A player is only as good as his legs. He can play with a sore arm, finger, or hand, but it is impossible for a player to play effectively with a sore toe, foot, ankle, knee or leg. Our running and leg drills strengthen the legs, prevent injuries, develop a more agile player and increase stamina. Many players weaken in the late innings because their legs are not in shape. This weakness causes poor control and weak fielding and batting.

The old adage, "An ounce of prevention is worth a pound of cure," is worth thinking about in conditioning work. Clean dry socks and good shoes are important for healthy feet. Keeping the nails trimmed and the feet clean can prevent athlete's foot, ingrown nails and infected blisters. Watch for blisters and take care of them immediately. Any of the above problems could ruin a career in baseball.

The throwing arm must be conditioned gradually and should be kept in partial throwing condition during the off-season. Our throwing drills were developed to strengthen the arm, prevent injuries, increase velocity, help the control and keep the arm in good muscle tone all year.

Conditioning for baseball should take place through the entire year. We, therefore, have divided our conditioning program into two phases; (1) OFF-SEASON OR WINTER CONDITIONING and, (2) SPRING TRAINING AND PRE-GAME CONDITIONING. Many of the drills can be, and are, used through both phases.

OFF-SEASON OR WINTER CONDITIONING

In addition to using off-season drills, players should participate in other sports or activities. One of the best activities, we believe, is handball or paddleball, using the glove or paddle to hit the ball with the fielding hand. This develops the fielding or glove hand for baseball.

Running, tennis, Ping Pong, soccer and swimming are also good activities for keeping in good physical condition. Swimming develops the shoulder muscles. Using the overhand stroke develops muscles almost identical to those used in throwing a ball. It is advisable, however, to keep throwing a baseball between swimming sessions. Tennis and Ping Pong are good for the fielding and hitting eye. Basketball, tennis and running are good for leg development and lateral movement. A majority of the major league players were good basketball players.

Preparation for a baseball season requires players to work on their own, physically and mentally, from the day the last game is played until the first day of official practice. At a minimum, players should work on their own at least a month prior to the opening of the official pre-season practice sessions.

OFF-SEASON work should be divided into five categories: A) STRETCHING, B) RUNNING AND LEG DEVELOPMENT, C) THROWING, D) WEIGHT WORK, and E) BAT SWINGING.

A) STRETCHING

The best way to avoid a pulled muscle is to go through stretching exercises prior to any workout. Stretching also helps eliminate fatty tissue and strengthens muscles. A fifteen-minute stretching session is good for the body. Keeping the muscles stretched all winter is important to help prevent sore arms and legs in early practice. Muscles, such as those used for throwing during the season, are fully stretched and extended by the end of the baseball season. If these muscles are not exercised and stretched during the off-season, they will contract and become weak. The tendency in early spring workouts is to throw too hard too soon. This sudden stretching and extending of the muscles can cause harm to muscles that have been inactive for an extended period.

The following stretching drills can be used during the off-season and can be used during the baseball season for daily stretching exercises.

1. RAISE YOUR HANDS   by Dr. Robert "Bob" Bauman

PURPOSE

For better health, whether you are an athlete or John Q. Public, you should raise your hands high above your head in the morning and in the evening. This improves circulation and is good for the heart, lungs and chest muscles.

PROCEDURE

Stand erect and extend your arms and hands up as far as possible directly above your head on the count of one. On the count of two, drop your arms and hands to your sides. Continue this exercise for 20 repetitions. It should be done in the morning upon rising from bed. Once a day is sufficient, but it must be a daily ritual.

2. SIMULATED HANGING STRETCH
by Dr. Robert "Bob" Bauman

PURPOSE

To stretch the arms, shoulders and back without hanging dead weight from a bar or door. (Hanging dead weight on a throwing arm is not advisable.) An excellent exercise for between innings if a pitcher does not feel loose. This is not preferred as a daily routine. Drill #1 takes priority over this drill.

PROCEDURE

Stand in a doorway and on the count of one extend your arms and hands up as high as possible, placing your hands against the upper side of the wall of the doorway or frame. On the count of two lean forward as if to fall through the doorway. Your hands will press against the side of the wall or upper door frame, keeping you from falling through the doorway, and stretch the proper muscles for baseball. On the count of three push yourself back through the doorway. On the count of four drop your hands to your sides.

Continue this sequence for six repetitions, once daily, either in the morning or the evening.

3. SHOULDER-LOOSENING AND FLEXIBILITY DRILLS

PURPOSE

For loosening tight shoulder muscles, to make them more flexible and to keep them flexible.

PROCEDURE

A. The first drill is performed by the player placing his fingertips on top of his shoulders, right hand to the right shoulder, left hand to the left shoulder, extending his elbows and rolling his shoulders front to back and back to front, twenty times each way.

B. The second drill is executed with the use of a baseball bat. In front of his body the player grasps a bat at each end, keeping the arms fully extended, passes it up and over his head and down behind the shoulders and down near the buttocks. He then returns the bat back over his head to the original starting position. He must never take his hands off the bat and he must keep his arms fully extended. Five repetitions at any one time should be sufficient. This is an excellent stretch prior to going to bat in a game.

C. The third drill substitutes a rope for a bat. Tie knots in the rope at distances shorter than a 35-inch bat. Do this exercise by tying the knots as close together as you can and yet keep your arms fully extended as you pass the rope up over your head, back to your buttocks and return to the starting position as you do with the bat in the above. Tie the knots closer as you become more flexible in the shoulders.

4. ABDOMEN REDUCER

PURPOSE

To keep a slim waistline and give a player better and faster action. A heavy waistline causes "lazy hips" in batting and pitching.

PROCEDURE

In your spare time and at your own convenience, suck in your stomach and hold it in for a slow count of six. Repeat about 25 times daily and watch your waistline reduce. A good time to do it is when you are driving and you stop at a light. Suck in your stomach as many times as possible.

5. ISOMETRIC ROPE DRILL

PURPOSE

To strengthen the throwing arm and back.

PROCEDURE

The isometric rope drill should be executed only once a day during the off-season. During the season it should be done after practice.

Attach a piece of rope five feet long around a door knob or other stationary object at approximately the same height and wind the other end around your wrist or hand. Then follow the steps listed below:

1) Assume a pitcher's position with both body and arm as you would in your first in stride motion to pitch. Pull against the rope with maximum effort for a slow count of six. (Note Illustration No. 1, Figure No. 1.)

Illustration No. 1   Isometric Rope Drill

2) Assume a position halfway through your delivery and repeat pulling against the rope with maximum effort for a slow count of six. (Note Illustration No. 1, Figure No. 2.)

3) Finally, set your arm and hand at the downward follow-through position and repeat the pull and count. (Note Illustration No. 1, Figure No. 3.)

6. LIGHT BULB TURNING STRETCH
by Dr. Robert "Bob" Bauman

PURPOSE

To keep the throwing muscles stretched during the winter months.

PROCEDURE

Raise up your toes, reach up as high as possible, imagine you are reaching to turn a light bulb into a rusty socket. Turn the bulb into the socket and turn it out again. Ten turns in and ten turns out with one arm, then repeat with the other arm.

7. THIGH STRETCH

PURPOSE

To prevent a charley horse.

PROCEDURE

Standing up, lift one foot up behind you, bringing the foot up to around your buttocks. Grab the instep of your foot with the hand on the same side as the foot that is off the floor. Pull that leg up behind you close to your buttocks. Keep other leg straight. As you pull the leg up with your hand, lean your torso forward as far as possible and nearly parallel with the floor. Hold and pull the foot up, stretching the thigh muscles in that position for a slow count of six. Continue with the other leg. This exercise should be repeated twice. After each stretch shake the leg, making the muscles bounce. (Illustration No. 2.)

Illustration No. 2   Thigh Stretch Drill

8. HAMSTRING STRETCH

PURPOSE

To prevent pulling a muscle when running.

PROCEDURE

Standing in an upright position with feet together, reach down toward your toes, with your fingers touching your shins. Walk your fingers down your shins as far as possible, gradually stretching the muscles that are so often pulled in early spring practice. When both hands can be placed flat on the floor, you are getting nearly maximum stretch out of the muscles. This exercise should be repeated twice. After each stretch shake the leg muscles making them bounce like Jello.

9. GROIN STRETCH

PURPOSE

To prevent pulled muscles in the groin area.

PROCEDURE

In a catcher's crouch position, place the heel of the left hand against the inside of the right knee and the left elbow against the inside of the left knee.

Illustration No. 3   Groin Stretch Drill

Illustration No. 4   Groin Stretch Drill

Squeeze in toward the center with your legs. Hold this pressure against the elbow and hand for a slow count of six. Either hand and elbow may be used for this part of the stretch. (Note Illustration No. 3.)

Staying in the crouched position, now cross your arms to grab a hold on the outside of the knees. Push your legs apart as hard as possible as you hold the legs in both hands for a slow count of six. Repeat both exercises twice. After each stretch, stand up and shake the muscles on the legs, making them bounce like Jello. (Note Illustration No. 4.)

B) RUNNING AND LEG DEVELOPMENT

Running is one of the best conditioners known to athletes; it can be done indoors or outdoors. The legs contain our largest muscles and need hard work to develop stamina and better execution in most fundamentals of play.

10. RUNNING   by Jim Gibbard

PURPOSE

To condition the whole body, particularly the legs.

PROCEDURE

Running at least one mile three times weekly should keep any player in top condition during the off-season. This mile run can be done outside or inside. The ideal running drill is to run the mile in six minutes or less. Then walk a lap of the track or about 250 yards. Take a short break then run a half mile at alternate speeds, using 50-yard dashes. Include eight 50-yard dashes with jogging between the dashes to cover the half mile. This half mile should be done in about four minutes. Thus, the total running time should be about 10 minutes.

Do not attempt to run the full mile at a full jogging speed the first two weeks. Only injury can be the result of this foolish procedure. It is a gradual process of jogging and walking at your own pace to finish the mile. By the end of two weeks, you should begin to establish a speed pattern for both the mile run and the half-mile alternate dashes and jogging. The reason for doing the dashes after the mile run is to make certain your legs are warm and loose. This prevents pulled muscles.

11. JUMP ROPE

PURPOSE

To develop the feet and legs and loosen the shoulder muscles.

PROCEDURE

Jumping rope is wonderful exercise for quickness of the foot. Make a game out of it much as the professional boxers do in their workouts. Five minutes of rope jumping plus running is ample. If you do not run, you should jump longer.

C) THROWING

Whenever possible a player should continue to throw a ball during the off-season a minimum of once a week.

12. WEEKLY THROWING

PURPOSE

To keep the arm muscles from becoming weak and contracting, thus keeping good muscle tone in the arm all winter.

PROCEDURE

It is best to throw three times a week if possible. Fifteen to 20 minutes per session is sufficient to keep the arm flexible and ready for the strenuous early practice and games in the spring. Maximum velocity is not important, but some hard throws should be included in the workout. It is very important to work on and concentrate on control.

D) WEIGHT WORK

We do not advocate heavy weight work or training. We are not trying to develop bulging muscles, but are working for good muscle tone and flexible muscles. We believe in supervised limited weight work to accomplish a specific purpose. We want to develop the muscles necessary to throw a ball, swing a bat, field a ball and run.

13. OVERLOAD: FOR THE QUICK BAT   by Mike Marshall

PURPOSE

To develop a more powerful swing, a quicker bat and better bat control.

Authors note: This drill was devised by Mike Marshall for Danny Litwhiler and the Michigan State University Spartans as the result of a question asked of Mike, "Which arm is the power arm, the front arm or the back arm?". Mike's answer was, "Let's find out!" As a result of his study we settled on the "Overload: For The Quick Bat" as a means to develop more power and distance. Believe me, it works.

PROCEDURE

Method and Equipment:

(1) We want to simulate the baseball swing versus gravity.

(2) High school boys use a 7½-pound hand barbell. Older players use a 15-pound hand barbell.

(3) Increase at 2½-pound intervals.

(4) Remain at each weight for at least four days.

(5) Move to the next weight only when the weight becomes easy to throw through ten repetitions.

(6) Ceiling weight is 25 pounds. For high school boys the ceiling weight should be 15 to 20 pounds depending on the physical size of the boy.

(7) An 18 to 20-inch high bench, long enough for a person to lie down is used during this exercise.

The hand barbell is a single unit for high school age using two-5-pound weights, two 2½-pound weights, two 1¼-pound weights, a hand bar with clamps and a wrench to secure the weights. College age boys use the same equipment but add two 10-pound weights. A pad should be used to place on the floor under the barbell. This prevents sudden jar to the arm and harm to the floor and barbell.

PROCEDURE

(1) Lie on your side on the bench with the front arm of the baseball swing upward. *Example:* Right-hand swingers lie on the right side and lift the weight with the left arm. Left-hand swingers lie on their left side.

(2) Support the head with the opposite hand and the elbow resting on the seat of the bench. (Note Illustration No. 5, Figure No. 1.)

(3) Lock the bottom leg to the side of the bench with your toe and the top leg on the other side of the bench with your heel. (Note Illustration No. 5, Figure No. 2.)

(4) The barbell is positioned directly in front of the shoulder and resting on the pad. The bar portion of the barbell is held parallel to the body line. (Note Illustration No. 5, Figure No. 1.)

(5) Use three slow repetitions to loosen the area being stressed. If any sharp pain is felt, drop the weights and stop weight training for the day.

(6) After three warm-ups, attempt to explode the barbell upward. Nothing will be gained if the weights are moved easily or slowly.

Illustration No. 5   Overload: For the Quick Bat (1)

Illustration No. 5   Overload: For the Quick Bat (2)

(7) If possible, do seven of these explosive movements. As soon as the
weights are extended upward, lower them to the pad easily. When
they touch the pad, explode them again. (Note Illustration No. 5,
Figures No. 3 and No. 4 for path of the barbell.) The barbell
moves directly vertical from its original position on the pad. The
barbell never extends up over the body to the arm's maximum
extension height. (Note Illustration No. 5, Figure No. 5.)

Illustration No. 5
Overload: For the Quick Bat (3)

Illustration No. 5
Overload: For the Quick Bat (4)

Illustration No. 5   Overload: For the Quick Bat (5)

Do no more than one exercise of 10 repetitions during a four-hour period. A maximum of two exercises is recommended. We prefer once in the morning upon rising and once upon retiring.

If soreness develops, discontinue the weight program and immediately tell the coach or trainer where the soreness is located. Do not confuse stiffness with soreness. Any good exercise will cause some stiffness.

The total procedure takes no more than one minute once you are on the bench and your hand is on the barbell. Do not lift other weights with the same motion. (For complete exercise, note Illustration No. 5, Figures No. 1, 2, 3, 4.)

14. OVERLOAD: FOR THE FASTBALL   by Larry Hamm

PURPOSE

To develop more velocity yet retain control.

EQUIPMENT

One regulation 5-oz. ball, one 7 oz. ball, one 9-oz. ball, one 10-oz. ball, one 11-oz. ball, one 12-oz. ball, and a net to throw the weighted balls against. Do not throw weighted balls to a catcher. They could harm his hand and ruin his glove. The balls are manufactured by Worth Sports Company.

PROCEDURE

This is a six, eight or ten-week program, depending on the maximum weight you wish to use.

Throw three times per week with at least one day's rest between throwing days. Use each ball for two weeks beginning with the lightest (7 oz.) and ending with the heaviest weight you wish to use in the program for the last two weeks. Once you have reached the maximum weight, throwing twice a week or a minimum of once a week should keep your arm in good throwing shape, if you stay at that top weight. Should you miss a week, drop back one ounce and work back to the maximum weight. High school players should stop at 10 ounces. College players can go up to 12 ounces.

Do not throw a curve ball with any weight over 7 ounces. Never snap the curve at maximal exertion. In fact, do not throw any weighted ball at maximal exertion. Three-quarter speed is the proper speed. Throw the weighted balls at a maximum distance of 60 feet, 6 inches. You can begin the throws at a shorter distance and move back to 60 feet gradually.

    (1) Warm up by throwing a regulation ball (5 oz.) until ready to throw hard.

(2) Ten (10) throws at sub-maximal exertion with the seven (7) ounce ball. As the weight goes up, throw five times with the last weight used prior to throwing ten throws with the new weight.

(3) Twenty (20) throws at maximal exertion with the regulation (5 oz.) ball, or until control comes back. This completes the weighted ball program for the day.

Outfielders, infielders, and catchers can use this same program. They may like to simply toss the heavy balls against a net or a Toss Back machine. This is a machine with a net stretched tight with rubber bands. When a ball hits it, the ball rebounds back to the thrower.

When throwing the heavy balls, it is very important to concentrate on the proper wrist movement. Make certain that the same arm and wrist delivery is used as when throwing a regulation ball. As the balls used are heavier, there is a tendency to push the ball. This would be harmful to the thrower.

15. WRIST CURLS WITH A BARBELL   by Don Fauls

PURPOSE

To develop muscle tone in both arms, but not develop bulging muscles.

PROCEDURE

Get a barbell or any 10 to 15-pound weight that is easy to control. Standing with the arm at the side in full extension, palm up, weight in hand, flex the arm slowly to complete flexion. Return to full extension. Do this 10 times. This exercise strengthens the interior arm muscles above the elbow. (Note Illustration No. 6A, Figure No. 1.) Then, in the same basic position, but with the lower arm in the midway position (thumb pointing up), repeat the above exercise 10 times. This also strengthens arm muscles above the elbow. (Note Illustration No. 6A, Figure No. 2.)

To strengthen muscles in the back of the arm, above the elbow: Raise the arm above the shoulder with the elbow bent (flexed), straighten arm 10 times. (Note Illustration No. 6A, Figure No. 3.) To strengthen muscles of the arm below the elbow: Rest elbow and lower arm on a table with the wrist extending over the end of the table, weight in hand, palm up, flex the wrist 10 times. These muscles are most important for action in throwing the curve ball or any breaking pitch. (Note Illustration No. 6B Figure No. 1.) Hold the weight with the thumb pointing up, spin the weight to the right and back to the left 10 times. (Note Illustration No. 6B, Figure No. 2.) This strengthens the rotator muscles of the wrist and elbow.

Turn the hand over, with wrist flexed, so that it faces the floor—extend wrist. Do this 10 times. (Note Illustration No. 6B, Figure No. 3.)

The above exercises are to be done only three times per week. Add one repetition to each exercise per week. The next week each exercise is done 11 times per day, three days a week, and so on, until 20 repetitions per day are reached. This can be continued indefinitely, at 20 repetitions; however, it is recommended that this weight work be done after practice, never before.

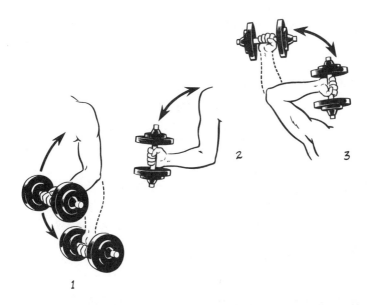

Illustration No. 6A   Wrist Curls with a Barbell

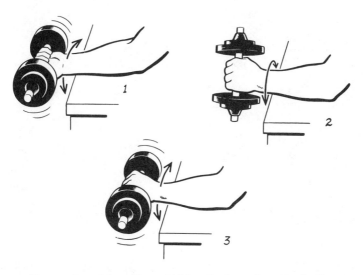

Illustration No. 6B   Wrist Curls with a Barbell

16. EXERCISE WITH THE MEDI BALL (Metal ball)
by Dr. Robert Bauman

PURPOSE

To condition the throwing arm and rehabilitation of persons after surgery or injury. To restore, revive and strengthen normal muscular action. Also, to prevent injury to the elbow from throwing a baseball. It is great for elbow stretching, and strengthening and increasing stamina in the muscles.

EQUIPMENT

One 3½-pound chrome-plated Medi Exercise Ball the same size and shape as a baseball.

PROCEDURE

(1) *Forward and Backward Swing. Starting position*—stand with feet apart, about two feet, with trunk bent forward and arms left or right hanging loosely with the ball. *Action*—swing ball forward and backward, using pendulum type swing, permitting the ball to do the work. Continue with them to 15 forward and backward strokes. (Note Illustration No. 7, Figure No. 1.)

Illustration No. 7   Medi Ball (1)   Illustration No. 7   Medi Ball (2)

(2) *Lateral Swing Side to Side. Starting position*—same as above. *Action*—with right hand, swing ball pendulum left to right 10 to 15 times. If holding the ball in left hand, begin swing from right to left. (Note Illustration No. 7, Figure No. 2.)

(3) *Circle Swing. Starting position*—same as above. *Action*—swing ball in clockwise direction making a circle about two feet in diameter depending on length of arm. Continue with 12 circles and then make 12 circles counterclockwise. (Note Illustration No. 7, Figure No. 3.)

(4) *Over the Head.* This exercise is done as one exercise by continuing on to (5) Arm Rotator as follows. You do not drop your arm between exercises. This builds stamina of muscles. *Starting position*—stand erect and face forward, bend elbow, bring to shoulder level and hold ball in hand to perpendicular position, head high. *Action*—raise ball straight upward until bicep touches ear, to count of one. Push a little higher to count of two. Push still higher to count of three. Relax to starting position. Repeat six times. After the sixth repetition remain erect and face forward and continue on to rotator exercise. (Note Illustration No. 7, Figures No. 4 and 5.)

(5) *Arm Rotator.* As you complete the above exercise with your arm in the above starting position, you now begin this exercise. *Starting position*—same position as above in No. (4)—*Over the Head*, (Figure No. 4.)

Action—move ball slowly forward to shoulder level with ball downward. Wrist, ball and elbow are now shoulder level. Raise ball slowly upward

Illustration No. 7   Medi Ball (3)   Illustration No. 7   Medi Ball (4)

Illustration No. 7   Medi Ball (5)

Illustration No. 7   Medi Ball (6)

Illustration No. 7   Medi Ball (7)

Illustration No. 7   Medi Ball (8)

keeping elbow at shoulder level and continue moving ball up and back as far as possible without bending body. Continue this forward and backward motion of ball six times. This movement should be smooth, no bounce. Never let ball or arm drop forward or backward from starting position. The complete exercise is done slowly and smoothly. (Note Illustration No. 7, Figures No. 6 and 7.)

(6) *Forearm Stretching and Strengthening. Starting position*—stand upright, place wrist under and back of elbow holding ball out in front of the body, ball in palm up. Keep elbow about shoulder level and arm stretched out. *Action*—bend wrist upward and downward slowly, now rotate forearm inwardly and repeat up-and-down motion of the wrist. Repeat exercise six times. (Note Illustration No. 7, Figure No. 8.)

17. USE OF ANKLE WEIGHTS AND WEIGHTED INNERSOLES

PURPOSE

To increase speed, strengthen legs, help recover from some injuries, and to act as a psychological booster.

PROCEDURE

The amount of weight on each foot should be no more than two or three pounds. Weights should be worn for a short workout of running and exercising before regular practice sessions, or on one's own time. Workouts with ankle weights during the winter months are beneficial and should be encouraged.

Weighted innersoles are on the market and very practical for this work. Some coaches find them more practical than the spat-like ankle weights. It is advisable not to practice baseball fundamentals wearing ankle weights. They could cause unnatural motion and cause injury. Use them for straight running or walking.

E) BAT SWINGING

Swing any bat, but particularly a heavy bat of 50 ounces or more, and you can develop a more powerful swing.

A heavy bat can be made by drilling a hole in the hitting end of the bat and filling the hole with lead as described in Chapter 16, Drill No. 262.

Using the metal doughnut or the cylindrical bat weights is also good. It is also possible to order an exceptionally heavy bat from a bat company that specializes in training aids, such as Worth Sports Company.

The "Power Swing," a plastic fin-like object which slips over the barrel of the bat, is good and is used by many coaches and players. The fins cause resistance to the air as they are swung through the air, thus giving the swinger the feeling of weight.

18. WEIGHTED BAT SWING

PURPOSE

To develop a powerful swing and force the arms away from the body when contacting the ball.

PROCEDURE

Swing a bat 50 times left-handed and 50 times right-handed every day during the off-season or at least three times a week. Switch swinging helps develop both arms.

Do not swing wildly and blindly. Always look at an object, keeping your eye on the object during the completion of the swing. This teaches you to hold your head still in the swing. You should assume the object you are looking at is a pitched ball.

If you use the "Power Swing" 20 swings every day should be ample.

19. HANGING TARGET SWING AND STUFFED STOCKING

PURPOSE

Designed to help the player in swinging a bat, this drill also helps him to keep his head and eyes on the ball while swinging. The drill should improve his ability to hit pitches at different heights.

PROCEDURE

A. *Stuffed Stocking on String*. The target is a rag or paper-filled stocking suspended by a string from the ceiling of a room. It is best to have several of these at different heights, so that players can get practice hitting at balls of various heights, inside and outside. The main idea is not to hit the stocking, but come as close as possible so as to just hit it. Hitting it dead center will soon destroy it.

The player should have two bats of his own model, and one of these should be filled with lead in the large end. First, the player should swing the leaded bat, then the regular bat. He should swing as many times as he can. Fifty to 100 swings a day are not too much for off-season work.

An ideal place for a ball player to set up this drill is in a garage or basement.

B. *Stuffed Stocking*. Stuff a stocking with rags or paper and tape it loosely. This object can be hit indoors without damaging anything. It is excellent for indoor swings, getting your eye on the ball and correcting batting flaws.

C. *Boxer's Heavy Punching Bag* by Walter Rabb

Hang the punching bag in the strike zone. Mark the bag with stripes, 1) Shoulder high, 2) Belt high, and 3) Knee high.

The coach pulls the bag to him and lets it swing into the batter's strike zone. As the bag approaches the zone the coach calls out a number for him to hit.

For example: The coach yells "one," the player would hit the stripe shoulder high. If he yells "two," the player would hit the middle stripe and if he yells "three," the player would hit the bottom stripe. The force of the heavy bag against the swing of the bat will develop more drive in the player's swing.

20. BASEBALL BAT FIGURE EIGHT

PURPOSE

Designed to loosen up the wrists, arms and shoulders. This drill also helps develop the muscles for power hitting.

PROCEDURE

(1) Take a bat in one hand by grasping it near the knob at the end of the

Illustration No. 8

Figure Eight (1)   Figure 8 (2)

handle and extend it horizontally to one side. Now use the bat as you would an Indian Club, making a figure eight with it. Start with a small figure eight, using mostly wrist movement and increase to large windmill figure eight, using full arm extension movement. Then repeat with the other hand. Repeat both drills for several minutes. (Note Illustration No. 8, Figure No. 1.)

(2) Now, put the bat in both hands in front of the body and begin the figure-eight movement. Continue for several minutes. (Note Illustration No. 8, Figure No. 2.)

21. ISOMETRIC BAT DRILL

PURPOSE

To increase and develop the hitting power of the batter's swing. This drill should be practiced before and after workouts. It can be continued during the off-season as well as during the season.

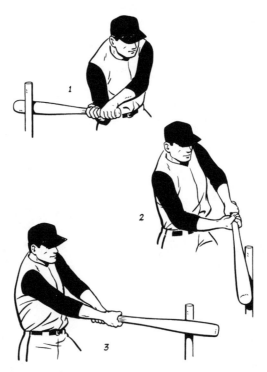

Illustration No. 9   Isometric Bat Drill

PROCEDURE

Desired results will be obtained when the exercises described here are executed with maximum effort.

With a bat in his hands the hitter addresses a solidly placed pole as he would face home plate when he is ready to hit.

(1) *First Position*. Standing one step in front of the pole, the batter places the barrel of the bat against the pole simulating a stopped swing at its very beginning. He then tries to pull the bat through the pole for a slow count of six. (Note Illustration No. 9, Figure No. 1.)

(2) *Second Position*. In this position, the batter stands even with the pole, places the barrel of the bat against it as though it were in the mid-swing position, and presses against the pole at maximum effort for a slow count of six seconds. (Note Illustration No. 9, Figure No. 2.)

(3) *Third Position*. Finally, the player assumes a stance one step behind the pole, places the barrel of the bat against it in a three-quarter swing position and pushes with full effort against the pole for a slow count of six seconds. This is the approximate position of the bat when it meets the ball properly. (Note Illustration No. 9, Figure No. 3.)

22. HITTING A TIRE

PURPOSE

To develop a more powerful swing and strengthen the wrists and arms.

PROCEDURE

(1) *Suspended Tire*. Suspend a tire on a rope, hanging the tire in the strike zone. At the bottom of the tire also tie a rope and fasten the rope to a stake or fixed weighted object. To make the tire spin when it is hit, swivels can be attached to the ropes and then fastened to the tire. The heavier the tire, the more resistance to the swing. Fifty swings daily will improve a player's power swing.

(2) *Tire Against the Wall*. If you want a fixed object to hit, you can cut a tire in half across its diameter. Take one half and fasten the cut ends to a 2″ × 4″ or 4″ × 4″ piece of wood. Fasten the wood at strike-zone level to a wall, leaving the tread of the tire extending out from the wall. The batter swings the bat toward the wall against the tire. Fifty swings daily should develop a more powerful swing.

SPRING TRAINING AND PRE-GAME CONDITIONING

In off-season drills we stress physical conditioning. We therefore ask that our players report for our first official practice session in pretty good physical condition. For our SPRING TRAINING AND PRE-GAME CONDITIONING, we first stress physical conditioning, using game-like drills which also teach fundamentals of the game.

A well-conditioned player and team are important to good play. However, conditioning can become a bore to the players and the coach. It is very valuable to the development of a good team or players to make conditioning interesting and game-like in execution. Once a player has pride in his physical condition he will be a real asset to the team. Several hard workers can have a positive effect on the whole team, making it a hard-working team. Luck is a by-product of hard work. A well-conditioned team forces the opposition to make mistakes.

If practiced correctly, our conditioning drills will build a team that is physically and mentally ready to enter a season in excellent shape and keep in good shape the entire season.

Stretching is of prime importance. A player's first obligation to himself and the team should be to go through a stretching program prior to any throwing, running or hitting.

23. RECOMMENDED DRILLS PRIOR TO WORKOUTS

The following stretching drills are recommended prior to a workout. Drill No. 1—Raise your Hands, Drill No. 2—Simulated Hanging Stretch, Drill No. 3—Shoulder Loosening and Flexibility Drills, Drill No. 6—Light Bulb Turning Stretch, Drill No. 7—Thigh Stretch, Drill No. 8—Hamstring Stretch and Drill No. 9—Groin Stretch, and of course some jogging, quick starts and dashes after the stretching exercises. For throwing, Drill No. 16—Exercise With the Medi Ball is recommended. For batting, Drill No. 18—Weighted Bat Swing and Drill No. 20—Baseball Bat Figure Eight.

24. INSTANT ARM AND BACK STRETCH

PURPOSE

To give the ball players a quick stretch prior to play or workout. It is advisable to go no further than the exercises recommended here unless directed and supervised by a competent trainer.

PROCEDURE

(1) With both of your hands, hold another player's fingers on his right hand. As you pull his hand until his arm is extended, have him relax his entire arm, hand, and fingers, while you shake the arm vigorously. He must pull away from the person doing the shaking. Alternate with the other hand, allowing only a few seconds for each hand and arm.

(2) As you approach the player's back, he reaches up and interlocks the fingers of both hands behind his neck. Standing at his back, reach under his armpits, passing your left arm up under his left arm and your right arm under his right arm. Your arms are now out in front of his shoulders and your hands interlock on top of his hands behind his neck.

Ask the player to completely relax his entire body, take a deep breath, then blow it out. When he has exhaled completely, pick him up, allowing his body to curl over your chest as you lean backward. Give a short bounce to his body, and the spinal column will loosen up with a popping or snapping sound. One good bounce should be sufficient.

(3) To strengthen the back and also to loosen it, lie on the end of a bench with only hips and legs on the bench. Another person sits on or pins the legs to the bench as the player moves his torso up and down as done in sit-up exercises. The player should lie first face down then face up.

This exercise, if done daily, should be done in a series of ten push- or pull-ups, each, face up and face down for the first week and increase to 15 the next week and so on up to 25 daily. This should be sufficient to strengthen a weak or injured back.

25. FOOTBALL PASS DRILL

PURPOSE

Especially good for pitcher conditioning, but very good for the rest of the team. It makes running fun.

PROCEDURE

The coach assumes a position near the edge of the infield behind the second base area. Take a starting position for all players on the right field foul line on the outfield edge of the infield grass. Each player has a ball in his hand. At the signal to start, a player runs past the coach, tossing him the ball as he passes by. After the player runs along the edge of the infield and progresses to the vicinity of the left field foul line, the coach yells "cut," which is the signal for the player to cut toward home plate or the left field fence and receive a "football pass" from the coach. (Note Illustration No. 10.)

When each player has had his turn, he lines up along the left field foul line and retraces his path past the coach, giving him the baseball again and receiving it in the same manner near the right field line.

This drill progresses from a slow jog at short distances to long, hard-running end zone passes beyond the foul lines. Twenty to 25 of these passes per day should be enough.

Illustration No. 10
Football Pass

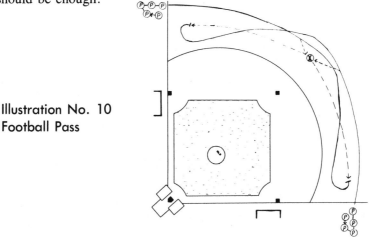

26. ROLLING SEMICIRCLE (Pick-ups)

PURPOSE

Valuable to all as a conditioner and especially beneficial to pitchers, it can be used at any time during the practice period. Players should wear their gloves while performing the drill.

Illustration No. 11   Rolling Semicircle (Pick-Ups)

PROCEDURE

A semicircle with a radius of approximately 12 feet is run around the coach or another player. The coach, or another player, who is facing the fielding player rolls the ball on the ground for him to field and return. Each time, the coach returns the rolling ball to a position at the opposite side of the semicircle. This is repeated 20 to 25 times for each player. After one week of practice, the number should be stepped up to 50 times for each player. After two weeks, the players should alternate, taking 50 pick-ups two times each for 100 pick-ups daily.

Note: Two players can easily pair off and work with each other on this drill without the aid of the coach. (Note Illustration No. 11.)

27. FIFTY-FIFTY

PURPOSE

An excellent team or individual conditioner with which to end a day's practice, this is really a series of activities to be performed as follows:

PROCEDURE

A) Jog 50 yards and walk back to the starting point. Repeat five times.

B) At starting point, place hands on hips, raise up on toes, breathe deeply, hold breath as long as possible. Then exhale rapidly.

C) Monkey squat and bounce 10 times. This is performed by doing a deep knee bend, one squat with both hands touching the ground in front of the body, followed by holding this position and bouncing in this squat position.

D) Stand erect on one leg. Relax and shake other leg vigorously to feel the muscles vibrate and bounce along the bone. Repeat with the other leg.

E) Again, sprint 50 yards and walk back to the starting point. Repeat five times.

F) Repeat deep breathing as above. Monkey squat 10 times and shake legs after each squat.

G) Run fast for 50 yards and walk back to the starting point. Do this five times. There is nothing wrong with jogging back after the run instead of walking back.

Increase the number of everything in this drill as the season advances and as the players are better conditioned.

28. TOUCH GRASS RIGHT AND LEFT

PURPOSE

To help all players to move properly to their right and left while running in a low crouched fielding position, and to serve as a good conditioner.

PROCEDURE

A) Line up pitchers, infielders, outfielders, and catchers with gloves on in the outfield area. Have players in columns, five to six feet apart, four or five to the column, with columns 10 to 12 feet apart. Players face the coach.

B) Coach gets players in fielding position by commanding, "hands on knees," then, "get set," which means hands off knees in fielding position.

C) On command, "break left," or "break right," each player uses a crossover step and moves 10 to 12 steps in the commanded direction while touching his glove to the grass with each step. Team stops, gets set and returns in the opposite direction when coach commands, "hands on knees, get set, break." Coach can point instead of using voice to indicate direction.

D) Repeat until team looks tired.

E) Give short break of about one minute, then give Monkey Squat and Deep Breathing as described in Drill No. 27—Fifty-Fifty. Give another short minute or two break.

F) Get team ready for breaking back on fly balls first to one side then the other. They do not touch the ground with their gloves or touch the grass in this part of the drill. They do use a crossover step and keep their eye on the coach as they break back.

Now command, "break back to the left" or "break back to the right."

G) Players walk back to starting position and repeat to the opposite side. Repeat this right and left until the team looks tired. (Illustration No. 12.)

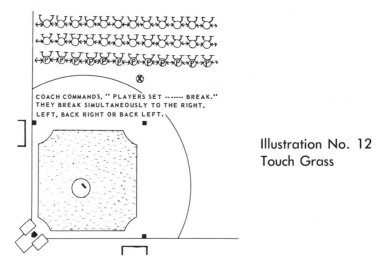

COACH COMMANDS, " PLAYERS SET ------- BREAK."
THEY BREAK SIMULTANEOUSLY TO THE RIGHT,
LEFT, BACK RIGHT OR BACK LEFT.

Illustration No. 12
Touch Grass

29. SHIFT AND TOSS

PURPOSE

To improve fielding ability, this drill may be executed before, during or after the regular practice period.

PROCEDURE

Start two players at the left field foul line about 25 feet apart. One player rolls the ball out in front of the other player who fields the ball and returns it on the ground out in front of the player who tossed him the ball originally. This continues over to the right field line. This drill is done at a medium running speed and continues back and forth several times. (Note Illustration No. 13.)

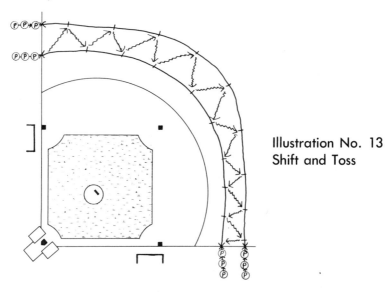

Illustration No. 13
Shift and Toss

30. DEVELOPING SOFT HANDS AND REACTION DRILL
by Dick Siebert

PURPOSE

To teach the players how to give with the ball and field the short hops.

PROCEDURE

A) *Hop Drill*. Two players stand 10 to 15 feet apart and throw grounders at each other, bouncing them right at the player's feet. Each backs up a few steps after a few throws until a maximum of 30 feet is reached. First use two hands to field the ball, then one hand. This is a time to have fun and get fancy with the glove. Spear the ball backhanded and once in awhile with the glove held around the back of the leg or between the legs. As a means of making the game more interesting and lively, the participants may want to compete for Cokes or some conditioning exercise such as push-ups or laps around the park—the player making the most errors being the loser.

B) *One-hand Drill.* Same as above, only the fielder hooks the thumb of his throwing hand into his belt behind his back. The thrower rolls the ball hard to the side of the fielder to within one step of the fielder. This teaches the fielder to react quickly and keep the face of the glove open.

31. DIVING DRILL WITH PITCHING MACHINE AND TENNIS BALLS

PURPOSE

To teach the players how to react for balls hit sharply to their right, left, and directly at them.

PROCEDURE

Equipment: One mechanical pitching machine such as ''Jugs'' and 25 to 50 old tennis balls.

Place the fielders in front of a net or screen. Place the pitching machine 60 to 75 feet in front of and facing the fielders. Turn the pitching wheels up as fast as possible and feed the tennis balls into the machine when the fielders are ready to field the ball.

A) Set the machine to shoot the tennis balls at a fixed target. Line the fielders up to the left of the target. Get your first fielder ready. As you place the ball into the spinning wheels the fielder will be ready to reach or dive to his left to field the fast-moving tennis ball. After he has his turn he moves over to the right side. The next fielder steps up in position to field the ball and move over to the other side. This continues until all the fielders have fielded from the left side and moved over to the right side.

B) Now the fielders get set and dive or reach to their right side and move to the left side. Continue this movement back and forth for at least 10 to 20 dives from each side, depending on how much time you have for this drill.

C) Now put a fielder in front of the target area so the machine will be throwing the tennis balls directly at him. The machine should be pointed so the balls shoot at the fielder on a short hop.

The coach can set the machine to throw line drives or bounces for any of the above drills.

Extreme Caution must be used not to use baseballs in the machine for this drill. Serious injury could result from using a hard and heavy baseball. Don't even have any baseballs around the area where a foolish player might sneak a baseball into the machine as a supposedly practical joke.

32. STEP ON BENCH

PURPOSE

To develop and condition legs for a long baseball season. This was a daily routine in spring training for Johnny Vander Meer who pitched two consecutive no-hitters for the Cincinnati Reds.

PROCEDURE

Stand in front of a bench 17 to 19 inches high. Alternately place feet on the bench in rhythmic movement of the legs and arms.

Do this 25 times for each foot. This can be done daily during the pre-season training. It is advisable to discontinue this program during the regular season play and use running drills instead. (Note Illustration No. 14.)

Illustration No. 14   Step on Bench

33. RUBBER BALL SQUEEZE

PURPOSE

To develop the strong hands, wrists and forearms necessary to be a better player.

PROCEDURE

This drill involves squeezing the rubber ball, digging the fingers in and flexing the muscles of the hand, wrists and forearm. The number of repetitions should be increased as you continue with the drill.

Inexpensive, convenient, and not time-consuming, this drill is used by many major leaguers. Recognizing its value, some players carry a rubber ball with them and perform the drill daily.

34. ARM STRENGTHENER AND CONDITIONER

PURPOSE

To strengthen the arm and condition it for the season.

PROCEDURE

After a warm-up period of calisthenics on the first day of practice, the squad should be arranged in pairs, with half the squad along the first base line and the other half from the third base line to the second base line across the pitcher's mound. In this manner, the pairs of players face each other at a distance of approximately 45 feet. They now play catch and gradually move back to the third and second base line and are throwing 90 feet.

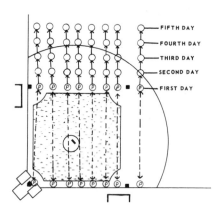

Illustration No. 15
Arm Conditioner

From this distance, partners throw to each other until their arms are loose, which usually takes about five minutes. Then they are ready to throw three hard ones, but there should be some easy tosses between the hard throws. This ends the drill for the first day. It should take only eight to ten minutes.

On the second day, players should line up in the same manner, but work back to a distance of 100 feet and proceed as on the previous day. It is advisable to work back to 100 feet as you are getting loose, as you should each day of throwing in this drill.

This drill should be continued for two weeks with the distance increased by 10 feet each day to a maximum of 150 feet for pitchers and infielders. Catchers can move back to 175 to 200 feet. Outfielders move back to 250 feet or more. (Note Illustration No. 15.)

35. THE PEPPER GAME

PURPOSE

The pepper game can be beneficial to fielders and batters. It provides practice for the batter in keeping his eye on the ball and place hitting. It is especially good for hitters on days when rain or wet grounds cancel batting practice. The drill gives the fielder practice in fielding and should sharpen his reflexes. It never involves more than three fielders and one hitter in any one group. The ideal group is two fielders and one hitter.

PROCEDURE

Fielders should line up about 20 feet from the batter and two to three yards apart, so that they will have room to make plays to either side. The batter attempts to alternate hitting the balls to the fielders. After the batter has hit 20 or 25 balls to each player, the player at the head of the line becomes the batter, and the original batter becomes a fielder at the foot of the line. Rotate fielders and hitters. Another way to work the drill is for the fielder at the head of the line to become the hitter when the group has fielded 25 balls without an error.

The pepper game is one of the few times when a player should attempt to get fancy with his glove. He should try out all of his novelty catches and really enjoy himself, but at the same time he should try to improve his fielding skills and strengthen his weaknesses.

For motivation and to make the pepper game more interesting, the group could play for Cokes. If the fielders catch 25 balls without error, the batter owes each fielder a Coke. However, if a fielder makes an error he owes the batter a Coke. If the batter hits the ball over the fielder's head, or fails to hit the ball, he owes the throwing fielder a Coke.

CHAPTER **2**

TEAM DRILLS

There are individual drills for various positions, but the following drills are ideal for all players. Many are designed to develop the same fundamentals for each player. Discuss individual drills with the player involved and advise him how to work on his own. However, you should work closely with the team on combination drills, seeing that that they are worked with zest and do not last too long.

36. RHYTHM WARM-UP—CATCHING AND THROWING

PURPOSE

To develop rhythm in the catching and throwing motion.

PROCEDURE

The drill is executed with pairs of players playing catch at approximately 50 feet. After a rhythmic pattern is developed, the players throw from a greater distance and add Drill No. 37.

In the development of a rhythmic pattern, the right-handed player should concentrate on the following factors:

    a. Step forward with the right foot as the ball approaches and catch it just as the right foot touches the ground.

b. Transfer the ball to the right hand as soon as it strikes the glove.

c. Step forward with the left foot, and at the same time release the ball, originating the throw from the right foot.

d. Then the player should back up a few feet to the position where he originally started the throw, since he usually moves forward a few feet in the process of catching and throwing.

For the left-handed player, the movements are reversed. That is, the left foot comes forward when catching, and the throw originates from the left foot.

All the steps mentioned should be repeated until a satisfactory rhythmic pattern has been developed. When distance is needed along with rhythm, use the crow hop as described in Drill No. 39.

37. PRE-WARM-UP—QUICK GRIP AND THROW

PURPOSE

To develop the habit of catching the ball, gripping it properly, and throwing as quickly as possible. The grip should always be across the seams at the widest space on the ball. (Note Illustration No. 16.)

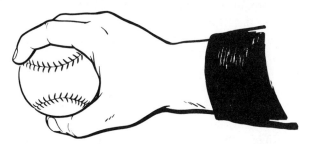

Illustration No. 16   Pre-Warm-Up Quick Grip

PROCEDURE

Have players use this drill while playing catch as a warm-up for the regular practice session or preceding a game. Players should begin the drill at 40–45 feet apart and should gradually back up to a maximum of 90 feet as their arms loosen. Outfielders should lengthen this distance at about 120 feet.

The right-handed player should catch the ball while stepping to meet it just as his right foot strikes the ground. He then quickly grips the ball across the seams in his right hand and throws as he strides and shifts his weight to the left foot. The feet and hands are reversed for the left-handed player. The whole action is one continuous motion with the ball being snapped out of the glove and gripped as quickly as possible. The player, in order to increase control, should always throw at an object.

38. CONTROL DEVELOPMENT

PURPOSE

To increase or develop the player's control of the ball when throwing.

PROCEDURE

All players should concentrate on the factors involved in this drill every time they throw. The principal factor is that of throwing at an object such as the catching partner's head, shoulder, stomach, or knee. Vary the object. For example, throw two or three times at the partner's head, then follow with two or three throws at each part of his anatomy mentioned above. The player should fix his eyes on the object at which he is aiming. *Never throw, unless you throw at something*, is a cardinal rule of baseball.

39. CROW HOP AND THROW

PURPOSE

To improve the throwing accuracy of both infielders and outfielders in the overhand throw, the crow-hop-and-throw drill should be practiced diligently. However, there are instances when time will not permit the crow hop before the fielder makes the throw. Therefore, he should be able to make the play without the crow hop when necessity demands it.

PROCEDURE

A. With infielders in position, hit ground balls to a specific fielder, who fields the ball correctly with his feet spread, left foot slightly forward and knees bent. (Reverse the foot position for left-handed players). The player then begins to straighten up, keeping his feet in the same position with his weight evenly distributed. He springs his weight forward, hopping to and landing on his right foot. As he throws overhanded, the infielder steps forward with his left foot. After he releases the ball, his right foot strikes the ground in a follow-through motion. He always steps toward the person to whom he is throwing. Hit 25 to 50 balls to each infielder.

B. Place outfielders in position. As you hit balls on the ground to the outfielders, the right-handed fielder fields the ball as described above, but as he comes up he shifts his weight to the left foot, steps forward on his right, and lands on his right foot. As the right foot comes down, the fielder hops on it (the crow hop) and steps forward with his left as he throws. Immediately after the release of the ball, the right foot hits the ground on the follow-through.

If the ball is caught in the air and on the move, the fielder tries to catch the ball in stride just as his right foot hits the ground, hops on his right foot, and throws, with the left foot hitting the ground on the stride. After the ball is released, the right leg comes on through in the usual follow-through. Hit 25 to 30 balls to each fielder. (On fly balls, left-hander uses opposite steps.)

C. Pitchers should use the same procedure as the outfielders and include a step before the crow hop. For left-handers in the above positions, the processes must be reversed as mentioned before.

It should be emphasized that on a close play the fielder may have to forget the crow hop and throw the ball in the best manner possible. This often happens on a slow ground ball to an infielder.

40. PEPPER GAMES

(Note Condition Drill No. 35.)

41. MULTIPLE BALL DRILL

PURPOSE

To orient the fielders so they can throw without looking first. Also, to give the fielders additional work.

PROCEDURE

This drill is performed with a full team on the field. Each fielder has a hitter to hit balls to him, and each hitter has a pick-up man to catch the ball

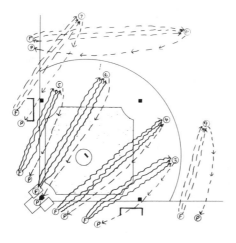

Illustration No. 17
Multiple Ball Drill

thrown to him by the fielder. Each hitter has from five to eight balls so that he can hit rapid-fire to the fielder. The fielder fields the ball and tosses it to the pick-up man. However, if the fielder misses the ball, he lets it go because the hitter will continue to hit to him without waiting for the fielder to retrieve a missed ball. (Note Illustration No. 17.)

After five minutes of this, the batter hitting to the first baseman stops and the first baseman moves to first base to receive balls thrown from the third baseman. The third baseman now takes rapid-fire ground balls and throws to the first baseman who returns the ball to the hitter's pick-up man. Continue this for five minutes, repeat for the shortstop, then for the second baseman. Players not taking part in this phase of the drill will continue fielding rapid-fire in their position.

The drills then move to the third baseman who throws to the second baseman, who makes the double play, all rapid-fire. Continue this phase of the drill for five minutes and repeat first with the shortstop, then the second baseman.

By the time the drill has passed around the infield, the outfielders should have their arms loose and the drill can be completed by having them throw to the bases and to the cut-off men.

42. POP FLIES WITH ALL PLAYERS IN POSITION

PURPOSE

To acquaint all players with the proper way to handle pop flies.

PROCEDURE

This drill should be practiced as much as possible on three types of days—windy, cloudy, and sunny. A new ball should be used so that players will be acquainted with pop flies in a game-like situation.

In order to make the situation realistic, all players should be in their respective positions, with the catcher in full gear. First, the coach should hit a few pop flies near the mound and home plate. This gives infielders and catchers an opportunity to play this type of ball. Flies near the mound provide the pitcher with practice in getting out of the way of the infielders playing the ball, and helping the infielders by using his voice. Flies should also be hit around and behind first base so that the first baseman and second baseman can get practice in fielding pop flies. When pop flies are directly behind the first baseman, they belong to the second baseman. This is also true for third base where the shortstop plays pop flies behind the third baseman.

The coach then hits those tough pop flies between the infield and the outfield. In calling for these balls the only person to yell (loud and clear) is the

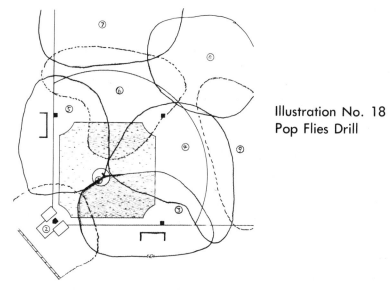

Illustration No. 18
Pop Flies Drill

outfielder. Every ball belongs to the infielder until the outfielder yells him off it. The infielder merely moves back under the ball while waving his hands up high if he can catch it. He listens for the outfielder to say, ''I got it!'' or, ''Take it!'' several times. (Note Illustration No. 18 for pop fly area.)

A point should be emphasized here. Fly balls between outfielders are run by the centerfielder. If both outfielders yell at the same time the centerfielder takes the ball, and the other outfielder drops back yelling, ''Take it! Take it! Take it!'' Using the Jugs Pitching Machine is ideal for this drill. It beats hitting fungos.

43. HIT-AND-RUN BASE RUNNING

PURPOSE

To practice the hit-and-run and base running drill. This drill also provides numerous opportunities for practicing cut-off plays.

PROCEDURE

With base coaches and the defensive team in position, place a runner on first base. A batter gives the hit-and-run sign to the runner who acknowledges it. Although the pitcher tries to get the ball over the plate and mixes up his pitches, he does not try to strike out the batter. The batter must hit the ball, regardless of the pitch, even if he must throw his bat at the ball so that he may protect the runner. The batter tries to hit behind the runner or to the opposite field. A left-handed hitter tries to hit through the hole left by a shortstop covering second. A right-handed hitter tries to hit toward the second base hole.

There should always be a man on first base. If the runner at first advances to second or third, he should stay there. The hitter takes first regardless of whether he is safe or out. Each player on the team should get his chance at bat. The runner on a hit-and-run breaks on the pitch and *looks up at the hitter* as soon as he hears the crack of the bat. He must know if the ball is a fly ball or ground ball, to avoid being doubled off on a fly ball. Outfielders and infielders make all plays on runners if the ball is hit.

If a catcher is used, he should make every effort to protect his throwing hand since hit-and-run plays generally produce many foul-tipped balls. (Note Illustration No. 26, Drill No. 79 for Hit-And-Run Procedure.)

44. CUT-OFF PLAYS AND LIVE RELAY THROWS

PURPOSE

To acquaint the entire team with all possible relay and cut-off plays in a game. It is also to determine the best possible way to make relays and cut-off plays according to the abilities of the team, and to improve upon these abilities.

The ideal cut-off situation has every base covered and key bases backed up on every play. On every fair hit ball and often on foul fly balls, all nine men have actual or possible participation in the play. The ideal cut-off play for one team may not be ideal for another. Perfect cut-off plays require perfect players, but every team does not have perfect players so work must be done to find the ideal way for each team. (Note Drills No. 173D, 186, 189E.)

A. THREE-DAY ORIENTATION SESSIONS   by Ray Borowicz

PROCEDURE

Almost the first thing we prepare is our long and short relays, which takes three days to accomplish—the first day we "dry run" and patiently try to place men in various positions for relays. We distribute "hand out" sheets fully explaining positioning and what we are going to try to accomplish. These sheets are handed out the night before to the whole squad. We use the double cut-off scheme with the shortstop and second baseman going out as a team for all long relays (except in the extreme left field corner where the third baseman and shortstop go out and in the right field corner where the first baseman and second baseman go out).

I call out various situations that first day and fungo to the outfield and we try to get proper positioning. The second day we set up spare people (pitchers, subs) as live base runners. We put a runner on first base and a runner at the plate. I call out one out, the score, and hit and run, and I fungo the ball to the outfield at outfielders or between them. I instruct runners to almost run recklessly at times to expose fielders to all sorts of possibilities on defense and ready them for it. We again correct and refine where necessary with what the live runners have brought out.

We do the usual things, man on first, or men on first and second, men on first and third, tag-up play at third on fly ball; each time we do this we call out the situation and use the live runners on base and from the plate, so the defense knows what must be done to cut down the extra base and prevent men getting into scoring position.

The third day we refine further, work out individual differences and this day we look for something a little short of perfection and more often than not we attain it. It is the *live runners* in this drill that accelerate our skills on cut-offs. It is great help in coaching and preparing the team defensively. An additional plus is the conditioning of all the members of the team.

B. FIFTEEN-MINUTE RELAY PRACTICE   by Cliff Gustafson

PROCEDURE

One of my favorite defensive drills is the outfield throwing drill. I feel most coaches probably neglect this phase of the game. We usually have the outfielders throw to the bases during routine infield-outfield practice, but this throwing work often becomes pretty casual as there are no base runners to challenge the outfielder. Bear in mind that an outfielder may go several games without getting a chance to throw out an advancing runner, then suddenly, we need a good strong throw and wonder why we didn't get it. Therefore, I feel we need to give outfielders regular competitive throwing work to keep them sharp. This drill is very simple and takes only 15 minutes, so it can and should be done regularly.

We put runners (utilizing pitchers and reserves as runners) on second and third base as well as home plate. We have two sets of outfielders and a full defensive infield set up. The coach will stand at home plate to hit fungos to the outfielders. We explain before each drill how we are running it so everyone involved will be aware of his job. In case of a fly ball, we assume there are no outs and the runner on third will be tagging up and trying to score. The outfielder, obviously is supposed to throw him out at home, but must use judgment on deep fly balls and throw to third if he has no chance for the runner at home.

In case of a base hit, only the runners at second and home plate are involved and we assume there are two outs—thus giving the runner at second a chance to get a good jump, even if the hit is a line drive or a looper that might get caught. The outfielder charges the ball quickly and tries to throw the runner out at home plate. Again, he must use judgment and throw to second if he has no chance for the runner at home plate. This will prevent the batter-runner from going to second on the throw to the plate. The fungo hitter may occasionally hit a "tweener" extra base hit so the outfielders get to practice hitting their relay and cut-off men. The fungo hitter also mixes up the fly balls and base hits to involve all runners and also alternates to all fields to keep all outfielders alert.

The infielders act as cut-off men on all plays. Thus, we are actually gaining practice in several phases: outfielders throwing to bases, outfielders hitting relay men, outfielders utilizing judgment, infielders practicing cut-offs and relays, pitchers and extra players getting in some running for conditioning as well as practice tagging up and leaving third base properly, along with regular base running technique. This drill, though simple, provides fun as well as much needed practice on several phases that are easily overlooked.

45. SPECIAL DRILLS FOR CUT-OFF PLAY PROCEDURE

(Note Drills: Catcher—140; First Base—164-C&D, 170; Second Base—173-D; Shortstop—186, 189-E; Third Base—207-E.)

46. BUNT DEFENSE

PURPOSE

To acquaint the team with all possible bunting situations and to develop competency in defense against the bunts.

PROCEDURE

Place the entire defensive team on the field and use base runners for bunting plays. Have the pitcher throw a ball to the catcher. The coach rolls a different ball to the area for the bunt. Set up all bunting situations, calling the play for the ball which is put into play. In all bunting situations, in order to predetermine whether the batter might be bunting, the pitcher assumes his set stance. Then he either backs off the rubber or throws to first. In either case the batter, if bunting, may make some move to tip off the bunt. (Note Drills: Shortstop—191; Third Base—203, 204; First Base—168, 169-A; Second Base—176; Catcher—143, 145-D, Outfield—223, 223-B; Pitcher—105.)

47. GENERAL PICK-OFF PLAYS

PURPOSE

To teach the players how to make a pick-off play, not necessarily to pick a runner off, but to show it to the opposition to keep them honest.

PROCEDURE

This drill is worked best by putting all players in their respective positions. Runners should be placed in desired positions for the pick-off play. When the pick-off is attempted, all players must assume their proper positions for backing up the play. If a runner is picked off, let the play continue until he is safe or out. This is good rundown practice.

Be sure that the pitcher and the player making the pick-off give each other a sign. It would be wise to cue the other players in on the signs so that they can ready themselves to back up the play.

In picking a runner off second base, when the pitcher makes the throw, two methods are used—the *daylight* and the *count* methods:

1. *Daylight method:* The pitcher takes his stretch, looks toward second. After he sees daylight between his shortstop and the runner as the shortstop breaks for the bag, he looks back at home and immediately whirls and throws to second base for the pick-off.

2. *Count method:* The pitcher looks at the runner, looks toward the plate, counts 1-2, and throws to second on 3. The shortstop breaks for second as soon as the pitcher turns his head toward home.

The catcher's pick-off play should also be explained here. This play can be used with a runner on any base. The pitcher checks his runners, then delivers his pitch, which should be a pitch-out. When the ball is 12 to 15 feet in front of the plate, the player to whom the ball will be thrown breaks toward the base and waits for the throw from the catcher. (For more about pick-offs, see Pitching Drill No. 122, Second Baseman—185; Shortstop—196; Third Baseman—208; Catcher—132-A, 135; First Baseman—169).

48. ONE PITCH—SIX OUTS

PURPOSE

To improve fielding when there are numerous base runners. It sets up natural play situations and should be used during the first and second weeks of practice out-of-doors.

PROCEDURE

Except for the following, baseball rules are in effect:

a. The pitcher is on the offensive side; that is, he throws the batter a good ball to hit.

b. There are six outs instead of three for the team at bat.

c. Only one pitch is thrown to each batter. He is out if he takes the pitch without swinging, fouls it, or is put out by a defensive player. He is safe on a hit or an error. The defensive player making the play calls the outs and safes.

d. Runners stay on base until all six outs are made, thus setting up more defensive plays.

49. TWO PITCH—SIX OUTS

This game is utilized at the beginning of the third week of practice and should be played occasionally between regular games. It speeds up the number of innings, thus allowing more play in game-type situations.

Two pitch is played exactly as one pitch, except that the hitter does not have to swing at the first pitch if he does not like it. If he takes it, he must swing at the second pitch, or he will be called out. There is an opportunity to get a better ball to hit with two pitchers. By having to swing at the second pitch, they get good hit and run practice.

50. FULL COUNT—SIX OUTS

This team drill is played with baseball rules except for two differences. There are six outs instead of three and the defensive players act as umpires. The catcher calls balls and strikes, the infielders call outs and safes at the bases, and the outfielder can call balls deep down the foul line. It gives the players game-like conditions. Runners stay on base until all six outs are made, thus setting up more defensive plays.

The other important difference is that the team at bat gets six outs each inning before being retired. By allowing the offensive team six outs, more innings can be played; pitchers do not have to warm up as often, and both teams get more fielding chances and times at bat. The pitchers have more opportunities to make the important double play.

51. THREE BALLS AND TWO STRIKES

This game can be played with three or six outs. There are some high school conferences that use these counts to play regulation games. They say it makes batters swing and pitchers concentrate on getting the ball over. It also makes the game move faster. However, pitching statistics can be misleading when compared to the regulation statistics where the four balls and three strikes are used.

52. TWO STRIKES AND ONE BALL—SIX OUTS
by Ray Borowicz

We have been using this drill for some 15 years. Regular batting prac-tice is boring and non-productive and worse yet becomes a breeding place for bad habits, does not foster concentration, and brings on the use of mechanics different from those used in games, particularly against "lollipop pitches."

Our squad usually numbers 18 to 20 and generally at least six of these are pitchers. We select three squads of four each (need a minimum of four on each squad). In picking the three squads we try to balance them evenly with batting ability. Two catchers (a minimum) are never placed on the same squad; use two sets of catching gear to speed changing "sides." To begin, squad one stays in to "hit" and squads two and three take the field filling in the defensive spots. (We do *not* use pitchers in the field *unless* they play on days that they don't pitch).

The "Two and One" practice begins. The squad hitting gets three outs, and each hitter starts out with a two-balls, one-strike count (if he takes a strike he is automatically out, thus we encourage aggressiveness at the plate). One of the managers serves as umpire. The pitcher throwing first has warmed up on the side and is ready to go (a pitcher that follows warms up appropriately since we count pitches and replace the pitcher immediately after the number of pitches scheduled for the day is reached). While the squads change sides, the pitcher stays on the mound continually until replaced. After three outs, the second squad comes in to hit and after they use up three outs, squad three comes in to hit. After squad three makes three outs, squad one comes in to hit again and we keep repeating the cycle—sides are changed on the double (this hustle in changing sides is carried over to our games). In an hour and a quarter, each hitter can get in over five to six at-bats at a minimum and it is game-like conditions for all.

53. TWELVE-MAN GAME   by Bill Wilhelm

For the coach who wishes to play an intra-squad game and does not have the full number of 18 players, it is possible to play what we call a 12-man game. Divide your 12 defensive players, not including pitchers, into groups A, B, & C. Be careful to put catchers in different groups and at least five right-handed throwing infielders into groups of two for team A, two for team B, and one for team C.

You will find you have four offensive players to bat and eight defensive players playing a position that they could likely play sometime during your season. Team "A" is at bat as combination of team "B" and team "C" takes the field. Team "A" bats until they make three outs and then they assume a defensive position while the four players from team "B" become offensive players. Now the defensive team is team "A" and team "C." This practice continues as team "C" gets their turn at bat and can continue indefinitely.

Since pitchers are no longer offensive players in college, they are naturally excluded from hitting, but instead alternate on the mound getting three outs.

This is a good way to have a scrimmage game when you are short of players and it serves other purposes as well. First, in such a game lasting two hours, 12 offensive players will get to bat 50 percent more than if 18 players were coming to bat. Second, on defense some versatility is likely to be developed that may be very beneficial later. Third, hitters have the opportunity to see more different pitchers and pitchers have the opportunity to pitch to more different batters.

There may be some poor features to this drill, such as one group of four having to stay an unusually long time in the field or if you have only two catchers, one of them necessarily working two-thirds of the time on defense. There is also often the need for one of the offensive players to take the place of a defensive player who is scheduled to bat.

All in all, however, we have found this to be a very practical way of playing an intra-squad game when actually the required number of personnel are not available.

54. MULTI-PURPOSE DRILLS   by Richard "Itchy" Jones

Baseball practice should be very well organized and a coach should get as much out of his practice with his team as possible. I try to incorporate in our drills more than one execution at a time.

I am going to present a drill that we start practice with and that our players really like. The coach can utilize his entire team at one time and it serves as a meeting together period for practice. We call this drill the mass drill. Each player goes to his position and there may be more than one person per position. Two fungo hitters are used for the outfield. One down the left field foul line and one down the right field foul line. Shaggers are also with the fungo hitters. This drill is used almost every day for approximately 20 minutes. Five minutes is allotted for the four separate phases. (THE FUNGO HITTERS ALTERNATE SO THAT BOTH DO NOT HIT AT THE SAME TIME.)

Phase I

1. Fungo hitters hit directly to the infielders they are facing and the infielders throw the ball to the shagger who is catching for the fungo hitter who hits the ball.

Phase II

1. Third basemen field ground balls and throw to first base.
2. The shortstops field grounders and feed the second basemen who throw to first to complete the double play.
3. Second basemen work on their pivot.
4. First basemen work on their footwork and taking throws at the first base.

Phase III

1. The third basemen now field grounders and throw to the second basemen for the double play.
2. The shortstops are now fielding grounders and throwing across the diamond to the first basemen.
3. Second basemen are working on their footwork at second and taking throws from the third basemen.
4. First basemen are taking throws from the second basemen and the shortstops.

Phase IV

1. The third basemen will charge ground balls and throw to the plate for a force-out or tag play.
2. The shortstops are taking throws from the second basemen and first basemen and relaying the throw to first base to complete the double play.
3. Second basemen and first basemen are feeding the shortstops for double plays.

While the infielders are working on this drill for 20 minutes the outfielders are working on the following:

Charging ground balls.

Shagging fly balls and line drives to their left, right, and with their back to the infield. After fielding the ball they try and hit a cut-off man who is approximately 150 feet from the fielder.

During this 20 minutes, the catchers are working on their hitting in the batting cages, on pop flies and on blocking pitches.

At the completion of this drill we feel that all our players are good and loose and have had an opportunity to improve their defensive skills. The pitchers are the fungo hitters, serve as catchers, extra first basemen and shaggers during the mass infield-outfield drill.

55. SHORT HOP   By Moby Benedict

All you need for this drill is a solid wall, two or three players with fielder's gloves and a ball.

PURPOSE

To teach the players, particularly infielders, how to field the high-bouncing ball on a short hop.

PROCEDURE

One player stands close to the wall and throws the ball on the dirt or floor close to the wall. The ball hits the dirt or floor, rebounds against the wall, and bounces high in the air toward the other player. This player positions his body in front of the ball and allows the ball to make contact with the dirt or floor before he attempts to catch it. The ball must be fielded as close to the surface as possible, thus called the short hop. Fielding the ball a foot or more above the surface is not correct. It is fielded only inches off the surface. Never catch the ball in the air while using this drill.

56. BASEBALL GAME IN A TUNNEL BATTER CAGE
by Frank Pellerin

We have devised a game that is very beneficial to our overall program. It not only helps us to select and teach but also acts as a conditioning program at the same time.

To use this program you need a tunnel batting cage. Also, it is necessary to have a good indoor mound. We use the plastic molded type for ease in handling. It would also be advisable to have a protective screen for the pitcher.

The program was originally designed for pitchers but we found that there were many other benefits:

1. Pitchers and catchers get together on signals.
2. Batters learn their strike zone.
3. Catchers learn pitchers' strengths and weaknesses.
4. All players are hitting or pitching under pressure and as near game conditions as possible.

This program takes six weeks, therefore, starts six weeks prior to our first game and must be run on a schedule that has as few interruptions as possible. Due to space and time limitations, we start our program by rotating

16 pitchers. When our program is finished, we have eight varsity pitchers and eight junior varsity pitchers.

First Week

Pitchers and Catchers report for easy throwing and drills. They are informed that they have two weeks to get ready to pitch two innings or 30 pitches twice a week with two days rest. They are to work at their own pace and are never to throw hard if their arms are sore.

Second Week

Pitchers throw to hitters in cage with a catcher to get used to the mound and throwing in the cage. Fielding and pick-off drills are practiced.

Third Week

Pitchers are divided into two groups of eight. Group "A" will pitch on Tuesday and Friday. Group "B" will throw on Monday and Thursday. First two pitchers warm up together to simulate game conditions. Pitcher "A" enters cage with catcher and batter while pitcher "B" puts on jacket and observes. Pitcher "A" pitches to batter, catcher calls balls and strikes, fair and foul hit balls. If fair ball is hit, coach calls out or hit. Each batter gets three consecutive outs. Pitcher "B" enters cage after three outs while pitcher "A" observes. Each pitcher throws two innings or approximately 30 pitches. We do not like our pitchers to throw more than 15 pitches per inning. There are no extra base hits or errors. Runners are assumed to be on base and move up one base at a time on hits and walks.

Fourth Week

Same procedure only each pitcher throws three innings or 45 pitches.

Fifth Week

We now break into three groups of four pitchers each, as time will not allow us to continue with 16. We also start Saturday practice; our groups now go Monday and Thursday, Tuesday and Friday, and Wednesday and Saturday. We will throw five innings or 75 pitches this week.

Sixth Week

Same procedure, but we now throw seven innings or 105 pitches. We are now ready to go to spring training or to start the season. We have 12 pitchers who can go at least seven innings. Some have gone 10 or 11 innings our first day outside. This program will tell you which pitchers can pitch on a regular basis without sore arms. Incidentally, we have very few sore arms with this program. We feel that before you can consider a pitcher he must be able to do it quantitatively. Now we look at the quality. Our pitching statistics include innings pitched, hits, runs, strikeouts, walks or hit batsmen, wild pitches and earned run averages. These things should give the coach a good idea as to which pitchers can do the job. It is important to have the same coach or person do the judging on the hitting. This way you get a constant judgment even though you get some disagreement from the players.

Our hitting statistics include—at-bats, hits, strikeouts, walks and batting averages. We cannot allow bunting. We have very good correlation between the pitchers and batters who do the job inside with those who do the job outside.

This is one of the fairest methods we have found for evaluating our players. Try it, you'll like it. It is an excellent place to instruct or coach the players under game-like conditions.

57. GETTING THE MOST OUT OF A DAY'S PRACTICE
by Ken Perrone

PURPOSE

Winning games comes from being well organized and keeping everyone active. To organize practice and make it work, the coach and players must believe in their potential ability, work with enthusiasm and believe in organization. This is a selling job on the part of the coach. You are a teacher, salesman and coach. Believe it and work with enthusiasm.

PROCEDURE

I try to keep everybody busy every minute of the two-and-one-half to three hours of practice as follows:

3:00 p.m.

      a. Loosen Up—1) Exercises, 2) Throwing
      b. Play Pepper
      c. Condition Drill Pick-ups
      d. Ball-in-Dirt Drill

3:15 p.m.

SQUARE DRILLS FOR GROUND BALLS

      a. Catchers practice throws from home to second base.
      b. Pitchers and extra outfielders hit fungos or shag for fungo hitters.
      c. Fungo hitters hit to infielders in their positions. Each position has a

fungo hitter. The first baseman's fungo hitter is down the third base line about 20 feet from home plate. The third baseman's fungo hitter is about 20 feet down the first base line. The shortstop's fungo hitter is down the first base line about 55 feet. The second baseman's fungo hitter is about 55 feet down the third base line.

Each infielder is backed up by at least one outfielder. The fungo hitter hits ground balls to the infielder who fields the ball and throws it back to the fungo hitter's shagger. Outfielders back up for missed ground balls.

3:30 p.m.

FLY BALL SQUARE DRILL

Keep the players in the same position but hit fly balls to the outfielders. The outfielders catch the ball and throw it in to the infielders who act as cut-off men. The infielder relays the ball to the shagger of the fungo hitters.

3:35 p.m.

INFIELDERS SLOW ROLLER DRILL

Coach stands at home plate with a catcher. Infielders are in their proper positions. All other players assemble at home plate area.

One extra player stands in left-hander's batting box and breaks for first base as the coach hits the slow roller to the third base area. Third baseman fields the slow roller and attempts to throw out the runner. First baseman throws ball back to catcher for the coach.

Next extra player steps in batter's box and runs to first as the coach hits a slow roller to shortstop area. Shortstop attempts to throw out the runner. First baseman returns the ball to the catcher for the coach.

Next player steps in batter's box and runs to first as the coach hits a slow roller to second base area. Second baseman attempts to throw out the runner. First baseman returns the ball to the catcher for the coach.

Next player, with a pitcher on the mound, steps in the batter's box and runs to first as the coach hits a slower roller to the first baseman. The pitcher covers first for the put out at first.

If you have more than one infielder for a position, hit balls to the rest of the fielders in that position before you hit to the next position. The first baseman or first basemen, if more than one is in that position, should be taught the proper footwork on these throws.

3:50 p.m.

INFIELDERS DOUBLE PLAY SQUARE DRILL

    a. Catchers work at the backstop on ball-in-dirt drill.

    b. Pitchers out in first base foul area play pepper.

c. Outfielders out in third base foul area play pepper.

d. Infielders pair off as shortstops and second basemen. Each base is assumed to be a second base. You have a shortstop and a second baseman at first, at second, at third and at home plate. They all face the mound.

Each second baseman rolls a ball to the second baseman diagonally opposite him across the pitcher's mound. That second baseman flips the ball to his shortstop who throws the ball counterclockwise around the baseline to the other second baseman who is assuming the position of a first baseman to complete the double play.

After five minutes, the same procedure is used to make a double play, but the shortstop throws diagonally across the infield to the other shortstop who flips to the second baseman, who throws counterclockwise around the baseline to the shortstop to complete the double play. This lasts for five minutes.

4:00 p.m.

PITCHERS AND INFIELDERS IN POSITION

a. Pitchers field ball hit to them and throw to bases. Concentrate on pitchers using crow hop to throw to bases. Infielders cover the bases.

b. Catchers roll out with ball and call bases for pitchers to throw.

c. Outfielders work on pop-ups.

4:05 p.m.

PICK-OFFS AND RUN DOWNS

a. Two groups work on run downs, one between first and home and one between third and home.

b. Pitchers work on pick-off plays at second base.

c. With runners on third and first, have pitchers practice defense of double steal.

1. Pitcher steps back off rubber.

2. Back off the rubber and fake throw to first, whirl and check third or throw to third for pick-off.

3. If runner breaks from first, check the runner on third, whirl and throw to second base.

4. The second baseman or shortstop runs runner back to first but never takes his eye off the runner on third. First baseman follows the runner stealing second to get a short rundown. Don't follow too closely.

4:25 p.m.

OFFENSE

Keep two running groups, one at first and one at third.

a. Delayed steal—break just as the catcher makes the catch. Go full speed and slam on the brakes about fifteen feet from second base. If there is a play on you, attempt to get in a run down. If no play, go into second base.

b. Walk off steal—break when the pitcher takes his first look at you. Slam on brakes after ten-foot break. Get in run down. This will allow runner on third an opportunity to steal home.

c. First-and-second steal (hoping to set up a first-and-third situation).

1. Man on first breaks toward second as the pitcher releases the ball. He slams on the brakes after ten feet and scrambles back toward first attempting to draw the throw from the catcher. Runner slams on brakes short of first base so he cannot be tagged by first baseman.

2. The runner on second base takes a good lead and breaks for third as soon as the catcher releases the ball toward first base for the pickoff.

3. If the man on first gets caught in a run down, we then treat it as a first-and-third situation. Runner on third breaks for home when he has the infielder with the ball at a disadvantage such as a left-handed first baseman running toward second at full speed.

4:35 p.m.

PRE-GAME INFIELD-OUTFIELD DRILL

Take a regular infield-outfield practice every other day. Alternate every other practice using situation drills. Situations—use pitchers and extra players for runners. Set up defensive team.

a. No one on base, hit to right, left and center.
b. Runner on first, hit to all fields.
c. Runner on second, hit to all fields.
d. No one on base, extra base hit to all fields.
e. Runner on third, fly out to all fields.
f. Runners on first and third, deep fly to all fields.
g. Double plays.

1. Pitcher to second to first.
2. Pitcher to third to first.
3. Pitcher to home to first.

    h. Priority drill on pop flys and outfield-infield fly balls.

    i. Throwing procedure after an out.

       1. Strikeout—first to second to shortstop to third to catcher to first.

       2. Ground out—first to catcher to second to shortstop to third to catcher to first.

       3. Fly out—to relay man and around infield as above.

4:50 p.m.

BUNTING—Four Areas for Bunting

Put bunters at home, at first, at second and at third. Each bunter has a pitcher throwing to him. The pitchers stand near the pitching mound. Each bunter has two fielders to bunt to. If catchers are available you can have a catcher in full gear for each bunter. Catchers should catch with one hand only. Bunts are too easily fouled, which can injure the bare hand.

5:00 p.m.

SUICIDE BUNTING

Discuss proper time of breaking from second and third. Put all bunters at home plate and runners on second and third. Have a complete defensive infield including a catcher and pitcher. Players should switch positions as fielders, pitchers, runners and bunters.

The pitcher throws the pitch to the bunter and the suicide action takes place. Infielders cover the bases, runners move up as timed with the pitch, bunter bunts ball, pitcher breaks in as do the third baseman and first baseman. Catcher covers home and calls the play. The best timing for the runner's break from a base on a suicide bunt is to break when the pitcher's striding foot hits the ground.

Alternate this suicide drill with the defensive play of the third baseman and pitcher on bunts with first and second occupied.

5:10 p.m.

END PRACTICE WITH BASE RUNNING

Players take turns acting as base coaches.
    a. Close play at first.
    b. Round the base.
    c. Extra base hit.
    d. Hook slide at second.
    e. Pop-up slide at third.
    f. Head first slide at home.
    g. Catchers blocking plate at home. Caution players not to hit catcher hard. Teach catcher how to give base runner part of the plate and have runners slide for that area of plate.

Note: Twice a week review signals for:

a. Straight steal.
b. Delayed steal.
c. Walk-off steal.
d. Walk steal—steal as pitcher starts his set motion.
e. First and second double steal.
f. First and third double steal.
g. Suicide bunt.
h. Bunt.
i. Take.
j. Hit.
k. Hit and run.

58. KEEPING A TEAM SHARP FOR TOURNAMENT PLAY
by Hal Smeltzly

The intra-squad game is an integral part of every coach's practice plan. In most cases it is used to get a team ready for the season, or is occasionally used during the season when there is a break in the schedule and there is a need to have all of the players get in action.

Here at Florida Southern we have had the good fortune to be in a number of post-season tournaments. The Modified Intra-squad Game that is described was developed and used to keep our team sharp and ready for tournament play. We feel it has been a major factor in our winning 5 out of 7 Regional Championships and 3 out of 5 National Championships.

THE MODIFIED INTRA-SQUAD GAME

PURPOSE

The situation that prompted development of the modified intra-squad game format was simply that with 5 or 6 pitchers in a squad of 21, we had to play pitchers with no defensive ability in various positions in order to have two full teams. A modified intra-squad game took care of the problem of having balanced teams without using pitchers in the lineup, unless of course they have defensive skill. Pitchers will face every player in the game and can work as many innings as needed under normal game conditions.

PROCEDURE

First, I suggest that you develop a flow chart (see example below). From this chart you can develop all of the options that you feel are possible with the talent you have on the team. List players by position and in the order of their skill at that position.

DEFENSIVE FLOW CHART

1st	2nd	SS	3rd
Bahns	Stevens	Krinchicki	Hassey
Hassey	Strain	Strain	Strain
Clopton	Carsley	Stevens	Carsley
Powers		Carsley	Allenson

	OUTFIELD		CATCHERS

Left	Center	Right	Gustavson
Kemp	Stegman	Clopton	Allenson
Stephenson	Clopton	Kemp	Hassey

The second step is placing a defensive team on the form. (Note Illustration No 19.) Take four remaining players and make an offensive team out of them. The offensive team stays at bat for three outs. Try to use the players in this first offensive team who will be used in the second defensive team. Continue making up defensive teams until you have been able to work every player into at least one offensive team (See Illustration No. 19.) In the illustration you can see that each player will come to bat at least six times. You can work pitchers in as many innings as you think are necessary. In addition, you have an opportunity to put together defensive combinations that may be used in an actual game. The form allows you to keep as detailed an account as you need to accomplish your practice objectives.

This game was used to condition the 1975 United States Pan American Games team. The names of the players used here were members of the Pan American Team in Mexico City. (Note Form Illustration No. 19.)

Illustration No. 19

MODIFIED INTRA-SQUAD

DRILL NO. 58

START	Defensive Team			Offensive Team			
	E / A		E / A		H / BB / K / SB		
1 Bahns	/	Pitcher	/	1. Kemp	/	/	/
2 Stevens	/	Catcher Gustavson	/	2. Allenson	/	/	/
SS Krinchicki	/	Inning 1	/	3. Strain	/	/	/
3 Hassey	/	Number of Pitches		4. Carsley	/	/	/

Defensive Team		Offensive Team

LF Stephenson / F__ C__ CH____	TOTALS / / /
CF Stegman / SL__ TOTAL____	RUNS SCORED _____
RF Clopton /	

	E / A		E / A		H / BB / K / SB
1	Powers	/ Pitcher	/	1. Stevens	/ / /
2	Strain	/ Catcher Gustavson	/	2. Stegman	/ / /
SS	Krinchicki	/ Inning 1	/	3. Hassey	/ / /
3	Carsley	/ Number of Pitches		4. Bahns	/ / /
LF	Kemp	/ F__ C__ CH		TOTALS / / /
CF	Stephenson	/ SL__ TOTAL____		RUNS SCORED _____
RF	Clopton	/		

	E / A		E / A		H / BB / K / SB
1	Hassey	/ Pitcher	/	1. Gustavson	/ / /
2	Stevens	/ Catcher Allenson	/	2. Krinchicki	/ / /
SS	Strain	/ Inning 2	/	3. Clopton	/ / /
3	Carsley	/ Number of Pitches		4. Stephenson	/ / /
LF	Kemp	/ F__ C__ CH		TOTALS / / /
CF	Stegman	/ SL__ TOTAL____		RUNS SCORED _____
RF	Bahns	/		

	E / A		E / A		H / BB / K / SB
1	Bahns	/ Pitcher	/	1. Kemp	/ / /
2	Stevens	/ Catcher Allenson	/	2. Gustavson	/ / /
SS	Krinchicki	/ Inning 2	/	3. Strain	/ / /
3	Hassey	/ Number of Pitches		4. Carsley	/ / /
LF	Stephenson	/ F__ C__ CH		TOTALS / / /
CF	Stegman	/ SL__ TOTAL____		RUNS SCORED _____
RF	Clopton	/		

	E / A		E / A		H / BB / K / SB
1	Powers	/ Pitcher	/	1. Stevens	/ / /
2	Strain	/ Catcher Gustavson	/	2. Stegman	/ / /
SS	Krinchicki	/ Inning 3	/	3. Hassey	/ / /
3	Carsley	/ Number of Pitches		4. Bahns	/ / /
LF	Kemp	/ F__ C__ CH		TOTALS / / /
CF	Stephenson	/ SL__ TOTAL____		RUNS SCORED _____
RF	Clopton	/		

	E / A		E / A		H / BB / K / SB
1	Hassey	/ Pitcher	/	1. Allenson	/ / /
2	Stevens	/ Catcher Gustavson	/	2. Krinchicki	/ / /
SS	Carsley	/ Inning 3	/	3. Clopton	/ / /
3	Strain	/ Number of Pitches		4. Stephenson	/ / /

Defensive Team				Offensive Team			
LF Kemp	/	F C CH		TOTALS	/	/	/
CF Stegman	/	SL TOTAL		RUNS SCORED			
RF Bahns	/						

		E / A		E / A	H / BB / K / SB			
1	Bahns	/	Pitcher	/	1. Kemp	/	/	/
2	Stevens	/	Catcher Allenson	/	2. Gustavson	/	/	/
SS	Krinchicki	/	Inning 4	/	3. Strain	/	/	/
3	Hassey	/	Number of Pitches		4. Carsley	/	/	/
LF	Stephenson	/	F C CH		TOTALS			
CF	Stegman	/	SL TOTAL		RUNS SCORED			
RF	Clopton	/						

		E / A		E / A	H / BB / K / SB			
1	Powers	/	Pitcher	/	1. Stevens	/	/	/
2	Strain	/	Catcher Allenson	/	2. Stegman	/	/	/
SS	Krinchicki	/	Inning 4	/	3. Hassey	/	/	/
3	Carsley	/	Number of Pitches		4. Bahns	/	/	/
LF	Kemp	/	F C CH		TOTALS	/	/	/
CF	Stephenson	/	SL TOTAL		RUNS SCORED			
RF	Clopton	/						

		E / A		E / A	H / BB / K / SB			
1	Hassey	/	Pitcher	/	1. Allenson	/	/	/
2	Stevens	/	Catcher Gustavson	/	2. Krinchicki	/	/	/
SS	Strain	/	Inning 5	/	3. Clopton	/	/	/
3	Carsley	/	Number of Pitches		4. Stephenson	/	/	/
LF	Kemp	/	F C CH		TOTALS	/	/	/
CF	Stegman	/	SL TOTAL		RUNS SCORED			
RF	Bahns	/						

		E / A		E / A	H / BB / K / SB			
1	Bahns	/	Pitcher	/	1. Kemp	/	/	/
2	Stevens	/	Catcher Gustavson	/	2. Allenson	/	/	/
SS	Krinchicki	/	Inning 5	/	3. Strain	/	/	/
3	Hassey	/	Number of Pitches		4. Carsley	/	/	/
LF	Stevenson	/	F C CH		TOTALS	/	/	/
CF	Stegman	/	SL TOTAL		RUNS SCORED			
RF	Clopton	/						

		E / A		E / A	H / BB / K / SB			
1	Power	/	Pitcher	/	1. Stevens	/	/	/
2	Strain	/	Catcher Allenson	/	2. Stegman	/	/	/
SS	Krinchicki	/	Inning 6	/	3. Hassey	/	/	/

Defensive Team				Offensive Team			

3	Carsley	/	Number of Pitches	4. Bahns	/	/	/
LF	Kemp	/	F C CH	TOTALS	/	/	/
CF	Stevenson	/	SL TOTAL	RUNS SCORED			
RF	Clopton	/					

		E / A		E / A	H / BB / K / SB			
1	Hassey	/	Pitcher	/	1. Gustavson	/	/	/
2	Stevens	/	Catcher Allenson	/	2. Krinchicki	/	/	/
SS	Carsley	/	Inning 6	/	3. Clopton	/	/	/
3	Strain	/	Number of Pitches		4. Stephenson	/	/	/
LF	Kemp	/	F C CH		TOTALS	/	/	/
CF	Stegman	/	SL TOTAL		RUNS SCORED			
RF	Bahns	/						

		E / A		E / A	H / BB / K / SB			
1	Bahns	/	Pitcher	/	1. Kemp	/	/	/
2	Stevens	/	Catcher Gustavson	/	2. Allenson	/	/	/
SS	Krinchicki	/	Inning 7	/	3. Strain	/	/	/
3	Hassey	/	Number of Pitches		4. Carsley	/	/	/
LF	Stephenson	/	F C CH		TOTALS	/	/	/
CF	Stegman	/	SL TOTAL		RUNS SCORED			
RF	Clopton	/						

		E / A		E / A	H / BB / K / SB			
1	Powers	/	Pitcher	/	1. Stevens	/	/	/
2	Strain	/	Catcher Gustavson	/	2. Stegman	/	/	/
SS	Krinchicki	/	Inning 7	/	3. Hassey	/	/	/
3	Carsley	/	Number of Pitches		4. Bahns	/	/	/
LF	Kemp	/	F C CH		TOTALS	/	/	/
CF	Stephenson	/	SL TOTAL		RUNS SCORED			
RF	Bahns	/						

		E / A		E / A	H / BB / K / SB			
1	Hassey	/	Pitcher	/	1. Gustavson	/	/	/
2	Stevens	/	Catcher Allenson	/	2. Krinchicki	/	/	/
SS	Strain	/	Inning 8	/	3. Clopton	/	/	/
3	Carsley	/	Number of Pitches		4. Stephenson	/	/	/
LF	Kemp	/	F C CH		TOTALS	/	/	/
CF	Stegman	/	SL TOTAL		RUNS SCORED			
RF	Bahns	/						

		E / A		E / A	H / BB / K / SB			
1	Bahns	/	Pitcher	/	1. Kemp	/	/	/
2	Stevens	/	Catcher Allenson	/	2. Gustavson	/	/	/

	Defensive Team			Offensive Team			
SS	Krinchicki	/	Inning 8	/	3. Strain	/	/	/
3	Hassey	/	Number of Pitches		4. Carsley	/	/	/
LF	Stephenson	/	F C CH		TOTALS	/	/	/
CF	Stegman	/	SL TOTAL		RUNS SCORED			
RF	Clopton	/						

	E / A			E / A		H / BB / K / SB		
1	Powers	/	Pitcher	/	1. Stevens	/	/	/
2	Strain	/	Catcher Gustavson	/	2. Stegman	/	/	/
SS	Krinchicki	/	Inning 9	/	3. Hassey	/	/	/
3	Carsley	/	Number of Pitches		4. Bahns	/	/	/
LF	Kemp	/	F C CH		TOTALS	/	/	/
CF	Stephenson	/	SL TOTAL		RUNS SCORED			
RF	Clopton	/						

	E / A			E / A		H / BB / K / SB		
1	Hassey	/	Pitcher	/	1. Allenson	/	/	/
2	Stevens	/	Catcher Gustavson	/	2. Krinchicki	/	/	/
SS	Carsley	/	Inning 9	/	3. Clopton	/	/	/
3	Strain	/	Number of Pitches		4. Stephenson	/	/	/
LF	Kemp	/	F C CH		TOTALS	/	/	/
CF	Stegman	/	SL TOTAL		RUNS SCORED			
RF	Bahns	/						

59. CIRCLE DRILL   by Paul Tungate

PURPOSE

To encourage defensive players to stay down on ground balls. *Players Needed:* five or seven in a group (must be an odd number).

PROCEDURE

a. Players assume infielder's defensive stance. (Illustration No. 20.)

b. Give "A" the ball.

c. "A" throws ground ball to "C," then "C" throws ground ball to "E," and "E" throws ground ball to "B," then "B" to "D," then "D" back to "A." THIS DRILL CAN BE TIMED TO INCREASE SPEED

VARIATIONS

(I)

a. Give one ball to "A" and one ball to "B."

b. Follow same procedure as above except two balls are now involved

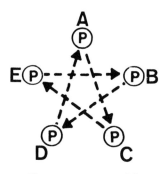

Illustration No. 20

creating more concentration on the part of the players. Start both balls at the same time.

c. Increase the number of balls as proficiency improves.

VARIATIONS

(II)

a. Proceed as in original drill except "A" throws ground ball to "C," "C" underhand tosses to "E" (toss as in a short to second double play, "E" throws ground ball to "B," "B" underhand tosses to "D," "D" throws ground ball to "A," "A" underhand tosses to "C," etc.

b. Increase the number of balls as proficiency improves.

VARIATIONS

(III)

a. Proceed as in original drill except players slide laterally in a clockwise or counterclockwise rotation. This will simulate going to right or left for ground balls.

b. Increase number of balls as proficiency improves.

60. UTILIZING SPACE AND TIME FOR COMPREHENSIVE PRACTICE DRILLS FOR 18 MEN   by Paul Tungate

PURPOSE

To keep everyone busy at the same time while utilizing a small area. *Players Needed* as follows: (Note Illustration No. 21.)

PROCEDURE

Assign and place all players to numbered circles as follows:

Player	Function
1	Batting
2	Swinging weighted bat
3	Bunting
4	Tossing to #3 (Use 3 balls)
5	Hitting line drives into net
6	Tossing to #5 (Use 3 balls)
7	Hitting line drives off knee into net
8	Tossing to #8 (Use 3 balls)
9	Feeding the pitching machine
10	Sliding on mat
11	Sliding on mat
12	Circle Drills
13	Circle Drills
14	Circle Drills
15	Circle Drills
16	Circle Drills
17	Throwing short hops to #18
18	Picking up short hops

a. Players stay at stations for five minutes and then rotate as follows:

Player #1 goes to position #18
Player #18 goes to position #17
Player #17 goes to position #16
Player #16 goes to position #15
Player #15 goes to position #14
Player #14 goes to position #13
Player #13 goes to position #12
Player #12 goes to position #11
Player #11 goes to position #10
Player #10 goes to position #9
Player #9 goes to position #8
Player #8 goes to position #7
Player #7 goes to position #6
Player #6 goes to position #5
Player #5 goes to position #4
Player #4 goes to position #3
Player #3 goes to position #2
Player #2 goes to position #1

b. At the end of 90 minutes, players have gotten in hitting, bunting, sliding and defensive fielding. This drill will give more hitting and fielding in 90 minutes than most practices will give in three hours.

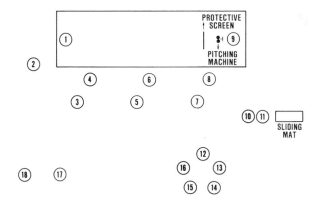

Illustration No. 21   Utilizing Space and Time
for Practice Drills for 18 Men

61. RUNDOWN DRILL   by Pat Daugherty

PURPOSE

To develop players offensively and defensively for rundown situations.

PROCEDURE

Using all players, place about five players in one line, five more in another line approximately 90 feet apart. You can run as many lines as you desire. Everyone keeps his glove on. We give a ball to the second man in one line and the first man becomes the base runner. The base runner takes a lead and the man with the ball yells "go" and the runner is chased hard by the man with the ball; the lead man at the front of the other line moves under control to shorten the rundown distance. When the runner is chased to a point of 12′ to 15′ in front of him, he yells "now" and the chaser gives him the ball and he makes the tag. After making the tag he flips the ball to the man behind him in his line and now becomes the base runner and the drill continues. (Note Illustration No. 22.)

There are some coaching points that are critical. When the chaser yells "go" to the runner, he must get either to the inside or outside of the imaginary baseline. Second, he must chase the runner as hard as he can run; no faking, just flat out running. He runs with the ball up in position so that when he gets the "now" command he can release the ball with a firm, accurate toss. The receiving man must come under control, but shorten the rundown distance as much as possible. He gets on the same side of the runner or the baseline that the chaser is on. When he sees the runner getting close enough (12′ to 15′), he

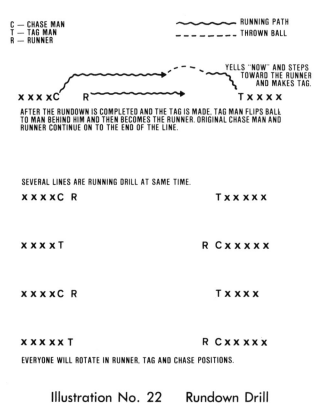

Illustration No. 22   Rundown Drill

screams ''now'' and at the same time takes a couple of controlled steps toward the runner, receives the ball and makes the tag. If executed properly, one throw will get the man.

We use this drill for five or ten minutes at the start of practice each day. We run three or four lines depending upon the size of the squad. One coach can do much coaching on rundowns with this drill. It is an excellent conditioning drill and there is very little standing around.

You can vary the drill by sending the runner hard. The man with the ball gets set and throws the ball to the receiver, simulating catcher's throw on a steal or a runner getting a great break, thus eliminating the initial chase.

62. PITCHER-INFIELD BASE RUNNING-FIELDING DRILL
by Ken Dugan

PURPOSE

To incorporate two game-like situations into one drill.

PROCEDURE

Put all your pitchers on the mound—one complete infield and catcher in position. Outfielders and extra players become base runners. Start the drill with a base runner-batter at home plate and a base runner on first base. There are two fungo hitters at home plate, one on the first base side who hits to that side and one on the third base side who hits to that side. They must coordinate their fungo hitting to hit at the same time.

The pitcher holds the runner close at first base and then throws to the catcher. As the ball passes over the plate, both fungos are hit simultaneously. The base runner-batter breaks for first, the pitcher covers first or fields the ball and throws to first. The third baseman or shortstop fields the ground ball and makes a play at second base on the runner advancing from first, who broke on the pitch to the plate.

CHAPTER **3**

BATTING DRILLS

Batting is one of the most important activities of any practice day and should take more time than any other activity. If a player has strength and works hard enough, he can improve his hitting. There are very few hitters who cannot be helped. These drills are designed to develop the individual in team practice and on his own time. During the off-season, numerous drills may improve a hitter, but when the season begins many, many swings at a ball are needed. Batting practice means exactly what it says. Pitchers must let the batter hit the ball in order to improve his timing and bolster his confidence. Working with a pitching machine is very valuable. A good machine should throw 95 percent strikes, throwing curves or fastballs.

One of the most important assets of a batter is knowing what to do when he is at bat. If he cannot hit well, he should learn to do other things such as bunt, hit behind the runner, spoil pitch-outs on stolen bases, help the runner on stolen bases and work the pitcher to tire him out and get a base on balls. These drills should help mentally as well as physically.

63. CHECKLIST FOR PROPER EXECUTION—BAT GRIP

(Note Screening Candidate Drill No. 246.)

Proper grip of the bat is probably one of the most overlooked procedures in hitting. When gripping the bat, the middle knuckles of both hands line up or are nearly lined up. (Note Illustration No. 23.) The middle knuckles of

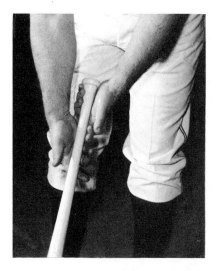 

Illustration No. 23   Bat Grip

the top hand can be lined up between the middle knuckles and the knuckles at the base of the fingers on the bottom hand.

The bat in the bottom hand (left hand for right-handed hitters) is held slightly diagonally and gripped with the fingers. The bat in the top hand is more or less straight through the hand much like the grip of a hammer, when swinging at the ball, and gripped with fingers. The pressure of the bat, when hitting the ball, is against the palm of the top hand just under the knuckle at the base of the index finger and in the cushion area between the thumb and index finger. It is practically the same grip as used on a carpenter's hammer.

The index fingers and thumbs are completely relaxed and held off the bat or very lightly against the bat. The grip prior to the swing is relaxed and with the middle, ring, and little fingers. When the swing is made, all fingers grip the bat firmly. At the start of the swing, the index fingers react like pulling the trigger of a gun, gripping the bat firmly.

64. BALL TOSS FUNGO BATTING

PURPOSE

To teach batters to extend their arms as the bat makes contact with the ball. This drill also gives them many swings and is good for quick reaction.

PROCEDURE

Needed for this drill are the following: a protective screen, two bats, an ample supply of baseballs, and two players. Tennis balls can be used also. A broomstick and plastic golf balls are ideal indoor practice items.

Illustration No. 24   Ball Toss Fungo Batting

The screen is set up about 10 feet from the batter. The other player, the feeder, kneels behind the screen and tosses balls overhand around its corner in such a way that they will enter the strike zone of the batter, who hits the ball. The batter should concentrate on a complete follow-through in his swing. (Note Illustration No. 24.)

A. On one knee. Right-hand batters kneel on the right knee and extend the left foot and leg out toward the pitcher. Left-handers kneel on the opposite knee.

B. For the first 25 to 30 balls tossed to him, the batter should use a 35-inch bat with a medium-sized handle. This bat should weigh about 50 ounces. Since the batter's arm should be fully extended when the bat contacts the ball, this big, heavy bat will force him to extend his arms and also help to develop the hitter's arms, forearms, and wrists.

C. For the next 25 to 30 balls tossed, the hitter should use his regular bat. However, the batter should continue to concentrate on extending his arms as the bat contacts the ball. This is a must for good hitting.

65. SOFT TOSS FROM SIDE DRILL   by Jim Frye

PURPOSE

To emphasize and teach the fundamentals of using the proper hip action, wrist alignment at contact, stroke angle and flight angle of the ball. This is our most often used hitting drill other than regular batting practice.

PROCEDURE

The feeder has a bucket of approximately three dozen balls and positions himself at about 45-degree angle from the hitter, and approximately 15 to 20 feet away from the hitter.

The hitter faces a net about 20 feet in front of him. This net has a white line horizontally about head high on it. He hits balls into the net as they are tossed softly underhanded to his strike zone by the feeder.

The feeder is on his knee as he tosses the balls. He watches the hitter reminding him not to hit the ball above the white line, and concentrate on line drives only.

We use the following progressions:

1. One-half bucket of balls using both hands with a regulation bat.
2. One-half bucket of balls with a 50-ounce bat for overload to increase bat strength and bat speed.
3. One-half bucket swinging a regulation bat in the top hand only, stressing bat control and wrist alignment.
4. One-half bucket alternating two strokes with the top hand and two strokes with both hands using a regulation bat.

66. SWING STRENGTHENER

Use Drills No. 13, 15, 18, 19, 20, 21, and 22.

67. DRY SWING TEAM BATTING   by Dick Siebert

PURPOSE

The development of the batter's ability to master different swings to meet a variety of pitches. It is especially valuable when no batting cage is available. This is one of our better full team pre-season batting drills.

PROCEDURE

Team members line up in a straight line with bats in hand, leaving sufficient room between batters for each to take a full swing without danger of hitting each other or each other's bats. Caution players about keeping hands dry to prevent bats from slipping out of their hands.

Stand behind the batters and call hypothetical pitches out loud to the batters such as "inside fast ball," "low outside curve," and "high fast ball." On your command, "ready, swing" each batter swings at the imaginary ball as though the pitch were thrown to him. Fifty to 60 swings should be sufficient. Remember to call every possible pitch the team might face.

68. MIRROR SWING

PURPOSE

To permit the batter to see his swing, check various phases of it, and by so doing, improve his swing. Constant practice can develop a more perfect swing.

PROCEDURE

The player stands in front of the mirror, facing it, and takes several practice swings, making them as natural as possible. He pays particular attention to wrist roll, level swing, eye movement, stride, arm, and head movement. However, he should try to watch only one thing at a time. In this manner, he tries to develop his swing to reach his maximum ability.

69. HANGING TARGET SWING AND STUFFED STOCKING

(Note Drill No. 19.)

70. BASEBALL BAT FIGURE EIGHT

(Note Drill No. 20, Illustration No. 20.)

71. SHADOW DRILL

PURPOSE

To teach players to swing at the ball without moving their heads forward or downward. Keeping the head and eyes on the ball in the swing is very important.

PROCEDURE

The hitter stands with his back to the late afternoon sun so that his shadow is cast on the ground in front of him. A spot is made on the ground where the shadow of the top of his head is cast. The player takes a normal swing with the bat. After the swing the player looks at his shadow to see if his head moved away from the spot. Although no movement is desirable, a small amount is not bad. The hitter continues to swing until he can swing normally with little or no movement of his head shadow.

Stand on the head shadow in order to note any movement and work with the player.

72. ISOMETRIC BAT DRILL

(Note Drill No. 21, Illustration No. 9.)

73. HIP ROTATION DRILL

PURPOSE

To teach the hitter hip rotation so that it becomes natural—a part of his complete movement in swinging at a pitched ball.

PROCEDURE

The batter assumes a normal batting stance. He places a bat behind him, horizontal to the ground, and locks it in position with the inner elbows. After the bat is in position, he turns his head and eyes and focuses on an object in the direction from which the pitch will come.

At this point he starts rotating his hip as far as possible: right-left or left-right determined by his swing, left or right-handed, keeping his head and eyes level and looking at the object selected as a ball thrown by the pitcher. His feet pivot as they would when swinging at a pitched ball. He does this 25 times in succession.

Next, taking the bat in his hands and assuming a batting stance, he incorporates a swing of the bat with the hip rotations, but he keeps his feet still. There would be 25 of these movements.

Finally, he takes 25 swings of the bat with good hip rotation and a normal batting stride.

74. BAT THROWING DRILL

PURPOSE

This drill is designed to improve the player's ability to literally throw the bat at the ball so that he will get more power into his swing. The drill should help the hitter to hit the long ball. It also gets the head of the bat out in front on the swing.

PROCEDURE

The player takes 10 to 15 old bats, with the knobs cut off, to the outfield for use in practicing the bat throwing. The knob ends, if left on, hurt the fingers when the bat is released. He must be sure that no one is on the field and that bats will not hit an object such as a post or fence. This drill can be used in a gym throwing into a net.

The batter takes a normal stance and loose grip on the bat. In order to get the best action in the swing of the bat, he should extend his arms and snap his wrists. After the wrists are snapped, the batter should release the bat so that it will fly into the field in the direction of an imaginary pitcher. If inside, it flies against or into a net.

This drill can be practiced daily. It is great to help one get out of a batting slump. The batter must be able to throw the bat with much force directly at the pitcher.

75. BREAKING FROM HOME

PURPOSE

To improve the hitter's technique and speed in breaking from home as soon as his swing is completed.

PROCEDURE

Line the team up near home plate, but caution your players to stay away from the area of a possible flying bat. As soon as a hitter finishes his swing, the next batter steps up to hit. Five or six rounds of this should be ample for one day of practice. Three or four days' practice of this drill should be sufficient during the early season.

The hitter takes his regular batting stance and breaks for first base at the crack of the bat on any hit ball—foul or fair. Time the runner to a mark half-way to first base. A right-handed hitter should strive for 2.5 seconds, a lefty should make it in two seconds.

Make every effort to get hitters to react quickly and break toward first as soon as the bat cracks. Some players would like to pause momentarily and admire their hit.

A defensive team can be used for this drill. Have the infield make plays only on ground balls. A pitching machine is best for this drill.

76. BATTING TEE

PURPOSE

To get extra work and swings in spare time.

PROCEDURE

The tee should be placed with the ball in front of home plate, either outside, inside, or center, but *never on* home plate. Hitters must learn to meet the ball in front of the plate.

The batting tee can be made by filling a 5-gallon oil can ¾ full of sand, placing one of three lengths of broomstick into the sand in an upright position, with a 6- to 8-inch radiator hose over the top of the broomstick. The ball is placed on top of the radiator hose. There should be three lengths of broomsticks: knee high, belt high, and letter high. Additional balls may be kept in the oil can for ready use.

When using the tee, balls can be hit against a canvas, mat, or hanging blanket, or they may be hit to a fielder. Some coaches use the tee to work infield and outfield drills. (Note Illustration No. 25.)

Illustration No. 25   Batting Tee Drill

77. PEPPER GAMES

(Note Drill No. 35.)

78. IMPROVING A POOR HITTER

PURPOSE

To develop the poor hitter. Since the inability to hit well usually is due to a combination of factors, all or some of the following drills should be used, many of them under your direction. The most common faults are taking the eye off the ball and overstriding. Use the following drills:

1. No. 13—Developing the Front Arm for Hitting
2. No. 19—Hanging Target Swing and Stuffed Stocking
3. No. 22—Hitting Tire
4. No. 63—Checklist for Proper Execution—Bat Grip
5. No. 64—Ball Toss Fungo Batting
6. No. 65—Soft Toss From Side
7. No. 68—Mirror Swing
8. No. 71—Shadow Swing
9. No. 74—Bat Throwing
10. No. 79—Place Hitting and Hit-and-Run Drill.

79. PLACE HITTING AND HIT-AND-RUN DRILL

PURPOSE

Although the principal purpose of this drill is to help the batter to come out of a slump due to some fault, such as overstriding or not keeping his eye on the ball, it is excellent as a drill for hit-and-run practice.

PROCEDURE

In his effort to hit to the opposite field, the hitter may choose one of the following methods:

A. He may swing late and hit the ball behind or over the plate, rather than in front of it, thus causing it to go to the opposite field.
B. The batter may step back from the plate (not toward the catcher) with his back foot, and then step in toward the pitch with his front foot, again meeting the ball over or behind the plate and hitting to the opposite field.
C. Luke Appling, the White Sox Hall of Fame player, in my estimation, was the best hit-and-run man ever to play baseball. Here is the method he explained to me. I found it very easy to learn and teach. (Note Illustration No. 26.)

Stand one foot from a net, screen or backstop. You then swing the bat as normally as possible into the screen and follow through on the swing. You will note that the hands will come through first and the barrel of the bat follows. After about 25 to 50 swings, you will begin to realize the action of the bat in the swing. You will feel the hands leading the head or barrel of the bat.

When you get this feeling, step away from the screen and take some normal swings at an imaginary ball. Then step up to the plate and attempt to use this knowledge to hit balls to the opposite field. If done correctly, you will not have to alter your foot stride from your natural stride. You will also note that the bat, when it meets the ball, is in about a 45-degree angle to the path of the ball, thus making the ball go to the opposite field. You will also note that you can hit the ball with power.

Illustration No. 26   Place Hitting and Hit-and-Run Drill

80. TEAM BATTING PRACTICE

PURPOSE

To have an organized system for holding batting practice.

PROCEDURE

A. *Early Season*. During the first few days the work should be on fundamentals, but no hard swings should be taken. The batters should be trying to get their eyes on the ball—a correct roll of the wrist and hips in the swing. Each player should take two bunts—one to first base area and one to the third base area, then five or six swings. They should rotate so that each player bats three or four times during the practice session, which should last for one hour. Pitchers should be included in this early batting practice if a designated hitter is not used in your conference.

B. *During Season*. During the season each player should take one or two bunts and four swings, then rotate so that each player gets in as many turns at bat as possible, still limiting the session to one hour. Pitchers scheduled to pitch the next day can be included in this drill if designated hitters are not used in your games.

If time does not permit a full round of four swings for the last turn, the number of swings should be cut. Perhaps a hit-and-run swing can be used here with each player getting several rounds. Some teams allow the batter to get an extra swing if he gets a hit when it gets down to one pitch or one swing per player.

Outfielders can start the batting practice, infielders next, and catchers next. They should rotate daily, thus cutting down arguments. Batting practice catchers run the practice by telling each hitter how many swings he has left.

81. BATTING PRACTICE DRILLS   by Demie Mainieri

PURPOSE

To teach bat control and concentration during batting practice. We find players do not concentrate and pick up bad habits in unorganized batting practice.

PROCEDURE

1. Each hitter lays down a bunt to third and a bunt to first. For each bad bunt, they lose one swing.

2. Each player has a given number of swings from 6 to 10.

    a. First two are hit-and-run with the runner stealing. The batter gives the hit-and-run sign to the runner and the runner answers it.

    b. The pitcher mixes in curves when the hitter is loose, however, not full speed.

    c. With a runner on third tell the hitter to score him. Remind the runner to tag on all line drives and fly balls and break toward home on all ground balls.

3. For the last two swings, the hitter goes to the opposite field. He continues to hit as long as he goes to the opposite field in fair territory.

CHAPTER **4**

BUNTING DRILLS

Bunting need not be a lost art; it merely takes time and work. The bunter must visualize the top half of the ball meeting the bottom half of the head of the bat, with the bat angled so as to bunt the ball near a foul line or in the area desired. He must also realize that being up in the front part of the batter's box gives him a better opportunity to bunt the ball into fair territory.

These drills teach angle of bunting, area of bunting, and the art of bunting. Some bunting can be practiced on the sidelines with other players. Pitchers in particular should learn to bunt if a designated hitter is not used in your conference. A sacrifice in the early innings may result in a run which will keep the pitcher in the game during the late innings. A poor-bunting pitcher will often be removed for a pinch-hitter.

82. CHECKLIST FOR PROPER EXECUTION

(Note Screening Candidates Drill No. 246.)

83. INSTRUCTIONAL BUNTING BAT FOR ALL BUNTING DRILLS

PURPOSE

To teach bunters how to bunt correctly, making the top half of the ball meet the bottom half of the head of the bat.

PROCEDURE

This bat is made simply by cutting away that portion of the bat facing the pitched ball which, if hit with the ball, would make a poor bunt and probably a pop-up. The part removed is part of the top and part of the bottom area around the trademark and the top half of the head of the bat. In order to get the feeling of normal weight, after the bat has been cut and shaped, bore a one-half-inch hole six to eight inches deep in the head end of the bat and fill it with lead. In order to keep the lead in and to prevent chipping, tape over and around the end of the bat. A nail or pin can be put through the bat and lead.

Practice with the bat causes the bunter to get on top of the ball. Bunters must be cautioned to keep the flat portion of the bat facing up and parallel with the ground at all times. (Illustration No. 27; Bat made by Worth Sports Co.)

Illustration No. 27   Instructional Bunting Bat

84. POSITION OF FEET AND BODY

PURPOSE

To develop in the players the habit of using the proper footsteps in the sacrifice bunt.

PROCEDURE

(The positions and the steps described are for the right-handed batter; those for left-handed batters are reversed.) The bunter should take a position in the batter's box up near the front of the box. The bunt will be more likely to be in fair territory.

A. *Square around* (Note Illustration No. 28). When the pitcher's striding leg comes up off the ground, the batter acts as though he intends to swing. Then, when the pitcher's striding foot strikes the ground, the batter should square around.

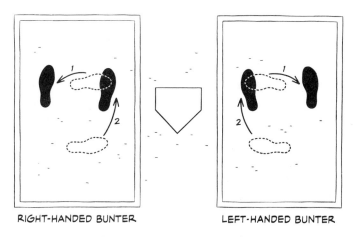

RIGHT-HANDED BUNTER   LEFT-HANDED BUNTER

Illustration No. 28   Square Around

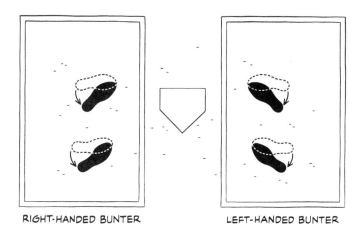

RIGHT-HANDED BUNTER   LEFT-HANDED BUNTER

Illustration No. 29   Pivot in Tracks

His left foot steps away from the plate and his right foot comes up parallel with his left, and he is facing the pitcher. The bunter's body is slightly crouched and his elbows are close to the body, relaxed. He has the bat held in front of him parallel to the ground. The bat is angled and gripped as described in Drill No. 85.

B. *Pivot in tracks* (Note Illustration No. 29). The bat position for the pivot-in-tracks is the same as in the square-around bunt position.

The batter remains in his tracks and on the balls of his feet. He pivots his hips, and his feet point toward the pitcher. His body faces the pitcher and he uses the same grip, angle, and bat position as in Drill No. 85.

85. ANGLE OF BAT

PURPOSE

To teach the bunter the proper angle to hold the bat in order to execute the perfect bunt.

PROCEDURE

Have each bunter take a turn at the plate and let him practice bunting until he appears to understand the proper angle to hold the bat.

The bat may be gripped by moving the top hand up near the trademark and bottom hand about four inches from the knob. (Note Illustration No. 30, Figure 1.) Or, it may be gripped by moving both hands up, holding the bat with the top hand about two inches from the trademark. (Note Illustration No. 30, Figure No. 2.)

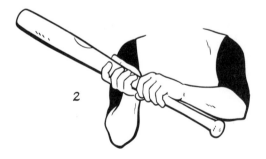

Illustration No. 30   Angle of Bat Drill

In the spread grip, the bottom hand holds the bat loosely and curls around the handle. The top hand cups the bat without curling the fingers around it. The grip is mostly with the thumb, index finger, and middle finger. The other fingers are tucked in and under the bat.

The two-hands-together grip has both hands gripped firmly but not tightly around the bat.

In all cases, hold the bat parallel to the ground, chest high and covering the plate, with elbows near the body. Let the ball contact the bat with the top half of the ball striking the bottom half of the "meat" of the bat.

A. *Right-handed hitter*

1. To first base area:
   Extend left arm and bend right arm. Get on top of the ball. (Note Illustration No. 31.) The bat should be held at about a 45-degree angle to the path of the ball.

Illustration No. 31   Illustration No. 32

2. To third base area:
   Point the head of the bat at the first baseman. The right arm is extended and the left arm crooked. (Note Illustration No. 32.) The bat should be held at about a 45-degree angle to the path of the ball.

B. *Left-handed hitter*

1. To first base area:
   The left arm is extended and the right arm crooked. (Note Illustration No. 33.) The bat should be held at about a 45-degree angle to the path of the ball.

2. To third base area:
   Point the handle of the bat at the first baseman, with the right arm extended slightly and the left arm crooked. (Note Illustration No.

Illustration No. 33   Illustration No. 34

34.) The bat should be held at about a 45-degree angle to the path of the ball.

86. SACRIFICE BUNTING TO PROPER INFIELD AREA

A. First Base Area:

PURPOSE

To develop bunting skills of players until they can bunt accurately into the first base area, thus taking advantage of a weak-fielding first baseman. This ability is also valuable when the third baseman is crowding the batter or when the first baseman is right-handed.

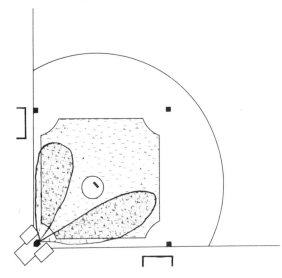

Illustration No. 35
Sacrifice Bunting

PROCEDURE

Give every player an opportunity to bunt 10 times in the drill.

1. Right-handed hitter: practice drill No. 85, A-1. (Note Illustration No. 35 for proper area.)
2. Left-handed hitter: practice drill No. 85, B-1. (Note Illustration No. 35 for proper area.)

Practice the drill until desired proficiency by players is attained.

B. Third Base Area:

PURPOSE

To develop the player's ability to bunt accurately and consistently into the third base area. Players bunt only strikes. A sacrifice bunt means exactly what it says; a bunter must sacrifice himself to make a good bunt.

PROCEDURE

Give every player an opportunity to bunt 10 times in this drill. (Note Illustration No. 35 for proper bunting area.)

1) Right-handed hitter: practice Drill 85, A-2.
2) Left-handed hitter: practice Drill 85, B-2.

Practice until desired proficiency by the players is attained.

87. STRINGS TO DENOTE PERFECT BUNTING AREA
by Ken Schreiber

PURPOSE

To designate the angle and area where we want bunts to be executed. Note that if you use this area indoors, you can use chalk to mark areas. (Note Illustration No. 36.)

PROCEDURE

Attach two strings approximately 70 feet long to nails. Drive one nail into the dirt at the first base corner of home plate, stretch the string out and drive the other nail in the turf approximately halfway between first base and the pitcher's rubber. Now drive a nail, attached to the other string at the third base corner of home plate, stretch that string out and drive the other nail into the turf approximately halfway between third base and the pitcher's rubber. This area is good for sacrifice bunts between the string and the foul line.

Now take a string and attach it to the two extending strings horizontally to home plate, 10 feet in front of home plate, and attach another string horizontally to home plate 25 feet from home plate. This area is the only safe area for sacrifice bunting if the ball is bunted back toward the pitcher. If the bunt goes beyond this area, the pitcher can possibly make a force play at second or third base. If the bunt does not get into this area 10 feet beyond home plate, the catcher can possibly make a force at second or third base.

We want the ball bunted on the grass of the infield in the designated area, except when we are practicing bunts for a base hit down the third base line. We then ask them to attempt to bunt down the line just fair. If it goes foul, you have another attempt to bunt or hit. If it stays fair, you have a base hit.

We use a pitching machine most of the time for this drill because we want accuracy in our pitches, thus saving time. We do, however, put a pitcher on the mound and use this drill for both offensive and defensive work.

We use the instructional bunting bat for this drill early in the season as described in Drill No. 83. (Note Illustration No. 27.) As we progress into the season, we use our regulation bats in order to get the proper feel of bunting.

We try to stress bunting the ball down the base line that the pitch dictates. For example, right-handed bunters bunt an outside pitch down the first base side and the inside pitch down the third base side.

We work on sacrifice, drag-push and suicide squeeze bunts and put runners on base to work on all game-like situations. However, we always discuss each situation and ask the bunter to place the bunt in the proper area. (Note Illustration No. 36.)

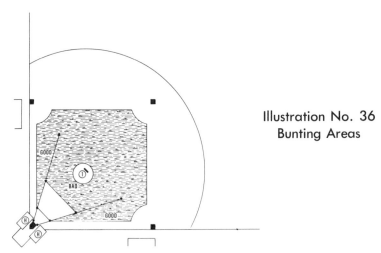

Illustration No. 36
Bunting Areas

88. BUNT FOR A BASE HIT—FIRST BASE AREA

PURPOSE

To teach batters the proper way to bunt for a base hit in the first base area.

PROCEDURE

Put the infield in position with a pitcher on the mound and a catcher behind the plate.

A. *Right-handed batter: the "push" bunt*. The batter stands at the plate, decoying a possible swing at the ball. As the pitcher cocks his arm in his delivery, the batter rotates his hips to the rear as if to take a full swing. When the ball is released by the pitcher, the batter takes a crossover step, stepping with his right foot toward the second baseman. As he steps, he also sets the angle of the bat with the end of the handle pointing halfway between third base and home plate. The batter must meet the ball before his right foot hits the ground. Holding the bat in this position, he "pushes" the ball past the pitcher and directly at the second baseman. (Note Illustration No. 37.)

Illustration No. 37   Illustration No. 38

B. *Left-handed batter: the "drag" bunt*. The batter stands at the plate, decoying a possible swing. As the pitcher cocks his arm in his delivery motion, the batter rotates his hips to the rear as though he would take a full swing. When the pitcher releases the ball, the batter takes a crossover step, stepping with his left foot over his right foot. As he steps, he also sets the angle of the bat so that the big end points halfway between third base and home plate. The batter should meet the ball before his left foot hits the ground. Holding the bat in the bunting position, the hitter "drags" the ball down the first base line with him, toward the second baseman, past the pitcher. (Note Illustration No. 38.)

89. BUNT FOR A BASE HIT—THIRD BASE AREA

PURPOSE

To develop hitter's ability to bunt safely to the third base area.

PROCEDURE

When bunting for a base hit, the batter should bunt the ball as close to the foul line as possible. If the ball stays fair along the foul line, the player's chances of reaching first base safely are much better than they would be if he bunted the ball into the middle of the infield. If the ball should roll foul, the hitter has another chance.

A. *Right-handed hitter.* The hitter takes his normal batting stance. As the pitcher releases the ball, the hitter rotates the upper part of his body clockwise and draws his bat back simulating a swing. When the ball is about 20 feet from the plate, the hitter sets his feet and bat into position.

He assumes this position by stepping one stride backward with his right foot; that is, to the left of home plate, not back toward the catcher. As this movement is made, the weight is shifted again to the right foot.

The bat is set into position by sliding both hands up the handle from 6 to 12 inches. The head of the bat points toward first base, and the handle of the

Illustration No. 39

Illustration No. 40

bat is slid between the hitter's right side and his right elbow. It is parallel to the ground and slightly above the right hip.

Some hitters like to have their hands separated when bunting. If this is the case, the right hand should slide about 10 inches while the left hand slides about 6 inches toward the head of the bat. (Note Illustration No. 39.)

B. *Another method of bunting for a hit*. Follow the same procedure as "A" above for the feet and body, except that the hands and bat are held in front of the body toward the pitcher. The hands are held either together or spread. The bat meets the ball in front of the plate at an angle, with the head of the bat pointed toward first base. The right foot steps toward the ball as the ball meets the bat. (Note Illustration No. 40.)

C. *Left-handed hitter*. The left-handed hitter follows the same procedure as the right-handed player until the ball is about 20 feet away, except that his body rotates counterclockwise.

He sets his feet in position by crossing the left foot over the right toward first base when contacting the ball. However, some hitters like to take a short step forward with the right foot prior to crossing over with the left foot. In order to get the bat into position, the left-hander slides his left hand up the handle of the bat 6 to 12 inches. The handle of the bat is pointed toward first base when the bunt is being made, and the handle should be held away from the body. The hands can be spread or held together. (Note Illustration No. 41.)

Illustration No. 41

90. THE SQUEEZE BUNT

PURPOSE

To develop the bunting skills of players so that they can lay down a bunt when needed with such accuracy that it will be away from the pitcher.

PROCEDURE

A. *Safety Squeeze*. Set up a game-like situation with defense in position and a runner on third. The pitcher takes a wind-up or a set stance, then throws to batter. The runner at third advances when the bunted ball is on the ground. He returns to third base on a missed ball or a pop bunt.

This is similar to a sacrifice bunt (Drill No. 86), but the main thing is to bunt the ball away from the pitcher. Bunt only strikes.

B. *Suicide Squeeze*. Set up the same situation as in the safety squeeze. The batter gives the runner the sign, and the runner acknowledges it. The batter *must* bunt the ball even if it is thrown at him, for this will protect the runner coming home from third base.

The ball is bunted anywhere on the ground, but the runner does not break for home until the pitcher strides and his foot hits the ground, just as his throwing arm and hand are by his head, in a vertical position. The runner breaks at that time, but *never before*.

Pitchers and weak hitters should do a lot of bunting of this type; however, all players should practice this bunt situation.

91. FAKE BUNT AND HIT

PURPOSE

To help players develop the ability to fake a bunt in a bunt situation; where the infield is in too close for safe bunting, swing instead of bunt.

PROCEDURE

The batter squares around to bunt or pivots in his tracks, as in Drill No. 84, to fake a bunt. The hands are together, but fairly high on the bat. As the pitcher releases the ball, the batter rotates his hips slightly toward the catcher and takes a short swing, stepping with his front foot toward the ball as he swings. The batter should never attempt to take a full swing because this may make him pop up or miss the ball.

92. FAKE BUNT AND STEAL

PURPOSE

To draw the infielders out of position and cause the catcher to lose sight of the ball.

PROCEDURE

On the pitch, the runner breaks for the advance base attempting to steal. The batter squares around as described in Drill 84. He lines up the bat for contact with the ball. Just as the ball approaches the bat, the batter raises it so that the ball passes just under the bat. This causes the catcher to lose the ball momentarily. Stay in this position after the catcher catches the ball. He will have to throw over your bat. Do not move in over the plate because the umpire may call you out for interference.

93. WET GROUNDS BUNTING TIME   by Ric Lessman

The idea of this drill is to practice the sacrifice bunt technique while practicing defensive positioning and movement against the sacrifice. The drill is actually played as a game with three outs to a half inning with the sides changing upon the completion of each half inning. As each inning begins, place runners on the bases related to a particular bunt situation. For example, an inning may begin with a runner on first, or runners on first and second, and at times a runner on third. Every hitter and every situation is played as a bunt situation regardless of the number of outs made. As outs are made through force outs, put outs at first, strikeouts or pop-ups, place new runners on the bases creating new situations.

An example of a typical half inning would be the coach places a runner on first—the pitcher makes a pitch to a hitter—who bunts the ball down the third base line. The third baseman fields the ball and throws the hitter out at first base. The runner on first base moves to second base on the sacrifice. Now, with an out and a man on second, the coach places another runner on first creating a first and second bunt situation. The pitcher makes the first pitch to the next hitter who bunts the ball down the third base line. The pitcher fields the ball and throws to the third baseman for a force out at third base.

With two outs, the coach now moves the runners to second base and third base. On the second pitch to the third hitter, the squeeze play is put on with the hitter bunting the ball to the pitcher whose only play is to throw to first base. This is the third out and the sides change. One bunting team can compete against another team.

This drill not only assists the team to develop offensive bunting skills and defensive bunt situations, but it gives hitters a look at live pitching and pitchers a chance to throw against hitters in a game situation. It also gives pitchers a chance to practice pitch placement to prevent a successful squeeze play. This bunting drill can also be used in the gym during cold weather and, of course, during the season on the regular playing field.

CHAPTER **5**

PITCHING DRILLS

Pitching is often said to be 75 percent of the game. With this in mind, pitchers must work hard to get in shape. Their arms are only as good as their legs. Pitchers do considerably more running than other players. They must gradually get their arms ready for the season, but should begin throwing a few hard ones early in the season. They should spin the ball for the curve ball the first day, but should not break it off for a fast curve. The following drills are designed for good conditioning and mastery of the mound.

94. CONDITIONING A PITCHER FOR COMPLETING A GAME   by Al Ogletree

PURPOSE

To condition the arm and body by using a set pattern or schedule for throwing, plus using drills to attain good physical stamina. We use drills as described in Drill No. 10 for long distance running. Drill No. 27 for dashes and wind sprints, Drills No. 2, 3, 5, 6, 7, 8, and 9 for stretching and finally use Drill No. 26 to work the pitchers up to 200 pick-ups a day.

PROCEDURE

First we sell our pitchers on the four "C's": 1) Control, 2) Confidence, 3) Conditioning, and 4) Command of Pitches. This starts our first day of practice. To start, the pitchers throw just five or six minutes each on the first

111

day. We increase this every day, just a little, throwing every day but not hard, just to get the muscles in shape. The pitchers work on control, form, and their follow-through. Maybe in a few days they will start pitching to two or three hitters, then go to three or four, then six or seven.

By the end of the second week we start playing intra-squad games. While we're throwing early, we have the pitchers just spin the ball to simulate a curve. If they are throwing just fast balls, their arms feel good, but they also need to get the curve ball muscles in condition since you use different muscles for the curve.

We work on both at the same time from the start, but early in the season we just spin the ball for the curve and don't try to snap it hard. When a pitcher starts throwing intra-squad games his first time out, we usually have him throw for six outs without leaving the mound. The defensive team changes every six outs, too, to go with the pitcher in these early games.

The second time they pitch intra-squad, they throw nine outs, but we change pitchers every three outs. We keep track of the number of pitches they throw. If they happen to be in trouble, we make a pitching change. The first time out we limit them to 30 to 35 pitches, the second time 45 to 50, the third time 60 to 65, the fourth time 75 to 80, and the fifth time 90 to 95 pitches—which is about seven innings.

When they finish on the mound, if they need to throw more, they do it on the side so they can stop when they feel they have thrown enough.

The conditioning pattern we use is this. Throw six outs, take a day's rest; throw nine outs. Now changing sides every three outs, take two days' rest; throw 12 outs, take three days' rest; throw 15 outs, three days' rest; then throw 18 outs, take three days' rest.

Roughly our schedule is to increase every two or three days what the pitcher throws by three outs. If you get up to five or six innings pitched in intra-squad games by the time the season starts, the other two or three innings (to seven or nine inning games) will come naturally.

We always have someone counting every pitch in intra-squad games and scheduled games. Any time the pitcher gets close to pitching the number of pitches mentioned above, we watch him very closely. If he gets in trouble, we have someone else ready to help him out.

During intra-squad games, I stand behind the mound with our young pitchers and usually go over things with them during the game. Between innings, or even the next day, I talk to them. You suggest things to them, to try this or that pitch and a reason for using it at that time. For example, not every pitcher throws a change the same way. One will use a slow curve for a change, another will take something off his fast ball. So a lot of coaching is suggestion and having the pitchers try it.

95. CHECKLIST FOR PROPER EXECUTION

(Note Screening Candidates Drill No. 246.)

96. SPOT CONTROL PITCHING DRILL

PURPOSE

To teach pitchers to throw at specific targets, and to develop their control so that they can hit their targets.

PROCEDURE

Place the pitcher on the mound and the catcher in his position behind the plate, or have them assume the proper distance for pitching along the side lines. The pitcher then throws at his catcher's left and right shoulders, left and right knees, at his chest, and finally at his glove. (Note Illustration No. 42.)

The catcher keeps track of the pitcher's hits and misses.

Illustration No. 42

97. STRING TARGET

PURPOSE

To develop good plate control.

PROCEDURE

Place two poles, similar to volleyball standards, four to five feet apart on either side of home plate, so that a string fastened to each pole will cross above the direct center of the plate. Tie three strings to the standards at different heights—one at armpit height, at waist height, and knee high respectively. At the center of the strings, directly over the center of the plate, tie a vertical string from the top horizontal string to the bottom one. Then, tie two other vertical strings so that one will come exactly to the edge of one side of home plate, and the other string will be at the opposite edge, making the distance between these outside strings the width of home plate.

This produces a window-type target at which the pitchers can throw. It is a large rectangle the size of the strike zone divided into four smaller rectangles, one for each pitch: high inside, high outside, low inside, and low outside. The strings should be taut, and the catcher should wear a mask when catching behind them. He should also catch with one hand, keeping his throwing hand behind his back.

98. CONTROL PRACTICE IN GYM

PURPOSE

To help pitchers in developing better control and to give them work on control prior to outdoor practice.

PROCEDURE

A. *String Target*. The pitcher throws through strings to the catcher, who should wear a mask for protection. The catcher keeps count of the strikes and a number of pitches. (Note Drill No. 97.)

B. *Tape Target*. The pitcher throws at a tape target located on a wall or taped to a hanging mat. The pitcher keeps track of the number of pitches and strikes.

Hang a mat on the gym wall and tape a strike zone target on it as suggested with the string target (Drill No. 97). If the wall is constructed of concrete or other material which is sturdy enough to withstand the force of a thrown baseball, tape can be applied directly to the wall, or paint can be used.

C. *Beveled Board Target*.

1. Cut a piece of ¾-inch plywood to the size of the strike zone of a batter. It should be approximately 30 inches high and exactly 17 inches wide.

2. In the center of the plywood, running lengthwise, glue and screw a 2-inch square piece of hardwood, 30 inches long.

3. Cut two pieces of 2-inch thick hardwood, each 7½ inches wide and 30 inches long. Bevel these boards from 2 inches to ½-inch, the narrowest width. Now glue and screw these pieces to the plywood, on each side of the 2-inch square board, to fill out the plate width and strike zone, 30 inches by 17 inches.

4. Attach this beveled board to a wall, pole, or tree at strike-zone height, approximately 22 inches off the ground or surface.

5. Have the pitchers throw at the beveled board. Balls hitting the center will rebound directly back to the pitcher. Balls hitting the board on either side of the center will rebound as a ball would be hit to the right or left of the pitcher. This is excellent control-fielding experience if you get them to throw into a net or to a first baseman, after fielding the ball rebounding off the board.

99. PITCHER'S CONTROL DRILL

PURPOSE

To help the pitcher learn the strike zone and to be able to hit it.

PROCEDURE

Put a pitcher on the mound, a catcher behind the plate and a batter in the batter's box. Have the pitcher throw his different pitches to the catcher who calls the pitches and teams with the batter in acting as umpire. The batter does not swing or bunt at the pitches. In most cases, the batter and the catcher will agree on the pitch; however, if they disagree, the pitch probably is in a very good location.

Alternate between left-handed and right-handed hitters.

A) Have the catcher call 10 pitches, while the pitcher and the batter discuss the calls.

B) Have the batter call 10 pitches, while the catcher and the pitcher discuss the calls.

C) Have the pitcher call 10 pitches, while the catcher and the batter discuss the calls.

After each pitcher is warmed up for game condition throwing, have him throw for five minutes. Run this drill several times prior to the season's play. (Caution: catcher should wear full protective gear for this drill.)

100. EYE PATCH DRILL FOR CONTROL

PURPOSE

To develop better control.

PROCEDURE

If a pitcher is having poor control, he probably is taking his focus eye off the catcher or target. Every person has a focus or dominant eye. It can be found by pointing at an object as if the finger were a gun, aiming with both eyes open. Close first one eye, then the other. One eye will be aiming at the target and the other will be off the target. The eye on target is the focus eye. By putting an eye patch over the non-focus eye, the focus eye does the job for the pitcher. Have him throw easily like this for a short time, and then have him throw hard several times. Do this daily until he learns to hold his focus eye on the target and his control gets better.

101. PREVENTION OF STEAL DRILL

PURPOSE

To teach the pitcher how to keep the runner on first base from getting a good lead.

PROCEDURE

Put a pitcher on the mound, a catcher behind the plate, and a first baseman and a runner on first base.

*A) *Back off*. With a runner on first base, the pitcher comes to a set stance. (Illustration No. 43, Figure No. 2.) After the runner has taken a lead, the pitcher backs off the rubber and drops his hands. However, he does not move his striding foot. This maneuver, in most cases, will cause the runner to return to the base. Before the runner can get another lead, the pitcher steps on the rubber, gets set, and pitches.

B) *First baseman returns the ball to the pitcher on the rubber*. The pitcher comes set and then throws to first in an attempted pick-off. While throwing to first, the pitcher leaves his pivot foot in contact with the rubber.

1. WINDUP STANCE

2. SET STANCE

Illustration No. 43   Prevention of Steal

the first baseman returns the ball to the pitcher, who still has his pivot foot on the rubber. The pitcher comes set and pitches before the runner takes a lead.

*Success of plays A) and B) depends upon the batter staying in the batter's box.

102. PITCHER'S FIELDING DRILLS
(A) by Rod Dedeaux—(B) by Loyal Park

PURPOSE

The most overlooked defensive fielding position is the pitcher's. We would like to state that this is perhaps the most difficult position in all baseball to field properly. The neglect in developing skills probably is tied to the technical difficulties of practicing fielding from that position. The following drill covers two areas of the pitcher's fielding and combines with the teamwork of the catcher, third baseman and first baseman. It also adds bunting practice.

PROCEDURE

A) *Rod Dedeaux Method*

1. Line the pitchers single file from the pitcher's mound toward second base, each with a ball in his hand.

2. The third baseman takes the position assumed (per the individual coach's preference) for a sacrifice situation with a man on first and second. (Note Drills No. 156 and 203D.)

3. The first baseman assumes a normal fielding position. (Note Drills No. 165C and 168.)

4. A batter stands at home plate.

5. To the third base side of home plate, place a catcher and a fungo hitter. The first pitcher throws to the catcher and the fungo hitter, with a ball already in hand, hits a ground ball to the first baseman who throws to the pitcher covering first (Note Drill No. 165). The next pitcher throws to the plate and the batter bunts the ball down third base to assume a sacrifice bunt play. *Note:* A) In each case the first baseman or, third baseman does not throw the ball, but gives it back to the respective pitcher. B) By doing two drills, the tempo is speeded and almost twice as much work can be accomplished.

You can add live action to this drill by putting the catcher in his gear behind a batter who bunts several balls before changing batters. We recommend that the catcher keep his throwing hand behind his body and catches the ball one handed. However, using a back-stop only would work, but it is slower.

B) *Loyal Park Method*

1) Pitchers line up in three lines, one on the mound and one on each side of the mound. The pitcher on the first base side throws to first base. Pitcher on mound throws to second base. Pitcher on third base side throws to third base. Each pitcher has a catcher.

2) The pitcher throws the ball to his catcher. The catcher rolls the ball back toward the pitcher who fields the ball and throws to man covering respective base. Emphasis must be placed on proper methods of fielding the ball and planting the feet to throw.

3) Pitchers rotate to their right, moving from first base side of the mound to the mound, from the mound to the third base side, from the third base side to the first base side. Continue this rotation so that pitchers get to field ball and throw to first, second, and third bases.

4) The catcher calls out the base to which the pitcher will throw.

5) It is possible to use only pitchers in this drill. Rotation would then be: first base side to mound, mound to third base side, third base side to home, home to first base side of mound. Rotate after each pitch.

6) The catcher can roll the ball out short, go out and field the ball, and throw to the proper base.

103. PITCHER'S FOUR CORNERS DRILL   by Pat Daugherty

PURPOSE

To condition the pitchers physically and mentally. It is a great reaction drill. You will find that they get confused at the onset. What was home for the catcher on the first throw, may become first, second, or third on the second throw.

PROCEDURE

This is a drill that can be conducted indoors or out. All you need is a relatively square flat area, 40 to 60 feet. Can be more or less if you desire. We like about 60 feet. Place four pitchers in a square 60 feet apart and one pitcher in the center with a ball. Each of the four pitchers represents a base. The man who receives the pitch from the pitcher in the center automatically becomes the catcher with the other three men becoming the three bases. After the pitcher throws to the catcher, the catcher gives a loud voice command calling out a base. Say he yells "first base," he then rolls the ball back to the pitcher or down one of the lines. The pitcher fields the ball and throws it to first base. As the first baseman catches the ball, he automatically becomes the catcher and all other men take the relative position of infielders to this catcher. Give the pitcher time to get set. Then a new command is yelled to the pitcher and the ball is rolled to him and he makes the play to the base that was called. Now this becomes home.

We find this to be a great drill to get our pitchers to approach a ball properly, catch it correctly, get their feet aligned, get their body under control, take a crow hop and throw the ball to the base called. It is also an excellent conditioning drill for your pitchers. You can tire a pitcher out very quickly if he's not in shape. It is important that the person catching the ball from the pitcher yell a base loud and clear before he rolls the ball back into the "infield." If not, the "pitcher" will not have the chance to approach the ball at the proper angle.

Players may mix in line drives and pop-ups if they desire.

104. QUICK REACTION DRILL

PURPOSE

To get the pitcher ready for balls hit through the box and to teach him how to field the ball.

PROCEDURE

Have a pitcher assume a position in front of and near a backstop (with the backstop to his rear). The coach moves approximately 30 to 40 feet away from the pitcher. The coach then throws balls into the dirt to the pitcher's right, left, and directly at him. The pitcher fields the ball with his glove hand only. He keeps his pitching hand away from the ball.

105. FIELDING BUNTS

PURPOSE

To develop the pitcher's ability to field bunts properly in all areas and to make necessary throws after fielding them.

PROCEDURE

From the rubber, the pitcher delivers a normal pitch to the catcher. As the ball passes the plate, the coach, who is standing in the batter's box with a ball in his hand, rolls a ball to a bunting area. (Note Illustration No. 44.) After a pitcher has fielded bunts on both the first and third base sides, he is followed by another, until all the pitchers get an opportunity to field bunts.

In making the different throws, pitchers should use the following procedures and take a crow hop prior to throwing:

A. *Throw to First Base:*
   1. Right-handers throw from the position in which the ball is fielded.
   2. Left-handers field the ball, pivot clockwise, and throw when their left foot is set.

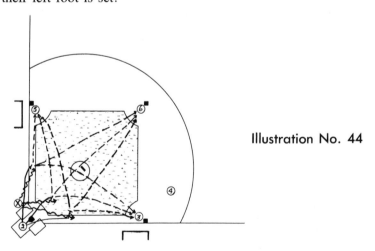

Illustration No. 44

B. *Throw to Second Base:*

Pitchers should get into position to throw as soon as the ball is picked up.

1. Right-handers field the ball with the right foot toward home plate and the left toward second base, pivot counterclockwise, and throw.

2. Left-handers field the ball with left foot toward home and the right foot toward third base, pivot clockwise, and throw.

C. *Throw to Third:*

Just the reverse of throwing to first base.

1. Right-handers pivot counterclockwise and throw as the right foot is set.

2. Left-handers throw from the position in which the ball is fielded.

D. *Throw to Home Plate:*

Give the ball to the catcher firmly, never too hard. It is usually a side arm or underhand toss.

1. On a force-out, throw the ball to the catcher shoulder high.

2. In a tag-out play, throw the ball knee high.

3. If the ball is fielded near home plate, the ball is scooped or shoveled to the catcher, using the bare hand only.

106. COVERING FIRST BASE

PURPOSE

To teach the first baseman and pitchers to work together on plays at first.

PROCEDURE

In this drill, pitchers, a catcher, and a first baseman are used.

A. *No Runners on Base.* Pitchers line up on the mound and the first baseman and the catcher get into their respective playing positions. As the pitcher throws the ball to the catcher, the coach hits a different ball to the first baseman. The pitcher breaks for first, running in an arc so that when he is 10 to 15 feet from the bag he is running parallel to the foul line. The first baseman gives the pitcher the ball about three feet in front of the bag. The pitcher's right foot always hits the base and he then pivots slightly toward the infield to avoid colliding with the base runner. (Note Illustration No. 45.)

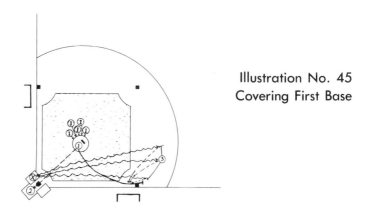

Illustration No. 45
Covering First Base

B. *Runners on Base:*

1. Right-handed pitchers:
   Right-handed pitchers make the moves as described above. However, when the pitcher steps away from the base with his left foot, he pivots on it counterclockwise, plants his right foot, and is ready to throw if the runner or runners attempt to take an extra base.

2. Left-handed pitchers:
   Same as above, except that as his right foot strikes the bag he pivots clockwise, landing on his left foot away from the bag and throwing from that position. All pitchers take turns with the drill in different play situations.

107. BACKING UP BASES

(Note Drills on relay throws—Drills No. 44-A and B-1)

108. WILD PITCH—PASSED BALL—COVERING HOME
by Chuck "BoBo" Brayton

(Note Catcher Drill 138—Passed Ball—Wild Pitch Drill.)

109. RUNDOWNS FOR PITCHERS   by Pat Daugherty

PURPOSE

To teach all the pitchers the proper mechanics in executing a successful rundown play.

PROCEDURE

If you have a squad of six or more pitchers and have no coaching help, you can use the following drill as a review or "brush up" tool with your pitching staff. When running through the various situations with pitchers, many times there is a great deal of standing around. During the season we will keep the pitchers out after everyone else has gone in, or bring them out 15 minutes early and run through all of our game situations with just our pitchers. Although it is simple, we feel that the drill adds conditioning to our pitchers; it gives them an appreciation of what the other team members do in a particular situation. The coach can watch the execution of each pitcher on every play he should make while on the mound, and finally they enjoy the drill. We have each pitcher put a ball in his pocket and start with a pitcher at each infield position. We have utilized as many as 18 pitchers in the drill. If you have a large squad, place two pitchers at each position. One pitcher takes his place on the mound. The coach is in the batter's box with a fungo. We try to cover the following with each pitcher when we run the drill:

1. Pitcher covering first base.
2. Pitcher being tail man on DP 3-6-1.
3. Bunt situation #1, runner on first base.
4. Bunt situation #2, runner on second base.
5. Bunt situation #3, runner on third base.
6. Pick-off at second base.
7. Moves to first base with runner on first base.
8. Pick-off at first base with runners on first and second or first and third.
9. Pitch out
10. Squeeze play
11. Move to first base with rundown responsibilities

You can add more of your own if you desire. After the pitcher throws the ball home, the coach fungos the ball to first base—pitcher covers—everyone now rotates around the infield much like the old game of work-up. We rotate from pitcher to catcher, to first base, second base, shortstop, third base, and back to the mound. After the whole pitching squad has made this play, we are back to the starting pitcher and we have the pitcher be the tail man on the double play from 3-6-1. After we all complete the DP, we move on to the next drill. Each pitcher uses and keeps his own ball. Everybody hustles from position to position and a great amount of work can be accomplished in a short period of time.

On bunt situations, the coach can simulate the bunter and then roll the ball to the desired area of the infield on pick-off plays, rundowns, etc. The coach can move to an area on the field where he feels he can do the best job of teaching.

110. PITCHER'S RHYTHM DRILL

PURPOSE

Although all pitchers have rhythm in their delivery, this should help them develop better rhythm. (Note Illustration No. 43, Figures 1 and 2 for correct windup stance and set stance.)

PROCEDURE

A. The pitcher is on the rubber assuming his windup stance. His pivot foot is on the rubber and the striding foot is behind the rubber. On the count of one, he shifts his weight to the pivot foot and his arms swing down and back behind the body. (Note Illustration No. 46, Figure No. 1.) On the count of two, he shifts his weight back to the striding foot and swings his arms up over the head, with the ball and glove meeting. (Note Illustration No. 46, Figure No.

Illustration No. 46

2.) On the count of three, the striding foot is kicked up and forward, the glove hand is brought down toward the hitter, and the ball hand is brought down behind the body. (Note Illustration No. 46, Figure No. 3.) With the count of four, the striding foot steps toward home plate, toe pointing forward and landing before the heel. The glove hand swings toward the hitter and falls to the side, and the ball is brought toward the catcher. (Note Illustration No. 46, Figure No. 4.) Finishing on the count of five, the pivot foot is brought up even with the striding foot, feet spread, and both hands forward in fielding position. (Note Illustration No. 46, Figure No. 5.).

B. The pitcher now assumes the set stance. (Note Illustration No. 43, Figure No. 2.) On the count of one, the striding foot is kicked up and forward, with the glove thrown toward the hitter and the ball brought back behind the body. (Note Illustration No. 46, Figure No. 3.) On the count of two, the striding foot steps toward home plate, toe pointing forward and hitting before the heel. The glove hand swings toward the hitter and falls to the side, and the ball is brought toward the catcher. (Note Illustration No. 46, Figure No. 4.) On the count of three, the pivot step is toward home plate, feet spread and parallel. Both hands are brought forward in fielding position. (Note Illustration No. 46, Figure No. 5.)

111. IN-STRIDE, SNAP THROW DRILL

PURPOSE

To help pitchers develop more snap in their wrist and elbow action when throwing. This drill is especially good for pitchers with a big sweeping arm motion.

PROCEDURE

With his foot on the rubber in the set position, and his striding foot at the distance of a normal stride toward home plate (approximately four feet), the pitcher throws the ball from a flat-footed stance, following through with his arm only. His feet remain in the same position.

112. BARE HAND DRILL

PURPOSE

To prevent pitchers or other ball players from throwing too hard during the first two days of indoor practice, and to aid in the toughening of the hands.

PROCEDURE

Have players pair off and throw to each other in the gym. Insist that no gloves be used for the first loosening-up period the first two days. If players are not wearing gloves, they will not throw hard enough to develop sore arms.

113. SNAP THROW WRIST DEVELOPER

A. *Pillow Throw Drill*. During the winter months or off-season, players can aid in the development of the wrist snap by throwing or snapping a ball into a pillow at close range. Three to four feet from the pillow is a good range for the throw.

B. *Rope for Snap Throw*. Take a rope that is three feet long and approximately one-half inch in diameter, and tie a knot in one end. With the knot end free, hold the rope back in the position the hand takes when going back to throw a ball. *Example:* The catcher holds the rope in his hand beside his right ear, and the rope hangs behind his back. He brings his hand and arm forward, making the rope snap out in front of him. His wrist action should be like that used in throwing a baseball. If the rope snaps, the wrist action is good. (Note Illustration No. 47.)

C. *Metal Ball or Medi-Ball*. Some players have made a mold of a regulation baseball and used it for molding a heavy metal ball. The ball is used during the off-season for the Pillow Throw (Section A above), and also for general arm and wrist development. However, the ball is not used for making

Illustration No. 47

actual throws, since this could injure the arm. For throwing, a ball can be made slightly heavier than a regulation ball. (Note Drill No. 14, and Drill No. 16.)

114. ISOMETRIC ROPE DRILL

(Note Drill No. 5.)

115. EARLY CURVE BALL PRACTICE

PURPOSE

To get pitchers' arms ready for throwing curve balls in games.

PROCEDURE

In the first day of practice, after loosening up properly, spin a few easy curves off the fingertips. Do this for no more than five minutes, alternating with straight balls. Repeat this for three or four days. During the fifth day, snap off a few curves. By the second week, pitchers should start throwing curves harder and for a longer time according to the individual, and by the third week they should have the curve ready for game conditions, but in limited amounts.

116. SIX-STEP PROGRESSION FOR TEACHING THE CURVE BALL   by Jim Brock

PURPOSE

To develop the best curve ball for each pitcher, concentrating on quick, fast breaking curve balls. However, the slow change of pace curve can be attained by using this drill. Furthermore, we do not teach the slider or slurve. At Arizona State, we work on the fast ball, change-up and the down-breaking curve ball. (The author has the same thoughts in teaching high school and college level pitchers.) Mastery of these three pitches is important for development to advance to higher classification baseball and be a successful pitcher. Proper rotation of the ball is the key to a good curve ball.

The proper curve ball rotation can be learned through a series of drills designed to teach the fundamentals of this pitch. There is no mystery about the curve ball, it is simply a matter of imparting 12 to 6 o'clock rotation to a baseball. A basic feel is needed for what you are trying to do. The pitcher must get down rotation; if he cannot get this rotation, and if it is not consistent rotation, he cannot become a good dependable curve ball pitcher.

PROCEDURE

To learn the fundamentals of good curve ball rotation, one must start with the real basics: breaking down the correct arm action from release point backwards to include the full arm action. A pitcher should move on to the advanced concepts only after mastering the basics of rotation described in the following drills:

STEP ONE

Red Line Drill. Ron Squire, former coach at Mount San Antonio Junior College, Walnut, California, came up with what he called the "TV drill," and it is the best way to begin learning the feel of good curve ball rotation. It is a mistake to move on until flipping the ball (as shown in Illustration No. 48, Figure 1 and Figure 2) is second nature to the pitcher.

Illustration No. 48   Teaching the
Curve Ball Step One (1)

Step One (2)

This action, properly done, "draws" a red line with the perfect down rotation of the baseball's seams. Often one hears, "I can throw a curve ball, but I can't flip the ball like that." Perhaps so, but in my opinion that kind of shortcut can lead to an inconsistent curve ball—the kind of curve ball where he is "hoping for the best." If it doesn't hang at the wrong time, maybe you win; but if it does hang at a key time, you get beat. In this "red line" drill, one should be able to hear the actual snap of the finger, as really all that's being done is the snapping of the fingers with the ball between the thumb and middle fingers.

STEP TWO

Ten Yard Flip. After mastering consistent rotation in the Red Line Drill, move on to the second step. In this, the pitcher applies the same finger snap only he flips the ball to another player about 10 yards away. When the ball rotates correctly, he can see the red line as the ball loops to his partner. Remember to look for the same red line from seam rotation as in the first drill. (Note Illustration No. 49.)

STEP THREE

Tennis-Ball Can. Step three in the progression promotes learning the feel of an overhand curve ball released by tossing a taped tennis-ball can. This drill should be performed with arm, wrist, and hand locked in the curve ball

Illustration No. 50   Step Three

Illustration No. 49   Step Two

release position, and then the arm is recoiled 6 to 12 inches, just before moving forward for release. The wrist is bent down, as shown in Illustration No. 49, to produce the perfect down spin, flipping the tennis can end over end. Don't attempt to produce a football pass spiral. The pitcher tries to draw a rainbow with the flight of the can, imparting as much spin as possible while limiting the velocity (Illustration No. 50.) The arm, wrist, and hand action are exactly the same as when releasing a curve ball with a baseball, only he is gripping the end of the can. It is fairly easy to increase the consistency and amount of rotation through practice. One problem with the can drill is that some of the more result-oriented players will be able to get good-looking rotation without the proper arm action, but you can be sure that correct release will always produce perfection rotation.

STEP FOUR

Locked Release. Needed for the fourth step is a regular-size wash tub and an 8-foot screen (as in Illustration No. 51.) Place the wash tub 6 feet behind the screen. The pitcher then throws from 30 feet in front of the screen. He throws over the screen with a trajectory in order to land the ball in the tub. This forces the pitcher to toss a soft rainbow, while stressing the same low velocity and high rotation used with the tennis-ball can drill. He should stand with his feet set apart as when landing in his stride. Also, the pitching arm should be locked in release position as in the previous drill. The thrown ball should rotate as many times as possible, but make a soft landing in the tub. The coach can stand behind the pitcher or the screen to evaluate the rotation.

Illustration No. 51   Step Four

STEP FIVE

Full-Arm Action. Step 5 adds the full-arm action from this same type of foot placement using the screen and tub setup. Two flaws of the good breaking pitch will show up at this point in the learning process. Illustration No. 52, Figures 1 and 2, illustrate "wrapping" and "cocking"; both are fundamental flaws. "Wrapping" the curve ball is cocking the wrist during the reach-back, and "cocking" is dropping the elbow and "short-arming" the curve ball just before release. Step 5 will help combat these by stressing proper fast ball arm action with the curve ball adjustment coming just before the point of release. The pitcher should be thinking "fast ball, fast ball, fast ball," then "curve ball" as the arm gets overhead. Also, alternating the fast ball with the curve ball, when working on curve ball fundamentals, will help the pitcher avoid "cheating" to get good rotation.

Illustration No. 52   Step Five (1)   Step Five (2)

STEP SIX

Uphill Slope. In Step 6 the same tub is utilized, but the pitcher places his striding foot on the top of the mound on an upside-down bucket, with his pivot foot on the level ground behind the mound (as shown in Illustration No. 53.) He then delivers a soft rainbow to the wash tub placed 50 to 60 feet away. The uphill foot placement forces the pitcher to keep his elbow up and forward, and also enables him to learn the difficult concept of staying on top of the curve ball. Again, good down rotation is helpful in landing the ball in the tub. The possibility for proper rotation is increased with this drill as it forces exaggerations of the vital curve ball fundamentals.

Any time a pitcher has a breakdown and loses good rotation, most likely his arm action and release are not fundamentally sound. By using suggested drills in pre-game warm-ups and form work on off days, he over-learns these concepts and decreases the chances of a breakdown of these important techniques when under pressure.

This six-step learning and over-learning progression for curve ball rotation should be followed by regular work on the breaking pitch with a catcher. Several points need to be stressed about these practice sessions. First, proper follow-through needs to be emphasized. Check and encourage the exaggeration of the throwing shoulder to opposite knee concept. This will serve as an excellent indicator of the amount of pulldown necessary to produce good rotation on the curve ball.

During the curve ball learning stages, the pitcher should alternate fast ball and curve ball and should break the curve ball into the dirt. Most young pitchers hesitate in breaking the curve ball down that low during practice; and to avoid bruises, catchers usually apply great social pressure to encourage the pitcher to get the ball up out of the dirt. Unfortunately, the learning process is motivated more rapidly only when the pitcher works on rotation by bouncing the curve ball, then gradually adjusting into the lower half of the strike zone while keeping the same consistent release. It is extremely difficult to get classic

Illustration No. 53   Step Six—Uphill Slope

rotation on a pitch above the waist, so starting high and adjusting down just will not work.

Perfecting the curve ball to the point of having three or four speeds, different arm angles, and various adjustments in the wrists is not necessary or wise. Most pitchers will be better off if they master one speed and one release angle that is best for them and then groove it. Actually, only two breaking pitches—a "strike" curve ball and a "strike-out" curve ball are needed. These two curve balls are thrown with the same release and speed, but the "strike-out" curve ball is used when ahead in the count and the pitcher can afford to break the ball at the knees or lower on the outside "black" of the plate. For the "strike" curve ball, he will need confidence that can be gained by using sound, repeatable fundamentals that have been developed through intelligent practice. The pitcher can use this type of curve ball even when behind in the count. This pitch is down, but clearly in the strike zone. This type of command of the curve ball is a must for success unless the pitcher has an over-powering fast ball.

Teaching the curve ball can be an enjoyable and rewarding experience for both the coach and the pitcher. We have found that the six-step curve ball progression really aids in both the learning process and the winning process.

117. PITCHER'S STRIDE DRILL

PURPOSE

To help pitchers develop the correct striding and stepping technique from the rubber toward home plate.

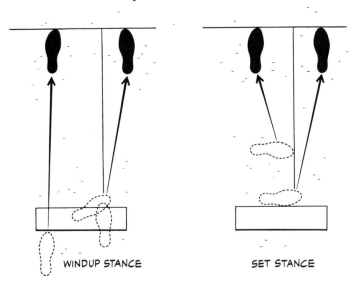

WINDUP STANCE   SET STANCE

Illustration No. 54   Pitcher Stride Drill

PROCEDURE

Place a pitcher on the rubber and a catcher in his box. With the pitcher's pivot foot on the rubber, draw a straight line from the foot toward home plate. Then have the pitcher throw a ball at normal speed to the catcher. Note that his striding foot, if he is right-handed, lands to the left of the line drawn from his pivot foot, but that it is to the right of the line if he is left-handed. At the point where his striding foot contacts the ground, draw another line at right angles to the first line.

Be sure that his pivot foot, on the follow-through, moves too, but not over the line which crosses the first line. (Note Illustration No. 54.) Observe that these drawings are for right-handers, and that the striding would be reversed for left-handed pitchers. Note also, pitcher's pivot foot is in front of the rubber, not on top of it).

118. PITCHER'S FOLLOW-THROUGH DRILL

PURPOSE

To help the pitcher learn to follow through properly, both from the set and the wind-up positions.

PROCEDURE

While on the mound, the pitcher takes his normal delivery as in Drill No. 110, (Pitcher Rhythm Drill) and uses the same stance. However, on the follow-through, he reaches down with his pitching hand and picks up dirt or grass on the outside of his striding foot. The feet remain in the same position as in Drill No. 117 (Pitcher Stride Practice).

119. DEVELOPING A FOLLOW-THROUGH FOR PITCHERS
by Dick Groch

PURPOSE

For pitchers who refuse to bend their backs or follow-through.

PROCEDURE

Each pitcher needs a catcher to throw the ball to and return it. The catcher returns the ball to a fielder standing aside or near the pitcher. The pitcher does not change his position.

The pitcher places his pivot-foot instep at the center of the seat of a standard height chair and places his striding foot out in front of the chair toward the catcher. The coach or another player holds the pitcher's instep flat on the seat of the chair. The shin and knee are not on the chair.

The pitcher now throws the ball about half speed to the catcher who is approximately 45 feet away from him. This drill continues for about 10 minutes. It can be used any time, but is best the day after pitching.

120. FORK BALL PITCHER'S HAND DRILL

PURPOSE

To teach the pitcher the correct method of gripping the baseball for throwing the fork ball.

PROCEDURE

While the pitcher is idle or on the bench, take a ball and place it in his hands in the position for throwing the fork ball. Force the ball between the forked index and middle fingers. This develops the proper grip and spread of the fingers for throwing the fork ball.

Daily work on this grip and forcing the ball between the fingers will develop a better and more comfortable fork ball grip. It will actually in time, stretch the skin muscles and tendons to create a much wider spread of the fingers.

121. IMPROVING LEFT-HANDER'S MOVE TO FIRST
by Dick Groch

PURPOSE

To improve the move to first base and hold runners close to the bag.

PROCEDURE

You need a first baseman, two players and a catcher. The two players are placed between home plate and first base and serve as targets for the "look" and "step" part of commands.

The coach gives the verbal commands. He takes care of the commands and changes them to best help the pitcher improve his move.

Put the left-handed pitcher on the mound, the first baseman who is number 1 on first, a player who is number 2 about 30 feet from first base, a player who is number 3 about 45 feet from first and 45 feet from home and the catcher who is number 4 at the plate.

The coach now gives verbal commands. The pitcher does not execute the pick-off or throw until he receives the entire command.

Following are a series of sample commands which can be used. When the coach completes his command, the pitcher begins to move his head from first to home several times prior to executing the throw.

Series 1— Look at 1, step toward 1, throw to 1.

Series 2— Look at 2, step toward 1, throw to 1.

Series 3— Look at 3, step toward 2, throw to 1.

Series 4— Look at 4, step toward 3, throw to 1, (and keep walking toward first base. This will be his good move.)

Series 5— Look at 2, step toward 2, throw to 1.

Series 6— Look at 3, step toward 3, throw to 1.

122. PICK-OFF PLAYS   by Loyal Park

PURPOSE

To teach the pitchers how to mechanically execute a pick-off play. (Note Drills No. 47 and No. 196.)

PROCEDURE

A. *Pick-off play by the pitcher*. Runner on first base. The pitcher uses three types of throws on pick-off plays:

(a) Quick move to first during his stretch move.

(b) A right-hander's best move to first after the completion of the stretch is a hop-and-throw motion.

(c) A slow deliberate move to first just to let runner know that the pitcher knows he is on base.

1. On a quick move to first, the pitcher starts his stretch and, at any time during the stretch move, he turns and throws to first.

Use this when the runner takes his lead off too fast, crosses his feet and legs and he takes the lead, or takes a lead without paying attention to what the pitcher does. The runner should wait until the pitcher completes his stretch before taking his lead. The pitcher should use his quick move with two outs as the offensive team may try to steal.

2. The pitcher completes his stretch and is set to pitch to plate. The pitcher looks at the runner; if the runner has too big a lead the pitcher makes as quick a move to first as he can, trying to pick the runner off.

On this move the pitcher makes a hop-and-step movement throwing the ball to first at the same time. He could also step back off the pitching rubber and throw to first as he steps off rubber. This move is used most to hold a base runner close to the bag to prevent stolen bases.

3. On a slow deliberate move to first, the pitcher just throws over to first to let the runner know he is aware of the runner on first base.

B. *Pick-off plays at second base.*
Pick-off plays to second base can be run in several ways:

1. Timed or count play on designated signal by shortstop or second baseman or catcher.

2. The daylight play—with shortstop.

3. The change of pace pick-off play also called the double-break play.

C. *Runner on second base or first and second bases.*
1. A right-handed pitcher turns to his left and a left-handed pitcher turns to his right.

   (a) This type of move looks as if the pitcher might be throwing to home plate. Also, it gives the pitcher a good chance to look at the target before throwing to home and is more deceptive on pick-off plays to second base. The runner must be cautious as the pick-off play may be on, or the pitcher may take a second look toward second, or he may be pitching to hitter.

   (b) Another turn: right-handed pitchers turn to their right, left-handed pitchers turn to their left to make throws to second base. The pitcher makes this type of move whenever he sees that the shortstop or second baseman covering the base has the runner beat.

   (c) We use this play (move in either direction) as part of our defense against the sacrifice play (first and second occupied, none out) to break up the sacrifice play with a force play at third base.

D. *The daylight pick-off play.*

1. The pitcher gets the sign for the next pitch from the catcher and completes his stretch before he looks back at the shortstop and runner on second base.

2. The shortstop gives the pitcher a signal for the pick-off play or the team has a rule that the daylight pick-off play will be run any time the pitcher and shortstop see DAYLIGHT between the runner and the shortstop the play is on.

3. The pitcher, seeing daylight between the runner and the shortstop, turns his head and looks toward the plate, counts one, turns and throws to the shortstop covering second base on the play.

4. The shortstop continues toward second as the pitcher looks toward home plate, covering the bag on the pitcher's throw to second base.

5. The daylight pick-off play is a fast play; the shortstop must break fast to be at the bag in order to handle pitcher's throw.

6. The second baseman stays out of the play so it will not be given away or interfered with. The second baseman backs up second base on the throw.

7. The daylight pick-off play can be used without a signal when the shortstop and the pitcher are looking at each other and they see daylight between the runner and the shortstop. The shortstop breaks for second base, and the pitcher turns and throws. He can turn in the direction of his throwing arm in making the daylight play.

E. *Pick-off play—catcher giving the signal to the pitcher as to when to turn and throw to shortstop or second baseman, whoever is covering the bag.*

1. The pitcher looks to the plate and gets the signal from the catcher for the type of pitch.

2. The pitcher also gets a signal from the catcher at this time that the pick-off play will be tried. The catcher touches his mask or rubs his hand across his shirt or any signal that the team wants to use.

3. The pitcher keeps looking at the plate until the catcher gives him the signal that the shortstop is breaking toward second. The catcher's signal to the pitcher to throw to second base can be any one of the following:

   (a) The catcher pulls his glove away from his bare hand.

   (b) The catcher picks up and throws dirt with his bare hand.

   (c) The catcher rubs his hand across his shirt.

   (d) The catcher touches his mask.

4. The catcher gives the pick-off signal to the pitcher when the shortstop breaks toward second base.

5. The pitcher, on getting the catcher's signal, turns immediately and throws to the shortstop or second baseman.

6. The shortstop breaks toward second base any time he thinks the runner has too big a lead and can be picked off. He goes all the way to the bag, looking for the ball to be thrown to him at any time. The shortstop must always look for a throw.

7. The shortstop can give a signal to the catcher that he wants to try for a pick-off when the runner is getting too big a lead off at second base.

F. *Timed or "count" pick-off play.*

1. A different signal is given by the shortstop, second baseman or catcher to the pitcher telling him who is taking the throw at second, when he looks back at the runner on second base or gets the sign from the catcher.

2. The shortstop can use one of these signals—touching tip of cap, belt buckle, or rub against shirt (any signal a team wants to use).

3. The pitcher gets the signal, looks back to second, then turns his head toward the plate. This starts the play with the count 1; the pitcher counts 2, 3, and turns to throw to second base.

4. The shortstop or second baseman, whoever is taking the play at second, breaks for second base on the pitcher's look to home plate. The shortstop or second baseman will be there in plenty of time to handle the throw and make the tag or prevent a bad throw into center field. (Work this play slowly when first starting practice. Count slowly even to 4, turn and throw. When the play is timed it will be made on 3 or 3½ counts. The pitcher will start to turn as he counts 3 and throws.) It is best to make a complete turn. It looks more as if the pitcher is going to pitch and also gives him a good look at the plate or target before he pitches to the hitter at the plate if the play is not on.

5. A pick-off play is worthwhile even if you do not pick the runner off.

G. *Change of pace or double-break play.*

The change of pace pick-off is run like the timed or count play with these differences:

1. The man who is to cover the bag on the play fakes the runner back to the bag. The man covering the bag starts back to his original fielding position. As the runner starts to take his lead again, the pitcher looks toward the plate, starting the play. The man (shortstop or second baseman) who is covering breaks for second base on the pitcher's look to home plate. The pitcher starts the count on the look to the plate as 1, then 2, and he throws. This method is faster, as the baseman covering the bag on the play will not have reached his original fielding position so the distance to bag is short. Regardless of how far the baseman covering the bag is away from the bag after he fakes the runner back toward second, he breaks to cover the bag on pitcher's look to plate.

2. The shortstop can fake the runner back to the bag when the second baseman is covering the bag or the man who fakes the runner back can also cover the bag after he fakes the runner back.

3. The right-handed pitchers can get the signal from the shortstop. Left-handed pitchers get the signal from the second baseman. The designated signal for the shortstop or second baseman remains the same, regardless of who gives the signal or who covers the bag.

4. The timing on this method has to be practiced until the play is timed

properly. Run it slowly at the beginning and increase the timing speed as the players involved get the play mastered.

H. *Pick-off plays—men on first and second bases.*
Situation: Runner on first and second bases; left-handed pitcher.

1. The runner on first base is taking an extra big lead. The first baseman plays behind the runner.

2. The pitcher gives the first baseman a signal for attempting a pick-off play at first base, or the first baseman gives the signal to the pitcher. The signal must be acknowledged by a return signal—both men can use the same signal so each knows that the play is on.

3. After looking back at the second base runner, the pitcher looks toward home plate. The first baseman breaks for first base. The pitcher makes a good pick-off move to first base.

4. The pitcher and first baseman are the only ones involved. The pitcher uses the same pick-off move as with a runner on first base only. The first baseman must break early enough so he will be at the bag to handle the throw.

5. The first baseman must be alert regarding the runner on second base.

Situation: Runner on first and second bases; right-handed pitcher.

1. Pick-off play at first base with right-handed pitcher.

2. Runner on first base takes a long lead from the bag.

3. The first baseman is playing in back of the runner.

4. The pitcher does not pay attention to the first base runner, but watches only the runner on second base. This is the usual procedure: The shortstop or second baseman can put on their pick-off play against the runner on second base. This should allow the first base runner to get careless.

5. The first baseman gives the signal to the shortstop that he wants a pick-off play to be tried on the runner on first base.

6. The shortstop gives the signal to the pitcher, who acknowledges that he has the play and will try it.

   (a) These signals can be simple, such as touching of cap or taking off his glove, by the first baseman, or touching his belt buckle.

   (b) The shortstop can use the cap signal to notify the pitcher that the play is on. He can also touch the belt buckle or rub across his shirt. Any of these signals is okay.

7. The pitcher must acknowledge the play by giving the signal to the first baseman that he will try the play. He does not look at the first baseman, only the shortstop.

8. Timing of play:

   (a) The pitcher continues to look at the shortstop and the second base runner.

   (b) The shortstop starts the play, gives the signal to the pitcher, as the first baseman breaks for first base.

   (c) The pitcher who has completed his stretch turns and throws to first on the shortstop's signal. This signal can be the dropping of his glove to his side. This gives the first baseman a slightly earlier break than the pitcher's move and throw to first base.

123. PITCHER'S SIGN DRILL

PURPOSE

To develop the pitchers' and catchers' understanding and clarification of signs to be used during a game. Shortstop and second baseman must be included in this drill.

PROCEDURE

Have pitchers and infielders line up facing catchers with approximately 60½ feet between them. While they are in a catching stance, have the catchers give the signs which will be used in a game situation. These should include signs for a fast ball, curve, change-of-pace, pick-off, pitch-out, and change-of-sign. After each sign given by the catcher, the pitcher or infielder should tell the catcher what the sign was, and there should be an agreement on all signs. However, if a pitcher has bad eyes and cannot see the signs given by the catcher, reverse the procedure and have the pitcher give the signs while the catcher calls out the correct answers.

124. BATTING PRACTICE THROWING SCHEDULE

PURPOSE

To see that all pitchers get enough work and that some pitchers do not get too much work.

PROCEDURE

A daily chart of how many minutes a pitcher worked should be made. It should include the pitcher's name, how long he worked, and on what days. When practice games begin, change the minutes into innings pitched. Work all pitchers equally for about two weeks. Then, after three weeks, separate starters from the others. This is done after pitchers are in fairly good shape.

See that starters get plenty of work; don't let them off with too little.

125. ALTERNATE BATTING PRACTICE PITCHERS

PURPOSE

To get the most possible batting practice out of a small pitching staff.

PROCEDURE

After two pitchers have loosened up, one of them throws 20 pitches to batters, and then the other pitcher throws 20. They pick up balls for each other when not pitching, and they also wear jackets when not pitching. These two pitchers alternate after every 20th pitch until each has thrown 60 pitches. In the meantime, two other pitchers should have been loosening up for their turns. They repeat the same procedure used by the first two. If there are two more pitchers, they loosen up and relieve the second pair after those two have pitched 60 balls each as described above.

Pitchers throw at half to three-quarter speed. After completing the first week of practice, each can change from 20 pitches to 10 minutes of pitching for a turn. Then, after pitchers are in good shape, they can take turns of 15 to 20 minutes each.

126. ROTATION OF PITCHERS

PURPOSE

To keep a daily rotation on all pitchers so that they obtain an equal amount of work.

PROCEDURE

When No. 1 pitcher who will start batting practice is warmed up sufficiently, he starts pitching to the batters. When he has about five minutes left to throw, No. 2 pitcher starts warming up on the side lines. While No. 1 pitcher is throwing, No. 3 pitcher is picking up balls for No, 1 and No. 4 is shagging balls into the outfield or is engaged in some other drill.

When No. 1 has completed his pitching, he immediately goes into another drill before he cools off. Then No. 2 goes in to pitch; No. 3 goes to the side lines to warm up, and No. 4 picks up balls for No. 2. This rotation keeps going until all pitchers have pitched their share of batting practice.

During the first week of practice, pitcher rotation should be about every 5 to 10 minutes, depending on the control and condition of the pitcher. Once they are in shape, they can throw from 10 to 20 minutes if they feel like throwing. Keep a daily chart of how much and how long each pitcher throws, and make sure all of them get a sufficient amount of batting practice pitching.

127. GAME POISE DRILL FOR PITCHERS

PURPOSE

To get the pitchers ready for opponents' jockeying and harassment and to prevent possible balks.

PROCEDURE

Put a pitcher on the rubber, and on command have him step off the rubber. Commands such as, "Time!" or "There he goes!" should be given.

1. In a set stance, not looking at the coach, the pitcher's pivot foot breaks off the rubber at the coach's command. Then put runners on bases and have them run when the pitcher is not looking at them. In all cases, the pivot foot must come off the rubber before the ball is taken out of the glove.

2. During some intra-squad games, have base runners harass the pitcher by yelling at him and giving many fake starts from the bases. (*Note:* With the exception of the fake starts, this is not recommended for regular games, since it is unsportsmanlike.)

128. USING SPEED GUN FOR PITCHERS

PURPOSE

To find the actual velocity each pitcher can throw a baseball. To see if any drills increased velocity. To find the best velocity for each pitch thrown by each pitcher.

PROCEDURE

Obtain a speed gun by purchase or loan. Most Police Departments own a speed gun and will, in most cases, work with a coach.

The Jugs Speed Gun can be used to check the velocity of a thrown baseball either coming toward the gun or going away from it. It is safer to get behind a pitcher at a very slight angle from the pitch. If you work directly behind the pitcher, he sometimes hides the pitch from the gun. The gun is very accurate and picks up the flight of balls thrown or hit in the vicinity of the pitch. It is best to work in a separate area.

A. Check velocity early in the year and again during the season to see if the pitcher or pitchers have gained velocity or lost some. Record the velocity because you will probably like to have it over a period of years. Check the velocity of all pitches and record them; 1) fast ball, 2) curve ball, 3) change-of-pace, and 4) slider.

B. Correct speed of all pitches—We have been checking speeds of major league pitchers, college pitchers, and high school pitchers who have been successful and some who have not been successful. This study has been going on since I discovered the use of a speed gun for baseball and presented my findings to Professional Baseball's Commissioner, Bowie Kuhn, who in turn notified all professional baseball clubs of the findings. Today, nearly every major league club owns at least one Jugs Speed Gun. They use it for scouting and teaching.

After studying successful pitchers, it was noted that pure speed or velocity was not the key to success. It was the change of speeds. Pitchers throwing in the high 70's with a good change and curve were throwing the ball past the hitters. Pitchers in the high 80's and low 90's were not throwing the ball past the hitters. This was true in major league baseball, minor league baseball and colleges. However, pure speed was successful in high school, but more successful when used with a good curve.

We are convinced that regardless of what velocity you throw, you must come close to the following alternate or change of speeds.

You must drop 10 miles an hour off your fast ball for the slider, 15 miles an hour off your fast ball for the curve, and 20 miles an hour off your fast ball for the change-of-pace.

For example, if you throw a fast ball 79 miles an hour, your slider should be 69 miles an hour. Your curve ball should be 64 miles an hour and your change-of-pace 59 miles an hour.

If a pitcher can throw 100 miles an hour I would recommend his slider to be thrown 90 miles an hour, his curve 85 miles an hour and his change-of-pace 80 miles an hour. Yet, there are successful pitchers in the major leagues who cannot throw the ball above 80 miles an hour. The figure 79 miles an hour above was clocked for a former successful pitcher of the New York Yankees who pitched a five-hit shutout against the Tigers after we checked his velocity and he adjusted the velocity according to the above stated formula. His change-of-pace, averaging around 59 miles an hour, threw the hitters off balance as did his curve of about 65 miles an hour. His fast ball at 79 miles an hour was thrown past the hitters. Their timing was completely off after looking at the change and curve.

When you throw your curve or slider too close to the velocity of your fast ball, you lose the effect the change of velocity should make. Also, if you throw the change-of-pace slower than 20 miles an hour off your fast ball it gives the hitter too much time to regain his balance and hit the ball with some solid power.

For comparison to check the velocity of your pitcher, the following information can be used. We have checked approximately 400 boys ages 9 through 18 years of age. The velocity shown is the maximum speed checked for each age group:

Age 9 (46 m.p.h.)—age 10 (54 m.p.h.)—age 11 (62 m.p.h.)—age 12 (63 m.p.h.)—age 13 (64 m.p.h.)—age 14 (69 m.p.h.)—age 15 (73 m.p.h.)—age 16 (76 m.p.h.)—age 17 (77 m.p.h.)—age 18 (87 m.p.h.). College pitchers (90 m.p.h.) and major league pitchers (79 minimum—94 maximum m.p.h.).

We have heard that one or two throw under 79 m.p.h. for their fast ball and several throw faster than 94. These would not be an average speed or a consistent speed but is their top speed thrown in three or more throws after warming up or in a game.

CHAPTER 6

CATCHING DRILLS

A pitching staff is only as good as its catcher. If a team has a good catcher, it will be a good team. He is the coach on the field and must run the team. His hustle and play can affect the whole team. The following drills develop the catcher so that he knows what to do, how to do it, and where to go during every play situation.

129. CHECKLIST FOR PROPER EXECUTION

(Note Screening Candidates Drill No. 246.)

130. CATCHING BODY POSITIONS   by Tom Smith

PURPOSE

To get the catcher to feel comfortable and at ease in different positions and to look the part of a catcher.

PROCEDURE

Place the catcher behind the plate in full gear. The coach works with him in assuming correct positions and gives him advice when needed.

146

A. *Giving Signals*. The feet are spread shoulder width with toes pointed straight ahead or slightly toed in, and are parallel. Knees are pointed straight ahead, and the back is leaning slightly forward. The catcher's right elbow is held near the body, and the glove hand is extended off the left knee with the palm facing first base, thumb upward, pointing toward the pitcher. In this position, the catcher gives signals with right hand fitted firmly up against and in his crotch. He may use fingers or hand positions.

B. *Catching Stance with Nobody on Base*. The catcher's feet are spread slightly more than described above. His right toe is parallel to his left heel. His tail is down, not up in the air, and the back is leaning slightly forward. The weight is on the toes. His arms are held away from the body and are half extended toward the pitcher. The right foot may be pointed slightly outward. (Note Illustration No. 55, Figure No. 1.) Although he can catch with the right knee on the ground, the catcher must be ready for the bunt or pop fly. The

Illustration No. 55   Catching Positions (1) (2)

catcher judges his distance behind the hitter by assuming his crouch and reaching up with his glove toward the batter's back elbow. The glove should miss his elbow by several inches.

C. *Catching Stance with Runners on Base*. With runners on base, the catcher must sit higher to be in better position to throw, and his feet must be wider apart for better mobility on a bunt or ball in the dirt, as described in Drill No. 131 below. The catcher will normally never catch on one knee with men on base, unless the score indicates it is safe to do so. (Note Illustration No. 55, Figure No. 2.)

D. *Giving the Target*. The palm of the glove is facing the pitcher, fingers up, thumb in. The catcher is in a sitting crouch as described above. In case a low target is needed, the catcher, in order to avoid a low crouch, especially with men in running position, simply turns his glove with fingers pointed down, thumb out, and the palm facing the pitcher. (Note Illustration No. 55, Figure No. 2.)

E. *Position of Bare Hand and Glove*. The right thumb is under the index finger, and the fingers are curled, but not clenched. The hand, which is held against the glove, turns counterclockwise as the ball approaches the glove. Then the back of the hand and fingers are facing the ball, not pointing toward it as it approaches. As the ball hits the glove, the hand covers it.

131. USING CHAIR FOR PROPER CROUCH POSITION
by Tom Smith

PURPOSE

To help the catcher easily assume the receiving position with men on base.

PROCEDURE

Place a folding chair behind the catcher and have him sit on the front edge of the chair. Now he should start moving his feet apart, leaning slightly forward as he does. Remember that the left foot will be forward of the right foot by a few inches and the right foot points outward, toward the first baseman, allowing the catcher the mobility needed to bounce out on bunts, or get in front of pitches in the dirt. The catcher's feet may spread up to twice shoulder width, depending on his physical characteristics, before he has the feeling he can support himself on the edge of the chair. Now the chair is removed, the upper trunk is tilted forward slightly and the arms are held forward and low, with a comfortable flex at the elbows, making sure that the elbows are never inside of the legs, which will restrict movement and receiving range. There you have it, the classic catching position. (Note Illustration No. 55, Figure No. 1.)

132. CATCHER'S SIGNALS

PURPOSE

To teach the catchers that a pick-off sign is necessary. To teach the catcher how to give signs.

PROCEDURE

A. *Pick-offs*. If the catcher wishes to pick-off a runner from first base, he must give a signal to the first baseman or the second baseman, whoever is going to receive the ball and make the tag. The player must answer the catcher's signal. For example, the catcher might pick up dirt and toss it toward the first baseman. The first baseman covers the letter of his hat acknowledging the pick-off sign. The catcher now gives the pitcher a pitchout sign, usually a fist sign.

If the catcher wants to pick-off a runner at second base, he will go through the same procedure as described above.

The same procedure is used at third base. Actually, any player can give the signal first, but it must be acknowledged by the other player.

The catcher can give any number of signs and the infielder can do likewise, but it is best to give a very simple sign that can be seen by both players easily. It should never be something that a player does naturally. Tipping one's cap might be a poor acknowledgment because many players unconsciously tug on the bill of the cap.

B. *For Pitchers*. Signs should not be complicated or hard to read. They must be covered so the coaches on the bases can't read them and they must be hard for the opposition to read when they are on second base.

With nobody on base, simply one finger for the fast ball, two fingers for the curve ball, three fingers for the slider, four fingers, or wiggle the fingers, for the change-of-pace will be good.

However, when the opposition has a runner on second base, that runner can relay the type pitch being thrown to the hitter if he knows the signs. It is, therefore, important to switch signs or have a series of key signs that will be hard for someone else to read.

There are various ways to accomplish deception:

1. The catcher throws four signs every time he calls for a pitch. The first inning the first sign thrown is the pitch. The second inning the second sign. The third inning the third sign, and the fourth inning the fourth sign. The fifth inning the series starts all over as if it were the first inning. If the catcher believes the runner on second is giving the signs to the batter, he can have a switch sign with the pitcher, such as taking his mask off and putting it back on while in a crouch. The signal would move up to the next sign. For example, if the signal was on the second sign thrown in the second inning it would move up to the third sign.

2. The up and down signs are very good and often deceiving. The second sign given is the key sign. If you want to throw a fast ball, your second sign could be one finger, two fingers, three fingers or

four fingers. Your third sign must be one or more fingers above the second sign. If you want to throw a curve or slider the second sign would be two or more fingers but the third sign must be less than the second sign. The change is an even call such as the second sign being the same as the third sign. This whole series can be changed by making the key sign the first, second or third sign. When you make the third sign the key sign, you will have to use a fourth sign to go up for the fast ball, down for the curve or stay the same for a change-of-pace.

133. ACROSS-SEAM OF BALL GRIP FOR CATCHERS

PURPOSE

To teach catchers to grip a baseball across the seams, at the widest spread of the seams, in order to reduce sliding and sailing of the ball when thrown by the catcher.

PROCEDURE

While playing catch, each time a catcher receives a ball he quickly grips the ball across the seams, removes it from his glove, and makes a snap throw. Without looking at the ball, he must be sure of this grip before throwing quickly. (Note Illustration No. 16, Drill No. 37.)

134. FOOTWORK DRILL—INTENTIONAL WALK

PURPOSE

To help the catcher develop the proper footwork for all plays.

PROCEDURE

A. *Throwing to Bases*. Place the catcher behind the plate and throw balls to him. Before each pitch, yell the play situation and which base or bases runners are on. After catching the pitch, the catcher sets his feet and hand as to throw, but does not actually throw the ball. During the drill, place a batter at the plate; the coach makes any necessary corrections in the catcher's footwork, as the catcher makes his moves with both left-handed and right-handed batters. (Note Drill No. 135.)

B. *Intentional Walk*

PURPOSE

To keep the catcher and the pitcher from balking and to show the catcher and pitcher where the ball is to be thrown.

PROCEDURE

Place the pitcher on the mound, the catcher in full gear behind the plate, and a batter in the batter's box.

The pitcher assumes a set stance and must come to a full stop prior to his delivery.

The catcher stays in his area until the ball leaves the pitcher's hand, then moves outside his area away from the batter to receive the ball. The pitcher throws at half speed, missing the plate by two or two and one-half feet, on the side opposite the batter. The batter should try to hit balls that are thrown close to him or across the plate.

Work with both right and left-handed hitters. The catcher takes a position in his area on the opposite side of the hitter and waves his right hand out away from the plate for right-handed hitters and his glove to the other side for left-handed hitters. (It is a balk if he steps out of the box too early.)

135. STEPS FOR THROWING   by Tom Smith

PURPOSE

To teach the catcher the proper steps for throwing to all bases.

PROCEDURE

Have the pitcher throw balls to the catcher to work the following steps:

A. *Throw to First Base*. Usually the throw to first base is a pitchout on the right side of the catcher.

The right foot steps out toward first base when receiving the ball. The catcher pivots on the right foot, steps with the left, and throws.

Another situation with a left-handed hitter is as follows: The right foot, which is about six inches behind the left foot, points toward first base. The batter is between the runner and the catcher when the catcher is crouching. When the pitch is caught, the catcher makes the throw to first base with a side-arm flip, very similar to that which the second baseman makes to the shortstop, by pivoting his hips instead of his feet. It need not be a pitchout.

B. *Throw to Second Base*. In this case the catcher does not use a deep knee bend, but he does keep his tail down, knees bent slightly in a crouch.

If the pitch is to the catcher's right, he steps out with his right foot, plants it, steps with his left foot directly toward second base, and throws. With a left-handed hitter, the first step is more forward than right.

When the pitch is straight in, the catcher takes a quick crow hop of only three or four inches toward second, and throws. The hop will be to the right foot and is started as he receives the ball.

If the pitch is to the catcher's left, he strides to the left with his left foot as the ball is being caught, crow hops to his right foot when the ball is caught, steps toward second base with his left foot, and throws. With a right-handed hitter, the first step is more forward than left.

C. *Throw to Third Base*. Throws for pick-offs should be two feet on the inside of the bag, and throws on steals should be knee-high on the bag.

1. Left-handed hitter:
    (a) If the pitch is down the middle or is to the catcher's left, he makes the catch, crow hops, and makes a snap throw.
    (b) If the pitch is to his right, the catcher steps laterally on his right foot and throws to third.

2. Right-handed hitter:
    (a) A pitch made to the right side or down the middle presents very few problems. The catcher simply steps out and toward the pitch with his right foot and throws as he steps toward third with his left.
    (b) On pitches to the left side, into the hitter, the catcher steps toward the ball with his left foot to receive the ball, but leaves the right foot in position. He then hops to his right foot, away from the hitter and toward third with his left foot on the throw. Don't throw over the batter or behind him.

D. *Blocked Ball at Home Plate—Throw to Pitcher Covering*. If the ball is in the dirt near the plate, the catcher picks it up with his bare hand and gives it a firm knee-high toss to the pitcher, who is covering the plate. Pick-up is made by first pressing the ball into the dirt.

E. *Ball at Backstop—Throw to Pitcher Covering*. The catcher approaches the ball as fast as possible, plants his right foot at the right side of the ball, and makes a quick knee-high throw to the pitcher covering the plate. The catcher should attempt to pick up the ball with two hands, but the position of the ball will determine this. The throw can be underhand, side-arm, or overhand, depending upon the time.

F. *Pick-off Play*. (Note Team Drill No. 47.)

136. BOXING GLOVE AND FOOTBALL FOREARM GUARDS
—BALL-IN-DIRT DRILL

PURPOSE

To teach catchers to block the ball, then to find it. (Illustration No. 56.)

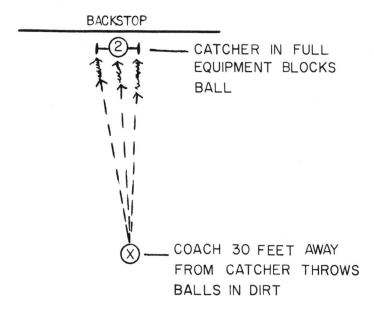

Illustration No. 56

PROCEDURE

Put the catcher in full game gear, including a protective cup and a boxing glove on throwing hand. This protects the fingers and hands. Also, put football forearm guards on each, arm, and place him against the backstop. Then, from a distance of about 30 feet, throw balls to his left, to his right, and in front of him, making all of them bounce in the dirt. The catcher's job in this drill is not to catch the balls, but to *block them*, and to keep them in front of him. (Note Illustration No. 57, Figure No. 1.)

A. *Balls to the Catcher's Right*. Have the catcher go down on his *left* knee, chest perpendicular to the path of the ball, with the face of the glove and palm of the hand at a 90 degree angle to the dirt. (Note Illustration No. 57 Figure No. 2.)

Figure 1

Figure 2

Figure 3

Illustration No. 57   Ball-in-Dirt Drill

B. *Balls to the Catcher's Left*. This is the same routine as above, except that the *right* knee is down.

C. *Balls in Front of the Catcher*. On these balls, the catcher should come down on both knees. It is important that the hand is open and the palm, not the fingers, is facing the ball. The face of the glove is angled in order to keep the ball in the dirt so it will not come off and up over the catcher. It will be between a 45 and 90-degree angle facing the ball. (Note Illustration No. 57 Figure No. 3.) (Note Drill No. 31 for use of tennis balls.)

137. SOFT-QUICK HANDS FOR CATCHER   by Ron Fraser

PURPOSE

To teach catchers how to give with the pitch and react quickly for normal-speed and distance-thrown baseballs.

PROCEDURE

Put your catcher in full gear and place him close to a backstop as in the above Ball-in-Dirt Drill.

The pitcher or coach stands 40 feet away from the catcher. When the catcher is set in his receiving position, the coach or pitcher fires the fast balls at nearly full speed to the catcher.

Start with pitches near the strike zone and gradually work low from one side to the other. Then work high from one side to the other. This is not a Ball-in-Dirt drill. It is a ball thrown in the air only.

The catcher should take at least 30 throws daily.

138. PASSED BALL—WILD PITCH DRILL
by Chuck "BoBo" Brayton

PURPOSE

To develop efficient communication between your pitchers and catchers on any ball that eludes the catcher, with a runner or runners on base. Many times a pitch or throw will take an erratic bounce after the catcher has attempted to block it, leaving him with no real idea as to its location. Should the pitcher attempt to guide the catcher simply by yelling, his efforts are often lost in the noise of the crowd. If he attempts to yell ''right'' or ''left'' this has no real meaning to the catcher and usually only adds to the confusion.

PROCEDURE

This drill can be done indoors or outdoors and can be set up anyplace. The pitchers are in a line near the pitching rubber and one takes his position to pitch without a baseball. The catchers are near home plate and one takes the receiving position. We place a coach or player with a baseball behind the catcher. The pitcher goes through his normal delivery to the plate *without* actually throwing the baseball. As the pitcher follows through, the person behind the catcher drops or rolls the ball in a variety of directions.

Since the catcher is entirely dependent upon the pitcher's help, the pitcher must react to the situation by pointing to the ball and yelling a sharp "THERE!" "THERE!" as he runs to cover home plate. A *straight* arm point is very important. You may experiment by having your pitchers make a normal or half-hearted pointing motion. Then have them use a hard full arm and finger extension—yelling a sharp "THERE!" "THERE!" as they point. You will see a significant positive difference in the catcher's reaction.

During the course of this drill the catchers and pitchers have an opportunity to practice other skills required to put a runner out at home plate.

The catcher gets to the ball as quickly as possible and always gets to the right side of the ball, thus establishing his throwing position by using one of three techniques, depending upon the situation. The techniques we coach are: sliding on the shin guards, dropping to one knee, and the infielder toss.

The pitcher gets to home plate as quickly as possible, aligning himself with the catcher so that he can receive his throw and make the tag without colliding with the base runner. (Note Illustration No. 58.)

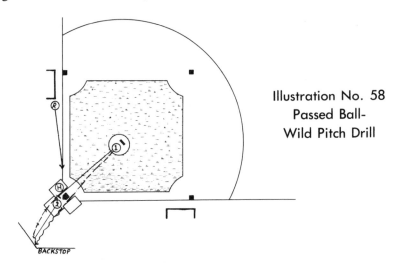

Illustration No. 58
Passed Ball-
Wild Pitch Drill

139. ARM STRENGTHENER TO DEVELOP
CORRECT THROWING FORM

PURPOSE

To develop the catcher's arm and throwing form.

PROCEDURE

The catcher assumes an upright stance with his feet parallel and spread a little wider than his shoulders. When warming up a pitcher and the ball is received, he brings his throwing hand up and straight back beside ear. Without moving his feet, using a sharp, snappy overhand motion, he throws the ball back to the pitcher. As he gets warmer, he can throw harder, and he can throw the distance from home to second base without moving his feet if some player will receive the ball.

This should be practiced every time the catcher warms up a pitcher or plays catch. (Note Drill No. 113-B, Rope For Snap Throw and Illustration No. 47 to improve catcher's throwing.)

140. CATCHER MAKING TAG PLAYS AT HOME   by Tom Smith

PURPOSE

To teach the catcher to make the tag properly while preventing injury to himself.

PROCEDURE

Place a temporary soft base in a grassy area. The catcher should be in full equipment and runners should be instructed to slide into this base. (However, the runners should not use spikes.) The catcher assumes his position in front of the base as if it were home plate. His left foot is on the middle front of the base, permitting runners to see the back half of it. When the runner can see the back half of the base, he is more likely to go for it and not try to make contact with the catcher to take him out of the play. Timed to barely beat the runner coming into the base, a ball is thrown to the catcher, who attempts to tag the runner.

Proper procedure for the tag: The catcher drops his knees just in front of the base and makes the tag, which can be made in two ways: (1) The catcher grips the ball in his right hand, with his hand and the ball in the pocket of the mitt. (2) He can grip the ball in his right hand and place it about six inches behind the pocket of the mitt with the back of the mitt facing the runner. By this method the runner hits the mitt and knocks it into the ball, thus taking the shock off the hand holding the ball.

In a game the catcher faces the throw and covers the plate as described above. He instructs the cut-off man to "let it go" or "Cut it." If he yells "Cut," he should also yell "Cut" and the base where he wants the ball to be thrown. For example, "Cut-two" means throw to second base.

141. CATCHER MAKING FORCE-OUT PLAY AT HOME

PURPOSE

To teach the catcher the proper procedure in making the force-out play at home plate. The catcher must remember that the runner is trying to knock him down and break up the play. The catcher takes a position in front of the plate, toward the play, with his right foot on the plate. As soon as he receives the ball, he crow hops off the base and makes his throw. His throw must be made out of the base path of the runner to avoid getting tripped and making a bad throw. His throw must be inside the first base line.

If the catcher does not have time to get off the base, he takes the ball on the move, steps on the base with his right foot, crow hops off to throw or throws directly off the plate.

PROCEDURE

Have all infielders throw from their positions to the catcher, who receives the ball, tags the plate as above, and throws to first, second, or third base, for an additional out. This can be performed in regular team infield practice drills.

142. DOUBLE STEAL PREVENTION

PURPOSE

To help the catcher develop skill in holding a runner on third while attempting to throw out a runner going to second base.

PROCEDURE

With runners on first and third, when an attempted double steal is made, the catcher quickly fakes to third with his head and shoulders, causing the runner to return to third, then throws to second base.

In every infield practice, before the catcher throws to second base, make him look at third base. This should be repeated until it becomes a habit. (Note Second Base Drill No. 177-B.)

143. FIELDING BUNTS

PURPOSE

To teach the catcher the proper way to field bunts and throw to the bases. (Note Illustration No. 59.)

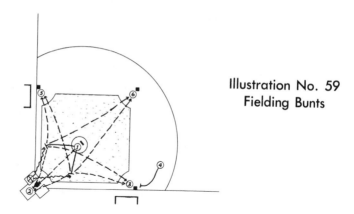

Illustration No. 59
Fielding Bunts

PROCEDURE

Put the defensive infield in position and runners on bases where needed. The coach rolls balls in front of the plate, and the pitcher lets the catcher make the plays.

A. *First Base Area*

1. Throw to first base:
   The catcher breaks out on the bunt, fields the ball with both hands as the palm of the glove hand faces the ball and properly stops the roll of the ball. He takes a crow hop, waltz step, or side step, bringing his right foot behind his left toward the middle of the infield, and throws three-quarters or overhand to first base. Caution should be taken not to throw directly down the base line. Avoid hitting the runner or making the first baseman field the ball into the runner.

2. Throw to second base:
   The catcher fields the ball as above, crow hops, and throws overhand to second base.

3. Throw to third base:
   The catcher works himself into a good throwing position before fielding the ball. He fields the ball as above, and then throws side-arm or underhand if he needs to in order to save time.

B. *Third Base Area*

1. Throw to first base:
   The catcher works himself to the left of the ball before fielding it with both hands, spins clockwise as described in A-1 above, and throws three-quarters or underhand to first base.

2. Throw to second base:

The catcher charges the ball, positions himself to the left of the ball, fields it, crow hops, and throws overhand to second.

3. Throw to third base:
In this situation the catcher charges straight at the ball, fields it as above, and if possible, throws overhand chest high to third. Alternate Drill No. 105 with the pitcher. When the pitcher fields the ball, the catcher should call the play. He should tell the pitcher the base to which he should throw.

144. POP FLY PRACTICE

PURPOSE

To give catchers needed practice in handling pop flies, which are always tough to handle in full gear, behind the batter.

PROCEDURE

With the catcher in full gear, the coach or another player hits pop flies for the catcher to field or a Jugs Pitching Machine is used. This should be done for 15 minutes two to three times weekly. Also, note Team Drill No. 42 for extra practice.

145. CATCHER COVERING FIRST AND THIRD BASES

PURPOSE

To teach the catcher how, when, where, to cover these bags properly.

PROCEDURE

A. *Backing Up Throw to First Base*. Hit the ball to an infielder and have a runner at the plate break for first base. The catcher breaks for a position near the fence or dugout, backing up the throw where an overthrown ball would go.

B. *With a Runner on First Base*. The catcher breaks for the above position if the play or out is made at second base. If the runner is not out at second, the catcher continues for the back-up of first base. If the ball is caught at first, he breaks back for home. If it is an overthrow, the pitcher must cover home, since the catcher will pick up the overthrow.

C. *Making a Pick-Off Play at First Base on Short Hit to Right Field*. Hit a ball in the hole between first and second basemen. Both of them make an attempt to field the ball. As the hitter, noting the first baseman is not near the bag, makes his turn toward second, the catcher, who followed the runner, covers first base for the throw from right field, and the pitcher backs up the catcher. (Note Drill No. 220-A.)

D. *Covering Third Base on a Bunt*. Put infielders in their respective positions and a runner on first base only. Bunt a ball to the third baseman. The catcher covers third base. The runner on first breaks with the pitch and continues to third on the bunt. The first baseman attempts to throw the runner out at third with the catcher taking the throw. The left fielder backs up third.

CHAPTER 7

GENERAL INFIELD DRILLS

Basically, there are certain fundamentals that all infielders must know and have the skill to execute. An infielder must know where he is on the field and be able to throw a ball to a base with his eyes closed. He must know what his team members can do and will do, and he must help them when the need exists. The following drills are designed to improve the skills of the infielder, and more specifically, to have him at the right place, at the right time, in condition mentally and physically, ready to play every day.

146. PROPER TECHNIQUE FOR FIELDING GROUND BALLS
by Tom Petroff

PURPOSE

To give infielders a stance that will initiate body movements for the player to get to any type ball, thrown or hit, in the shortest time and be ready to throw the ball or make another play. Furthermore, it should give the player more confidence and make him look like a ball player. This is a three-set progress drill.

PROCEDURE

SET (1) will initiate body movements, SET (2) will go into mechanical fielding position, and SET (3) will gather the ball, right his feet and complete the throw to the designated base.

SET (1) Initial Stance (Note Illustration No. 60) Position of body should be the same as taking a lead for a spring break toward a base.

Illustration No. 60

1. Feet placement—width of shoulders—toes pointing straight.

2. Knees bent—tail down, correlating with center of gravity.

3. Arms loose and bent about halfway at sides.

4. Head—eyes on the pitcher until pitcher picks up his stride foot. Eyes then focus on area in front of hitter where the ball will meet the bat. The flight of the ball from the pitcher to the batter is picked up by a side view in your peripheral vision.

5. As the pitcher gets his sign, the fielder is relaxed either standing or with hands on his knees. When the pitcher gets his sign and makes his first movement, the fielder's hand should be slapped into the glove to form a pocket. Hands then drop low as the fielder shifts his weight forward but remains in a low crouch.

6. When the pitcher picks up his stride foot and strides forward, the fielder picks up his feet in a 1, 2, stutter step (note Illustration No. 61, Figure 1), and comes to a complete stop and position before the ball reaches the home plate area. The weight is now forward, but the heels are not off the ground. This insures proper position to move to ball with quickness.

SET (2) Mechanical Fielding Position

1. Glove is carried low, barely touching the ground, and out in front of

(1)   Illustration No. 61   Fielding Ground Balls   (2)

the body. The face of the glove faces the ball at all times. Carrying the glove low is protection on bad hops. It is easier to come up on a bad hop than it is to go down. (Note Illustration No. 61 Figure 2.)

2. Keep eyes on the ball.

3. When the ball approaches the fielder, he moves in toward the ball, checking his movement to field the ball (right-hander) with the left foot forward, feet spread with the right foot back. (Left-handers have right foot forward.)

4. Watch the bounce and try to time your catch on the up bounce of the ball below or around the knees. However, the ball can be played on the down arc easily. The hardest play is about the middle of the arc on the top of its up bounce and just as it goes down.

5. When the ball hits the glove, let the hands move in toward the body, but not against the body. Give with the force of the ball bringing it in toward the waist area on the throwing side.

SET (3) Check Out Body Alignment

1. Move players by signal without batted ball and simulate batted ball with command of direction.

2. Players go in stance as described in SET (2). Command:

   a. ''Right back''—fielder drops right foot back and left cross-over (ball in hole simulation).

   b. ''Left back''—drop left foot back and right crossover.

   c. ''Right forward''—right foot steps to go forward on ground ball.

   d. ''Left forward''—left foot steps to go forward on ground ball.

   e. ''Straight forward''—either foot steps forward.

Using this part of the drill incorporates all three sets in the following manner. Line up all infielders and command: (1) ''Hands on knees,'' (2) ''Get set'' (incorporates set 1), (3) ''Right back,'' ''Break'' (incorporates set 2), (4) ''Field ball'' (incorporates set 3). Continue using all break positions such as left, back, forward, etc. (Drill No. 28 can be used for this drill.)

147. EARLY SEASON INFIELD FUNDAMENTALS DRILL
by Walter Rabb

PURPOSE

To provide all infielders a chance to handle a large number of ground balls in a normal fielding and throwing situation without danger of an early season arm strain.

To serve as an overall conditioning drill—particularly for the legs. To enable the coaching staff to evaluate new candidates for infield positions. To provide an opportunity for correction of faulty techniques of body control, glove handling, and various types of throws.

PROCEDURE

Weather and field conditions permitting, select a level, dry area of the outfield and establish a diamond with portable bases. Use approximately 75-foot base paths. Distances may be slightly shorter if necessary. A gymnasium floor can be used during inclement weather. More than one diamond may be used at the same time if space is available.

A. Place one or two infielders at each position with a catcher for each set. Have them completely warm from running and throwing prior to the start of the drill.

B. A coach or feeder either throws or hits ground balls to each fielder's left, then directly to him, then to his right. After several rounds of ''getting one'' at the first base, the same procedure is followed in working on double plays of all types.

The success of the drill depends to a large extent on the skill of the feeder in providing all types of ground balls and in making brief correction of the basic fundamentals of handling ground balls. Approval for good execution should be expressed and a great deal of enthusiasm and hustle developed and maintained.

C. The drill can be used to provide a lot of technique practice by the catchers on fielding bunts, looking runner back to third base, making the force and tag at home as well as getting the ball off quickly to all bases. Shortstop and second base are given repeated opportunities to make tags and return the ball to home base or to third on first and third base double steal simulations. It is an ideal drill to give third basemen work on swinging bunts without risk of arm strain. The length of the drill may be easily adjusted to practice schedule time and the current physical condition of the squad.

PROGRESSION

A. The normal progression is to move infielders from the short infield drill described to the regular infield, but using only the infield "in" and "halfway" positions during workouts. Another device to control arm strain while obtaining normal fielding and throwing execution is to have the first baseman move 10 to 15 feet toward second base.

B. The drill has proven particularly beneficial as a screening device for freshman infield candidates each fall practice. A good evaluation of quickness, balance, and basic techniques of handling ground balls can readily be obtained. Since the distances are modified, final judgment of arm strength and accuracy must wait for full distance infield work. A large number of candidates can be screened by setting up several fields around the outfield.

148. TOUCH GRASS RIGHT AND LEFT

(Note Drill No. 28)

149. ORIENTATION—RAPID-FIRE DRILL

PURPOSE

To help infielders learn where bases are located to the point that they can throw accurately without first looking for the base. It also keeps them alert.

PROCEDURE

Put an infielder in his position and a first baseman at first so that the infielder can throw to him. Have another player or the coach take five to eight balls and hit them rapid fire to the infielder. As soon as he has fielded, thrown to first, and before he is quite set, the hitter should hit another ball.

After the fielder has thrown 15 to 20 balls to first base, place a fielder at second base, and repeat the process, except that the throw goes to second base. Continue until the fielder is tired, and then replace him with another fielder until each is well oriented as to where bases are located. (Illustration No. 62.)

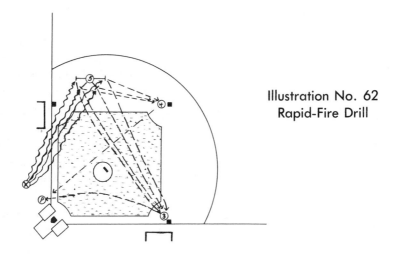

Illustration No. 62
Rapid-Fire Drill

150. INFIELD CIRCLE DRILL   by Paul Tungate

(Note Drill No. 59)

151. EQUILIBRIUM DRILL

PURPOSE

To teach players how to judge a fly ball after they have misjudged it. Also, how to keep their balance to make the proper play.

PROCEDURE

Misjudged Fly Balls: With infielders in position, the coach hits high fly balls to them, one at a time. When the ball has reached its greatest height, the infielder, for whom it was hit, turns completely around once before making the catch. After he is acquainted with the drill, he may turn around two or three times. Each infielder takes his turn. This is also a good drill for outfielders.

Fly ball practice should be given on three different type days. One day should have a clear sunny sky, one day a cloudy sky and one should be windy.

152. DEFENSING THE FIRST AND THIRD STEAL
by Russ Frazier

PURPOSE

To acquaint our infielders and pitchers with this confusing play of opponents and teach them the proper execution should this steal be attempted.

PROCEDURE

In defensing the early steal we have the second baseman break to a point in the baseline from first to second about 8 to 10 feet to the first base side of second base. The first baseman yells "Gone" when the runner breaks, and follows or trails the base runner to shorten the rundown. The first baseman should not follow too closely. The pitcher (right hander), steps back off the rubber with his pivot foot, and checks the runner at third at the same time. If the runner at third does not have an excessive lead, the pitcher whirls clockwise and throws the ball hard to the second baseman. The pitcher breaks to first base and covers first after he throws to the second baseman. A left-hander will step back off the rubber with his pivot foot, turn clockwise to check the runner at third quickly, then throw the ball to the second baseman, who should now be in the correct spot near second. The second baseman now has the play in front of him, and if the runner from third *breaks*, he throws home. If the runner at third *holds*, the second baseman tags the runner coming from first or gets him in a rundown while checking the runner at third. If the runner at third breaks at any time, the first base runner is forgotten and the play is made on the runner from third. The shortstop who is backing up second base yells, "Home" if the runner on third goes or, "Tag" if he doesn't go.

Defensing the delayed steal works similar to the early steal defense once the shortstop or second baseman gets the ball from the catcher.

When the runner on first breaks for second, the first baseman yells, "Gone" or "There he goes." The catcher looks the runner back to third and fires the ball to the second baseman or the shortstop, whoever is covering for the tag. It is best for the player receiving the throw to be off second base about four feet toward the mound. If he sees the runner on third breaking home or hears his teammate yelling "Home," he rushes toward the ball thrown by the catcher, catches it and fires it to the catcher for a play at home. If his teammate yells "Tag," he steps back toward the bag for the tag on the runner.

Our drills for both the offensive and defensive aspects of the early and delayed steals are as follows: we put our infielders and catchers in their respective positions, and the pitchers take turns on the mound. The outfielders are used as runners. We then vary the early and delayed steal situation without the pitcher's knowing which one we will use. By drilling in this way, we are able to work both offensively and defensively with the early and delayed steal situation. We later use outfielders at infield positions in order for the infielders to practice the offensive aspect.

153. RUNDOWN PLAY DRILLS

PURPOSE

To teach infielders the proper procedure for making the rundown play with the minimum number of throws. The secret is chasing the base runner going at full speed. (Note Illustration No. 63.)

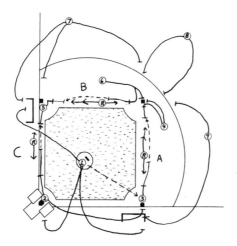

Illustration No. 63

PROCEDURE

Place infielders and outfielders in their normal positions and place runners on bases. Then pick or catch them off, with the outfielders backing up every play.

A. *Runner Between First and Second.* The pitcher picks the runner off at first base. The first baseman then runs him toward second base where the shortstop or second baseman is standing three feet in front of second with the other player backing him up at the bag. While the left and center fielders move in to back up the play at second, the right fielder comes in to cover first base, and the catcher, if there are no runners on base, moves down the line to back him up. The pitcher moves to help at first base.

When the runner is approximately 15 feet from the infielder standing in front of second, the fielder breaks toward the runner and yells, "Now." The first baseman throws the ball to him, and the fielder makes the tag.

B. *Runner Between Second and Third.* Have the runner caught off second base. The shortstop or second baseman chases him toward third base at full speed. The play is made in the same manner as in "A" above. With all fielders backing up the play, the third baseman breaks for the runner, as above, receives the ball from the player chasing the runner, and makes the tag.

C. *Runner Between Third and Home*. Hit a ball to the third baseman. When it is hit, the runner breaks for home and attempts to score on the play. The ball is fielded and thrown to the catcher, who chases the runner back toward third at full speed. He then throws to the third baseman, who is three feet in front of the bag. The same procedure is followed as in the above drills A and B. The shortstop covers third base behind the third baseman.

D. *Ball Hit to the Pitcher*. Have a runner on second or third, and let him break for the next base. The pitcher's job when he fields a ball in this case is to determine where the runner is going. If the runner sees that he is caught and hesitates, the pitcher should run directly at the runner to make him commit himself. When he does this, the pitcher throws to the fielder covering the base which the runner tries to take. However, if the runner is three-fourths of the way to the next base and does not hesitate, the pitcher throws to the base ahead of him. If he is only one-fourth of the distance to the next base, the throw should be to the base behind him. Then, the rundown starts when the ball is received from the pitcher, and it is completed as in the above drills. If possible, when the pitcher is running directly at the runner, he should attempt to get in a position between the advance base and the runner.

E. *Runner Between First and Home*. We don't expect to be caught between home and first in a rundown except if we make it an offensive play. When a ball is hit to first basemen near the line and in front of the bag, they often like to tag the runner. This is especially true when the other runners are on base. Should you have other runners on base, it would be to your advantage to try to get a stupid first baseman get you into a rundown or at least force him to make a delay of the out at first base until the other runner or runners might advance another base.

With a runner on first, second or third base, batter bunts the ball down the first base line. The first baseman fields the ball in front of the bag near the line. He must now decide whether to tag the runner who may have stopped, or throw to the second baseman covering first. His main concern is to keep the other runners from advancing another base.

The proper defense for a play such as this is for the first baseman to tag the base or the runner, as quickly as possible, or throw to a teammate covering first base. He should never take his mind off other runners, allowing them to advance.

154. MULTIPLE INFIELD PRACTICE

PURPOSE

To give infielders maximum ground ball practice and ball-handling experience.

PROCEDURE

Put all infielders, including extras, in position. Each fielding position has a fungo hitter who hits to that position only. Each fungo hitter has a shagger.

A. The fungo hitter hits a ball to the fielder in his position. If there are extra fielders, they take turns. Fielders throw the ball directly back to the fungo hitter's shagger or pick-up man. Hit to them in their position for several minutes. Then alternate as follows: (Caution—stop all play and hitting prior to each change.)

B. 1. Put a second baseman on second. The player or players at third now throw to second base, and the ball is returned to their fungo hitter. Extra second baseman continue to field balls hit to them, but they take turns receiving balls thrown from the third baseman. (Follow the drill as diagrammed, Illustration No. 64.)

2. Following the above drill, have the third baseman throw to an extra first baseman covering first. The first baseman returns the ball to the fungo hitter. Extra first basemen continue to field balls hit to them, but take turns covering the bag for thrown balls. (Follow drill as in Illustration No. 64.)

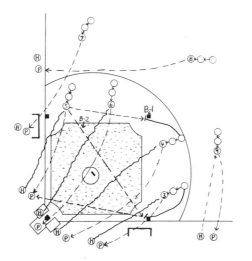

Illustration No. 64

C. 1. The fungo hitter hits a ball to the first baseman, who throws to third. 2. Fungo hitter hits ball to the first baseman, who throws to second base, which is covered by a shortstop, as in B-1 above.

D. 1. The shortstops throw to first base as their fungo hitter hits to them. 2. The shortstops throw to second base, second basemen throw to first to complete the double play.

E. 1. Second basemen throw to first as their fungo hitter hits to them. 2. Second basemen throw to shortstop at second, who throws to first to complete the double play.

Fungo hitters continue hitting to the players in their positions while Drills B through E are worked. Caution must be applied to use only one drill at a time. Fungos must not be hit to a player who is fielding a thrown ball while covering a base.

155. STUFFED GLOVE (Especially for double play)

PURPOSE

To teach fielders how to give with the ball when receiving a thrown or batted ball.

PROCEDURE

Take an old catching glove and stuff it so that it has no pocket. The material used should be something that will not form a pocket, such as a very firm piece of foam rubber. Have fielders practice fielding with the glove. Whereas, the good fielder gives with the ball when fielding it, the poor fielder kicks many balls out of the glove. Since many balls are missed while using this glove, fielders will get practice scrambling for the ball to throw the runner out. Fielders will also learn to use two hands on the ball.

It is an excellent glove for teaching the catcher to use two hands, and is excellent for use in double play practice.

156. DEFENSING THE BUNT WITH FIRST AND SECOND OCCUPIED   by Sam Esposito

PURPOSE

To be certain that if you do not get the runner at third, you throw the runner out at first. The most important thing is to make an out. Too often we get greedy and end up with everyone safe, and we're in big trouble. We attempt with this drill to teach all defensive players how to react in a game situation.

PROCEDURE

The pitchers are lined up behind the mound, each with a baseball, and a base runner on home, first and second. All infield positions are filled. Pitcher assumes the stretch position and delivers the ball to the catcher. The coach, then acting as the batter, bunts the ball in any direction. A good bat for bunting in this drill is described in Drill No. 83. Use the flat side to bunt the ball. This prevents many pop-ups.

On our defense for this situation, our shortstop is almost on second holding the runner as close to bag as possible. Our second baseman and first baseman are cheating . . . second baseman ready to cover first and the first baseman charging the bunt.

Now, the important part, the communication between our third baseman and pitcher. Our third baseman is instructed to be a few steps in toward home in front of the base line. On a bunted ball in his direction, he must make a decision as to whether to go in and field the ball and throw the runner out at first or go back to the bag for the throw from the pitcher, or catcher. We would like our catcher to call the play.

However, this is discretionary with the coach. Some coaches like the third baseman to make the call on the third base-pitcher side because he is the only person who knows if he is actually going to be able to cover third base or not. The catcher calls the play on all bunts back to the pitcher or the first base side of the infield. The third baseman, I feel, must draw an imaginary line between the third base line and the pitching mound. He fields any ball bunted between that line and the pitching mound and gets the runner at first. If the ball is bunted between the imaginary line and the pitcher's mound, he breaks back to the bag and the pitcher makes the play to third or first as instructed by our catcher.

Of course, you have to take into consideration how good a fielder the pitcher is and how much range he has. If the third baseman makes the throw or not, he must cover third as quickly as possible to keep the runner on second from rounding third too far or attempting to score.

157. DUTY DRILLS DURING INFIELD PRE-GAME PRACTICE

PURPOSE

To develop a well-organized infield practice, performed as snappily as possible.

PROCEDURE

Place infield players in their respective positions. The coach then hits medium-speed ground balls to the infielders, giving them confidence in their fielding. The coach hits to all positions, and the players take a typical infield practice with plenty of "holler and hustle."

The following are check points to note for each infield position:

A. *Catcher*

1. Equipment can be worn.

2. All throws should be hard, firm, and chest high.

3. He should receive balls behind the plate and throw from there.

4. On all throws to second base, he "looks" the runner back to third before throwing to second.

5. On bunts, the catcher should charge out and place his body in position to throw, as in Drill No. 143.

6. Good hard throwing in practice will discourage game-time stealing.

7. Practice Drill No. 141—Force-Out Play At Home.

B. *First Baseman*

1. Fields thrown balls and makes certain to tag the base on every play.

2. Throws hard and accurately to the catcher behind the plate.

3. Throws hard to shortstop and third baseman on the bag.

4. Throws should be overhand whenever possible, and they should be chest high.

C. *Second Baseman and Shortstop*

1. Snappy overhand throws whenever possible.

2. Cover the bases and back up plays when necessary.

3. Practice Alternate Double Play—Drill No. 183.

4. Practice Optional Double Play—Drill No. 194.

D. *Third Baseman*

1. Snappy overhand throws.

2. Covers the bag and backs up plays when necessary.

3. Fields slow bunts.

4. Crow hops to base for force-out at third and throw to first.

E. *Situation Play: Runners on First and Second*
When the ball is hit to first base, the first baseman throws for one out to the shortstop covering second, who throws to the third baseman to pick-off runner rounding third, as in Drill No. 194.

F. *Using Pitchers in Pre-Game Infield Practice*   by Ernie Myers
We use two pitchers who are scheduled to pitch the next two games and two first basemen for this part of pre-game infield practice.

When it is time for the ball to be hit to the first baseman, one of the pitchers runs to the mound. When the fungo hitter hits to the first baseman, one of the pitchers covers first base and the first baseman tosses him the ball. The pitcher, in a secondary play, throws the ball to the catcher at home plate. Repeat this drill with the other pitcher and first baseman.

The pitchers also cover first when the first baseman throws to second to get two. Extra pitchers back up the catcher, assist the outfielders or do additional drills along the foul line.

158. GAME CONDITION INFIELD PRACTICE

PURPOSE

To get all infielders acquainted with game condition plays. (Note Illustration No. 65.)

PROCEDURE

Have the infielders assume their respective positions, with a pitcher on the mound and a catcher behind the plate. Use outfielders and pitchers as base runners.

The pitcher throws a ball to the catcher. The coach, who stands near the plate, hits another ball to the infield—either a ground ball or a line drive. Just as the coach hits the ball, a player standing near the batter's box runs to first base. The infield tries to throw him out. However, if the runner is safe, he stays on base as in a game situation, thus setting up a double play situation.

The coach sets up various situations and hits to different positions as the runners run the bases.

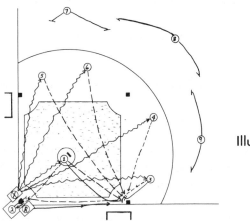

Illustration No. 65

CHAPTER **8**

FIRST BASEMAN DRILLS

A first baseman who knows how to catch the ball and play the bag properly can develop good infielders. If an infielder can throw the ball to first base without worrying about a perfect throw, he will field and throw better. A good first baseman can help the pitcher to keep runners close to the bag, resulting in a force-out at second. Pitchers should be able to throw to first with confidence. The following drills help a first baseman learn his position well and develop into a good fielder.

159. CHECKLIST FOR PROPER EXECUTION

(Note Screening Candidates Drill No. 246)

160. IN-PLACE REACH AND FIELD DRILL

PURPOSE

To give players an idea of how far they can reach and still field the ball while keeping their feet in place or by taking one crossover step. In addition to the purpose mentioned above, this drill also helps infielders and pitchers develop the quick reflex action so necessary for handling the hard smashes they are faced with during game situations. (Note Illustration No. 66.)

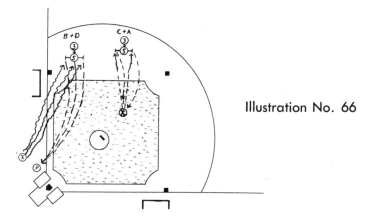

Illustration No. 66

PROCEDURE

Put infielders in fielding position, feet spread comfortably about shoulder width apart. Fielders should be crouched, knees slightly bent, weight distributed evenly on the balls of the feet, which are parallel and slightly toed-in or pointed straight ahead. Their arms should hang loosely out from and in front of the body, so that the glove and throwing hand are carried low. (Note Illustration No. 60.) After the fielders are in position, the coach should stand about 20 feet away with a supply of baseballs. (Note Drill No. 146.)

A. *Fielding Thrown Balls.* The coach throws line drives, one hoppers, and ground balls to the left and right of the fielders. The fielders must field the balls by reaching and keeping their feet in place.

B. *Fielding Batted Balls.* From 90 feet the coach hits the same type of balls he threw from 20 feet, and fielders must field them by reaching only, no stepping.

C. *Fielding Thrown Balls with a Crossover Step.* The same procedure is followed as in "A," except fielders are permitted to take one crossover step, since the coach throws the balls farther to the right and left.

D. *Fielding Batted Balls with a Crossover Step.* This is the same as "B," except that a crossover step is permitted, since the coach hits balls farther to the right and left. (Drills No. 31 and 161 can be applied here.)

161. DIVING DRILL WITH PITCHING MACHINE AND TENNIS BALLS

PURPOSE

To give infielders an opportunity to field fast-thrown or hit balls to their right, left and directly at them, in the dirt and on a line drive. Baseballs can be used for this drill, but there is less chance of injury using tennis balls.

PROCEDURE

Set the pitching machine up to throw the tennis balls at a specific spot either into the dirt or surface 35 to 40 feet away from the machine.

Now stand the fielders to the left of the spot and have the first player get set for the ball to come out of the machine. The player waits until the ball leaves the machine, then he dives and tries to make the catch. That fielder moves to the right side out of the play area. The next player moves into a set position and the coach shoots the next ball. He moves to the right and the process goes on until all have fielded the ball from the left side. They then field from the right side and move over to the left side each taking a turn for at least 10 dives from each side.

The next drill is to shoot the tennis balls directly in front of the player. Each player takes 10 consecutive shots from the machine. Then line up the players as for the first part of the drill. The coach now shoots line drives which the players attempt to catch by diving for them. Continue the drill as above on ground balls.

Finally, shoot balls over their head. Each player taking at least 10 each. This would be similar to a line shot off the bat, directly over an infielder's head. It is a jumping catch. The speed of the balls can be adjusted to the coach's wishes. However, the faster tennis balls are thrown, the better the results from this drill.

If you don't have a pitching machine, a fungo hitter can hit baseballs to the right and left of the fielders. The ball can be hit fairly hard, but for safety's sake the ball should not be hit directly at a player. The fungo hitter can stand 75 to 90 feet away from the fielder. (Note Drills No. 31 and 160.)

162. BREAK FOR AND COVER FIRST BASE

PURPOSE

To teach the first baseman how to find first base and to get to the bag quickly after the ball has been hit.

PROCEDURE

Place a first baseman in his fielding position and have balls hit to another infielder. When the ball is hit, the first baseman looks at and breaks for the bag. When he is about four feet from the bag he turns clockwise and hops to the bag, facing the fielder who is throwing the ball. The first baseman's heels touch the corners of the bag. (Note Drills No. 163 and 164.) To keep the first baseman from breaking for first too quickly, hit some balls near his fielding position. This will keep him "honest"—as he should not leave his position until he sees whether the ball is hit into his fielding area.

163. SHIFTING OF FEET WHEN TAGGING THE BASE

PURPOSE

To give the first baseman better balance in the fielding position on thrown balls.

PROCEDURE

Place the first baseman at the bag, and throw balls to his left and right, high and low. On balls thrown directly at a right-handed first baseman, his right foot tags the bag, and his left foot goes out toward the throw. It is reversed for the left-handed first baseman.

A. *The Well-Coordinated First Baseman:* The well-coordinated player should shift his feet on balls thrown to one side or the other. On balls to his right, his left foot tags the bag, and on balls to his left, his right foot tags the bag.

B. *The Uncoordinated First Baseman.* This player need not shift his feet. However, if he is right-handed, his right foot touches the base on all throws. And if he is left-handed, his left foot always tags the bag.

Illustration No. 67   Shifting Feet

Note: Prior to the throw, the first baseman breaks toward the base. His heels touch the inner corners of the bag. He strides to meet the ball. His striding foot hits the dirt just as the ball hits his glove. This keeps his other foot on the bag.

The foot tagging the bag should be turned sideways, with the inside of the foot facing the dirt and the toe of the foot tagging the bag. The first baseman never kicks the bag or at the bag on the catch, unless the throw pulls him off, but goes from the bag on the catch. (Note Illustration No. 67.)

164. FIELDING THROWS

PURPOSE

To teach the first baseman to get into position to field all throws.

PROCEDURE

Have all infielders in their respective positions. The coach hits balls to all infield positions, and the first baseman breaks for the bag to take the throw.

A. *From Second Base, Third Base, Shortstop.* In fielding balls thrown from the above three positions, the first baseman tries to face the fielder throwing the ball.

B. *From Catcher.* 1. On slow hits or bunts, the first baseman places his left foot on the bag and his right foot in the infield, giving the catcher a good target inside the base line. However, a good position for the first baseman for this throw is to be three feet inside the line, receive the ball and step to the left tagging the base with the left foot. Giving the catcher a target on the inside will help the catcher not to throw the ball into the runner.

2. On a ball that is in foul territory on the first base side—a passed ball or missed third strike—the first baseman puts his right foot on the bag and his left foot in foul territory, receiving the ball outside the base line.

C. *First Baseman as Relay Man.* The first baseman will take throws from right field on balls hit into deep right field foul territory. This is the only play in which a first baseman normally would go out as a relay man.

D. *The First Baseman as Cut-Off Man.* The first baseman acts as cut-off man on all throws to home plate from right and center fields. On throws from right field, he lines up the throw and is in the grass area between the mound and first base. On throws from center field, he gets near the mound, lining up the throw so the throw will not hit the mound.

165. PITCHER TEAMWORK DRILL

PURPOSE

To teach the pitcher the proper way to approach and cover first base, and to teach the first baseman the proper way to give him the ball.

PROCEDURE

Put a pitcher on the mound and a first baseman in position for the following plays. The coach rolls or hits the ball to the first baseman, who throws to the pitcher covering first base.

A. *Deep Throw*. The ball is hit to the first baseman's right, near the second baseman's position. The first baseman fields the ball and throws it to the pitcher approximately three feet before he hits the bag. The throw should be overhand and at medium speed.

B. *Close Throw*. The coach hits the ball to the first baseman near the bag, who tosses it to the pitcher, chest high, before he hits the bag. The throw is an underhand toss, with the palm of the hand facing the pitcher. When the first baseman tosses, he moves with the ball, stepping toward the pitcher in a follow-through. The ball must not hang in the air; the toss must be firm.

C. *Fielding Bunt*. The coach rolls the ball between the pitcher and the first baseman. If the pitcher sees that he can field the ball, he yells, ''I got it!'' and the first baseman gets out of the way, moving toward first. Normally, the second baseman covers first on this play. If the pitcher cannot get it, he yells, ''Take it!'' and breaks for the bag, allowing the first baseman to field the ball.

166. HOLDING THE RUNNER ON BASE

PURPOSE

To help the first baseman learn how to hold the runner on the base, then break from the bag on the pitch to be in position to field the ball if it is hit to his area.

The fundamentals involved in the drill are as follows: the first baseman takes a position with his left foot on or near the foul line. The right foot is on the inside corner of the base nearest the pitcher. The glove is held just off the right knee as a target for the pitcher. The tag is made in a sweeping motion back to the base. Let the runner come to the base rather than going to him. When no pick-off is attempted and the pitch is being made, the first baseman takes two quick steps toward second base and gets set to field the batted ball. An exception would be on a possible bunt. Then he must break toward home.

PROCEDURE

The pitcher holds the runner on the base, sometimes attempting to pick him off and sometimes pitching to the catcher. On the pitch, the first baseman takes two quick steps to get into fielding position. As the pitcher throws, the coach hits to the first baseman, who fields the ball and throws it to the pitcher to continue the drill. Add a bunt situation.

167. TEAMWORK WITH THE SECOND BASEMAN

(Note Second Base Drill No. 175)

168. FIELDING BUNTS AND THROWING

PURPOSE

To teach first basemen how to get into position to throw, and to throw accurately at the bases when fielding a bunt.

PROCEDURE

Place infielders in respective positions. The coach throws or rolls balls to the first baseman, who throws to one of the following bases:

A. *To Third Base*. Left or right-handed first baseman charges the ball, fields it on the run if possible, rounds off to get into position, and throws chest high to the third baseman for a force-out, knee high for a tag-out. Use a crow-hop throw if an emergency throw is not necessary.

B. *To Second Base*. The first baseman charges the ball, fielding it on the run if possible. The left-handed first baseman pivots clockwise and throws overhand if possible, using a crow hop if an emergency throw is not necessary.

The right-handed first baseman fields the ball with his back toward second base, pivots counterclockwise, uses a crow hop if possible, and throws overhand to second base if possible.

C. *To First Base*. The left-hander charges the ball, fields it, pivots clockwise, and throws to first base. The right-hander does the same, but pivots counterclockwise.

D. *To Home Plate*. Both right and left-handers charge ball, field it, and throw overhand or underhand, whichever is needed. The throw must be a firm, hard toss, chest high for a force-out, knee high for a tag-out.

169. TAKING THROWS FROM THE CATCHER
ON PICK-OFF PLAYS

PURPOSE

To teach the first baseman to break for the bag, catch the ball, and tag the base runner. It may be necessary to take throws on the run.

PROCEDURE

Have a pitcher on the mound, catcher behind the plate, a runner on first base, and a first baseman in his position. Use a pitchout for this drill.

A. *Bunt Situation*. Start the play with a prearranged sign between the first baseman and the catcher. The first baseman holds the runner on base before the pitch is made. The runner takes an exceptional lead and the first baseman moves toward home taking only about five steps on the pitch. The first baseman returns quickly toward the bag and receives the throw from the catcher.

B. *Runners on First and Second*. With runners on first and second, the first baseman is back behind the runner in his fielding position, and the runner at first is taking a big lead.

The pitcher delivers the ball to the catcher. When it is 10 to 12 feet in front of the catcher, the first baseman breaks for and straddles the base with his left foot in foul territory near the front corner and the right foot touching the opposite corner, and receives the throw from the catcher.

170. TRAILER PLAY

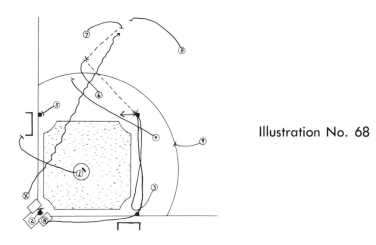

Illustration No. 68

PURPOSE

To give shortstop and second baseman practice in attempting a pick-off at second or holding the runner close to second base on extra base hits.

PROCEDURE

Put a team in its defensive position with a hitter at the plate. The coach, who is standing between third and home, hits an extra base hit to left or center field. At the crack of the bat, the hitter runs as though he had hit the ball.

As the runner is on his way to first, the first baseman drifts toward first base. When the runner goes on to second, the first baseman trails him at a distance of 10 to 15 feet, and covers second when the runner breaks for third.

When the ball is hit to left-center field, the left and center fielders give chase; the shortstop drifts out to become the relay man, and the second baseman goes out to back him up, thus leaving second base open. (Note Trailer Play No. 186 and Illustration No. 68.)

171. POP FLY DRILL

(Note Team Drill No. 42)

CHAPTER 9

SECOND BASEMAN DRILLS

Second base is a difficult position to play, and it takes practice and hard work to master it. The second baseman must have no fear of the sliding runner. To overcome fear, he must have confidence in his pivot steps. The following drills develop a confident, intelligent, well-conditioned second baseman. Teamwork with the shortstop is a key to success. There is no play like the double play to kill an opponent's rally. Work on it daily.

172. CHECKLIST FOR PROPER EXECUTION

(Note Screening Candidates Drill No. 246)

173. FIELDING AND THROWING

PURPOSE

To help the second baseman learn to get into position for fielding balls and to make the proper throws to bases.

PROCEDURE

The coach hits balls to the second baseman and sets up the following play:

A. *To First Base*.

1. The ball is hit to the second baseman's left. If he fields the ball while facing the infield or first base, he crow hops on his right foot and rotates his body clockwise, pointing his left shoulder at the first baseman. His throw is then a medium speed to the first baseman or pitcher covering first base.

2. The ball is hit to the second baseman's left side, to the deep field position, on the outfield grass toward the right field foul line. He catches the ball, pivots counterclockwise in a complete circle, and makes the throw to first base.

3. The ball is hit directly at the second baseman. He charges the ball in a normal way and throws overhand to first base, either flat-footed or with a crow hop.

4. The ball is hit to the right of the second baseman. He fields the ball and pivots or slides to his right foot, plants the right foot, and throws flat-footed to first. He may sometimes jump into the air and throw while at the top of his jump.

5. The ball is hit over second base—no runner on first base. This drill should be worked during regular infield practice. If the second baseman fields the ball and cannot throw the runner out, he should toss the ball to the shortstop, who throws to first base. This is very similar to a double play.

B. *To Third Base*. With a runner on second base hit a line drive or hard ground ball to the second baseman. The runner on second breaks at the crack of the bat. The second baseman fields the ball and:

1. If it is a line drive fly ball, the second baseman makes his throw to second base, where the shortstop is covering;

2. If it is a hard ground ball, he throws to third base to cut off the runner. He should use a crow hop to the right foot and an overhand throw to the knees of the third baseman.

C. *To Home Plate*. With the runner on third, hit hard ground balls and slow ground balls to the second baseman. The second baseman takes a position near the infield grass and fields the ball as he moves toward home. When he fields the ball, he makes an overhand throw to the catcher's knees, having him tag the runner out. On a slowly hit ball he may have to throw underhand or side-armed.

D. *Relays*. Hit balls into right field and center field for extra base hits, as in Drills No. 44 and 45. The second baseman goes out into the relay position for all plays, which means he sets up in a direct line between the outfielder and the base to which the outfielder throws. The outfielder should make the short throw head high and to the glove side of the second baseman. The second baseman should be moving toward the base to which he wants to make the long throw.

174. FIELDING SLOWLY HIT BALLS

PURPOSE

To teach the second baseman how to handle slowly hit balls on the run and to make accurate throws.

PROCEDURE

A. Hit a slow-bouncing ball to the second baseman in a deep position. He charges the ball, picks it up, and throws underhand to the first baseman.

B. With the second baseman in a position near the infield grass, hit slow balls or push bunts. The fielder fields the ball and throws to first. Daily work is needed on these drills.

175. TEAMWORK WITH THE FIRST BASEMAN

PURPOSE

To be sure that first base is covered and to prevent unnecessary base hits between the first baseman and the second baseman.

PROCEDURE

Use a pitcher, first baseman, second baseman, and catcher, with the coach as a hitter. The pitcher throws to the catcher, and the coach hits a different infield ball each time.

Ground Ball Between First and Second Base. When the ball is hit, the pitcher breaks for first base as described in Drill No. 106. Both the first baseman and the second baseman break for the ball. Knowing that the pitcher is covering first base, the first baseman takes all he can get. The second baseman runs the play by letting the first baseman take the ball or yelling, "I got it." If the first baseman fields the ball, he pivots and throws to the pitcher covering first. If the second baseman takes the ball, he throws from a clockwise or counterclockwise pivot, depending upon where he fields the ball, as in Drill No. 173 A-2.

176. FIELDING BUNTS

PURPOSE

To teach the second baseman to break for first base and receive the throw on a fielded bunt.

PROCEDURE

Use a first baseman, second baseman, third baseman, pitcher and a catcher. Bunt balls or toss them into proper bunting areas.

A. *Covering First Base.* Since it is a bunting situation, prior to the ball being bunted, the second baseman anticipates the bunt and takes a position closer to the infield than his normal playing position and slightly toward first base. When the ball is bunted, he breaks directly for first base as quickly as possible. (Note First Baseman Drill 164.)

B. *Receiving Throws.* Upon straddling the bag, the second baseman faces the player who is throwing the ball and receives it in the same manner as the first baseman in Drills No. 163 and 164. (Also note Drill No. 165-C.)

177. RECEIVING THROWS

PURPOSE

To teach the second baseman to get into proper position for throws to second base.

PROCEDURE

A. *Throw from the Pitcher on Batted Balls:* Place the shortstop and second baseman in position. Hit the ball to the pitcher with the second baseman covering second base for the force-out or double play. Prior to the ball's being hit to the pitcher, the second baseman and/or shortstop relays a sign to the pitcher telling him who is covering second base. The shortstop and the second baseman should alternate taking the throw. They back each other up on this play.

B. *Throw from the Catcher on Steals.*

1. On a steal of second base, cover as in Drill No. 178-D.
2. Place runners on first and third and attempt the double steal. The second baseman breaks to a position three or four feet in front of second base, toward the mound. As he is breaking into position, just before he receives the ball, or just after he receives the ball, he

looks for the runner on third base to break for home. The shortstop will also aid in calling the play by yelling, ''Home,'' or ''Second Base.'' If the play is at home, the second baseman moves in toward home, takes the ball on the run, and throws the ball to the catcher knee high. If the play is at second base, the second baseman stays in position, receives the ball, falls toward the bag to make the tag, and immediately comes up ready to throw home if the runner on third breaks for home.

C. For other throws see Drills No. 178 and 181.

178. COVERING SECOND BASE

PURPOSE

To teach the second baseman how to handle tag plays and to see that the bag is always covered.

PROCEDURE

A. During Drill No. 42, Pop Fly Drill, insist that the shortstop and the second baseman determine which one will cover second while the other is fielding a ball.

B. When a base on balls is given in a game, be sure that the shortstop or second baseman covers the base to prevent the base-on-balls runner from advancing to second base.

Illustration No. 69   Covering Second Base

C. When receiving throws from the outfield, the second baseman straddles the bag, facing the throw. He places his glove with the ball in it at the edge of the base facing the runner.

D. In taking throws from the catcher, the second baseman again straddles the bag, looking at the throw, receives the ball, and places it on the edge of the base facing the runner.

E. Taking the throw while straddling the bag, the second baseman places the ball in the web of his glove, and places the glove with the ball in it on the edge of the base facing the runner with the back of his index finger, thumb, and web toward the runner. He lets the runner slide into his glove. As soon as the runner hits his glove, he pulls the glove and ball from the play to avoid letting the runner kick the ball out of the glove. (Note Illustration No. 69.)

F. On hit and run, always take one step in toward the hitter before breaking for the bag. This helps to keep the fielder from breaking too soon, thus leaving a hole open for the hit and run.

179. ON-BASE-LINE-TAG DOUBLE PLAY

PURPOSE

To learn how to avoid being run down by the runner in the base line.

PROCEDURE

Hit slow balls to the second baseman, having him field them in the base line. Do this first without a runner, then with a runner.

When the ball has been fielded, the second baseman fakes a backhand throw to second base with his arm, hand, body, and head. In doing this he does not pivot toward second, but steps with his right foot and fakes a backhand toss to second base. He then turns toward the runner, tags him, and throws to first. The fake takes the runner's mind off the act of running the second baseman

Illustration No. 70

down. He will then become concerned with the shortstop. (Note Drill No. 180-B for action in faking throw and Illustration No. 70.)

180. SECOND BASEMAN AS A STARTER ON THE DOUBLE PLAY   by Woody Woodward

PURPOSE

To give the second baseman the knowledge, timing, and balance needed in the process of giving the shortstop the ball in the most accurate and best way on the double play. The double play is a difficult maneuver with a bad throw from the starter, but it can be made easier with a perfect throw.

A second baseman and shortstop must practice their own individual skills which are needed to complete the double play. They must work diligently together until they know each other's moves perfectly. This includes: how each player approaches the base; how he crosses the base; the manner of receiving his partner's throw and where he likes the throw. In order to effectively learn these moves, the player should know and appreciate the most difficult plays his partner must execute. For this reason at Florida State the shortstop and second baseman change positions and the second baseman and the third baseman change positions. I believe that learning all positions makes each one appreciate and understand the other players' jobs. They can then help each other make the difficult plays.

POINTS TO EMPHASIZE ARE:

1. The second baseman should approach the bag with his feet pointing toward third base and the upper part of his body facing the fielder making the throw. This will allow his hips to open up for an easier throw. The second baseman should anticipate bad throws from deep shortstop and third base. The distance makes it tougher to make a perfect throw.

2. The second baseman should not throw behind (right side of body) the shortstop as he crosses the bag. It is much easier for the shortstop to handle a throw in front of him or to his left.

Illustration No. 70 (*Continued*)

3. The second baseman and shortstop should keep the ball in full view and not hide it in the glove when starting a double play.

4. All infielders should work at making their throws chest high with something on the ball. Do not give your partner a soft toss.

5. Both hands should be carried chest high when receiving the throw. This will allow the infielder to release the ball quickly after the catch.

6. The shortstop should try to get the ball to the second baseman as soon as possible. The more time they take, the more time a runner has to reach the second baseman.

Following are the locations and methods for a second baseman to field a ground ball and give it to the shortstop to start a double play.

PROCEDURE

Hit some balls hard and some slowly to the second baseman in the following positions:

A. *Balls Hit Directly at the Second Baseman.* The second baseman should field the ball with his right foot slightly behind his left, legs spread, and both feet planted. He pivots his hips and throws overhand or three-quarters side-arm to the shortstop. There is no pivot of the feet. (Illustration No. 71.)

B. *Balls Hit to His Right, Near Second Base.* In this situation the second baseman fields balls nearly as above, except that his body may be facing more toward second base. The ball is tossed with a backhand, side-arm motion directly from the glove. The palm of the hand is facing the ground and rotates counterclockwise as the ball is thrown to the shortstop. (Note Illustration No. 72.)

C. *Balls Hit to the Second Baseman's Left.* The second baseman gets in front of the ball, catches it, and pivots in a snappy jump motion. His right foot pivots back behind his left, and his left foot pivots toward second base. The ball is thrown either side-arm or three-quarter from this position. (Note Illustration No. 73.)

D. *Balls to the Second Baseman's Deep Left.* On these balls the second baseman cannot get in front of them to make the pivot as described in "C" above. Often it is easier to pivot forward, counterclockwise, crossing the right foot in front of the left, planting it out toward the right field foul line, then throwing the ball as the left foot steps toward second. Sometimes a second baseman can make this throw more easily by pivoting on his left foot counterclockwise, jumping into the air, and throwing on the jump and pivot. (Note Illustration No. 74.)

Illustration No. 71   Balls Hit Directly at Second Baseman

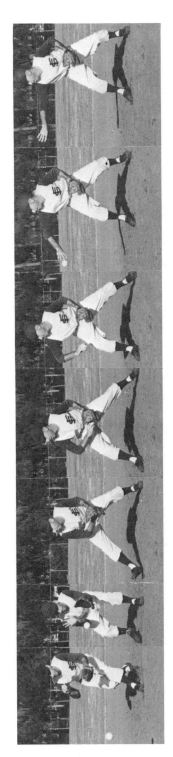

Illustration No. 72   Balls Hit to Right, Near Second Base

Illustration No. 73   Balls Hit to Second Baseman's Left

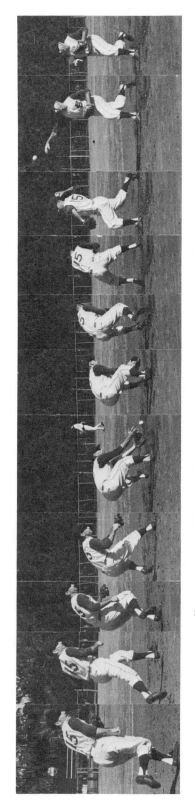

Illustration No. 74   Balls Hit to Second Baseman's Deep Left

194

181. DOUBLE PLAY DRILLS WITH SECOND BASEMAN AS THE MIDDLEMAN   by Woody Woodward

PURPOSE

To teach the second baseman all possible ways to receive a throw and make the pivot to complete a double play. (Note Detour Drill No. 182 and Drill 279, Illustration No. 110.)

PROCEDURE

Hit ground balls to the shortstop, who throws to the second baseman covering second base. The second baseman receives the ball and makes the pivot necessary to complete the double play by throwing to first base. The following are the recommended pivots. (Note Drill 180 under proposed points to remember for proper approach to the bag.)

A. *Method 1.* The second baseman moves toward second base, getting there as early as possible, steps on the bag with his right foot, and throws from there. As the left foot hits the dirt on the stride toward first base, the right foot comes up and over the sliding runner, with a slight jump off the left foot. This seems to be the most popular method and the quickest. (Illustration No. 75.)

Illustration No. 75   Right Foot Tag

Method 2. The second baseman steps on the bag with his right foot, crow hops from six inches to one foot off the bag on the right foot, and throws from that position. (Note Illustration No. 76.)

Method 3. The toughest play is for the second baseman to take the throw on the dead run, tag the bag, pivot and throw. This may occur on some hitters. A good procedure here is for the second baseman to step next to the bag on the side of his approach with his left foot, dragging it across the bag for the

Illustration No. 76   Right Foot Crow Hop

Illustration No. 77   Left Foot Drag

tag, then stepping with his right foot, and planting the right foot for an over-hand throw. (Note Illustration No. 77.)

Method 4. Here is the only pivot where the throw will originate from the left foot. The second baseman may have to take the throw a few steps before he hits the bag. The fastest and best way to make this play is for the left foot to hit the bag, with the second baseman throwing as he comes across the bag, leaping and throwing at the same time to get accuracy and something on the ball. (Note Illustration No. 78.)

Illustration No. 78   Left Foot Pivot

Method 5. The second baseman tags the bag with his left foot, backs up, and throws when his weight has been shifted to his right foot. Note that tag of the bag is completed before ball is received. (Note Illustration No. 79.)

Illustration No. 79   Left Foot Tag—Backing Off

Method 6. The second baseman steps on the bag with his left foot, steps and plants his right foot toward the mound, and throws from there.

Method 7. The second baseman straddles the bag and uses a shift similar to that of a first baseman. When the ball is to his left, his right foot tags the bag, and he throws. With the ball to his right, he tags the bag with his left foot, shifts his weight to his right foot, and throws.

B. *Receiving Throws from the Pitcher.* The coach hits the ball to the pitcher, who fields it, turns, and throws to the second baseman covering second. The second baseman attempts to straddle the bag so that he can shift to either side for the throw. Then he makes one of the above pivots to complete the double play.

C. *Receiving Throws from the Catcher.* When the coach rolls a ball out as though it were bunted, the catcher fields it and throws to the second baseman covering second. The second baseman receives the throw and pivots as above.

D. *Receiving Throws from the Third Baseman.* The coach hits balls to the third baseman in the deep position, close in, to his left, and to his right. The third baseman fields the balls and throws to the second baseman covering second. The second baseman makes a direct approach toward the throw, with toes always pointing toward third base when approaching the bag. He receives the ball, and makes the pivot best suited for completion of the double play.

E. *Receiving Throws from the Shortstop*. The shortstop fields balls hit by the coach and throws to the second baseman covering second. The second baseman gets to the bag as quickly as possible. He approaches the throw in a direct line, but tries to keep his body or shoulders angled slightly toward first base for an easier pivot, his toes always pointing toward third base when approaching the bag. He receives the throw, makes the best suited pivot and throws to first base to complete the double play.

F. *Timing the Double Play*. After the double play combination has been thoroughly developed, time the complete action from the hit of the ball until the ball reaches first base. A good double play is made in 3.5 to 4.5 seconds.

182. DETOUR DRILL

PURPOSE

To teach second baseman efficiency of motion in completing the double play as the middle man.

PROCEDURE

A. Put a second baseman on second base and a first baseman about 10 feet from the second base, directly in line with first and second base. In this phase of the drill the second baseman has no glove.

The shortstop tosses the ball to the second baseman, who steps on the base with his right foot and lets the ball hit his right hand. He merely keeps the ball moving toward first base—actually a detour of the ball to the first baseman.

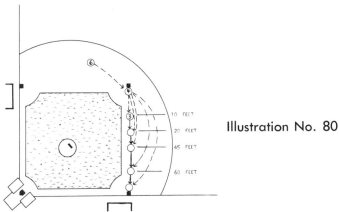

Illustration No. 80

B. The first baseman now moves 20 feet away from the bag, and the same drill continues.

C. The first baseman moves 45 feet away from the bag. Continue the drill.

D. The first baseman moves 60 feet away from the bag. The second baseman puts his glove on, and the drill is continued.

E. The first baseman covers first base, and the drill is continued. (Note Illustration No. 80.)

183. ALTERNATE DOUBLE PLAY WITH RUNNERS ON FIRST AND THIRD

PURPOSE

To learn how to get an alternate double play if the usual one is not feasible or cannot be made. (Note Illustration No. 81.)

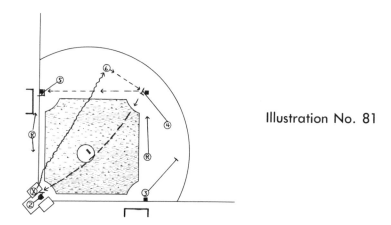

Illustration No. 81

PROCEDURE

Put the runners on first and third, with the infield halfway in, the pitcher on the mound, and the catcher behind the plate. Have balls hit sharply to an infielder or the pitcher. The player fielding the ball "looks" the runner back to third and throws to second base for one out. The runner breaks for home, and the fielder who covered second base throws to the catcher at the plate. The catcher tags the runner for the second out of the double play.

184. OPTIONAL DOUBLE PLAY

(See Shortstop Drill No. 194)

185. PICK-OFF DRILL

PURPOSE

To teach the second baseman duties on pick-off plays and to keep the runner close to second base. (Note Drills No. 47 and 122 for other pick-offs.)

PROCEDURE

Put the second baseman and shortstop in position, the pitcher on the mound, and a runner on second base.

A. *Fake Pick-Off*. The pitcher comes set and checks the runner at second. While the pitcher is looking back at the runner, the second baseman makes a short fake to the base. If the runner takes his eyes off the second baseman for a moment, the second baseman can break for the bag. The pitcher turns and throws for the pick-off.

B. *Set Up as in "A" Above*. The shortstop runs for the base. The pitcher, looking at second base, makes no move while the shortstop is out of position. The shortstop then moves between the runner and second base, then back to his position by going toward third base, passing in front of the runner. As the shortstop is even with and directly in front of the runner, the runner probably will move away from the bag with the shortstop. If the runner takes his eye off the second baseman, the second baseman breaks for the bag as the pitcher pivots and throws to second base for the pick-off.

186. TRAILER PLAY DRILL (Special Drill for Cut-Off Plays)

(Note Drills No. 44, 45 and 170)

PURPOSE

For protection on over-throws or bad throws to the relay man.

PROCEDURE

When working Drill No. 45 on extra base hits, the shortstop goes out for the relay throw, and the second baseman lines up 25 to 30 feet behind him for protection on bad throws from the outfield. When the second baseman goes out for the relay, the shortstop is the trailer. Second base is being covered by the first baseman, as in Drill No. 170.

187. POP FLY DRILL

(Note Team Drill No. 42)

CHAPTER 10

SHORTSTOP DRILLS

The opinion is often expressed that a team must be strong "down the middle." A weak shortstop results in a weak team. He should have a strong arm and be able to make plays to his left, right and moving in toward the ball.

Since the majority of double plays start at shortstop, he can make or break the second baseman. A good team will average a double play per game and complete a double play in less than five seconds from the crack of the bat until the first baseman catches the ball.

Designed to strengthen the shortstop's arm, to help teach him to be in the right place and make the right play, especially the all-important double play, the following drills should play a big part in the success of the infield.

188. CHECKLIST FOR PROPER EXECUTION

(Note Screening Candidates Drill No. 246)

189. FIELDING AND THROWING

PURPOSE

To orient the shortstop for all throws to all bases.

PROCEDURE

Place the shortstop in his fielding position and hit balls to his right, left, and straight at him. Be sure to hit both hard and slow balls.

A. *Throws to First Base*. He fields the ball with his left foot in front of his right. If the ball is hit slowly and straight at him, he scoops the ball outside his left foot, and throws in one motion. On a fast rolling ball, the ball is fielded directly in front of his body.

On balls to his right, the shortstop will go over to his right, and just as the ball is hitting his glove, he sets his right foot for sliding on the inside of his foot, plants this foot, and then throws without a further step.

On balls to his left, he fields them and pivots his right foot around behind his left, plants his right foot and throws.

B. *Throws to Third Base*. With a runner on second base, on balls hit directly to the shortstop and to his right, the third baseman covers third. The shortstop makes the throw without a step, with a clockwise pivot of the body, and knee high to the third baseman.

C. *Throws to Second Base*. (Note Drill No. 192.)

D. *Throws to Home Plate*. Hit both hard and slow balls to the shortstop. He should charge and field the ball, then throw overhand, if possible, knee high to the catcher. A crow hop improves accuracy.

E. *Throws on Relays*. The shortstop goes out for relay throws from left field, left center, and center field. He receives the ball head high on the glove side, moving toward the base at which he is going to throw. The throw is directly overhand, and in most cases it is a one-hop long bounce. A crow-hop step is used to make the throw. (Note Drill No. 44 for Relay Procedures.)

190. RECEIVING THROWS

PURPOSE

To help the shortstop learn the correct positions for, and how to handle, all throws.

PROCEDURE

A. *Throws from the Pitcher When Fielding Batted Balls*. Put the pitcher on the mound and the shortstop in his fielding position. Hit ground balls to the pitcher, who whirls and throws to the shortstop covering second base for a force-out or to start a double play.

B. *Throws from the Catcher*.

1. On an attempted steal of second base, the shortstop breaks for second on the pitch, and the catcher throws to the shortstop covering second. After this is practiced a few times, put a runner on first base and have him break for second on the pitch.

2. The attempted double steal. Work first without runners, then with runners on first and third bases. (Note Drill 178-F for hit-and-run situation.)

The pitcher delivers the ball to the catcher, who throws to the shortstop, who is three feet in front of second base, toward the mound. Moving in to meet the ball, the shortstop cuts off the throw and throws to the catcher knee high. On some throws, the shortstop pivots back and tags the runner at second. With runners on base, the shortstop must determine whether to make the tag or to cut off the ball and throw home for the tag at the plate. The second baseman can help by telling him, "Home!" or by saying nothing if the runner stays on third base.

C. *Throws from the Outfield.* (Note Drill No. 178-C and E.)

191. BUNTING SITUATIONS—COVERING SECOND BASE AND THIRD BASE

PURPOSE

To teach the shortstop to be in the proper position for all bunting plays.

PROCEDURE

Put the first baseman, second baseman, shortstop and pitcher in their respective positions. Have a player or coach bunt the ball.

A. When the ball is bunted with a runner on first base, the second baseman covers first, and the shortstop covers second base. The shortstop covers second for the possible steal or force-out.

B. 1. With runners on first and second base, the shortstop takes a position near second, holds the runner on, and fakes him back when he tries to take a lead. He must be certain not to break toward second base as the pitcher is delivering the ball.

2. With runners on first and second bases, the shortstop takes a deep fielding position, giving the runner a lot of room. The shortstop breaks for second base until he notes the runner is breaking back to the bag. The pitcher, who has been looking at second, makes a three-quarter speed perfect strike pitch to the hitter as the shortstop changes direction and charges to cover third base. The third baseman, pitcher, and first baseman cover the bunted ball. Whoever fields the ball throws to the shortstop who is on third base facing the throw.

192. DOUBLE PLAY WITH THE SHORTSTOP AS
THE STARTER   by Woody Woodward

(Note Drill No. 181 and apply to this drill.)

PURPOSE

To give the shortstop the knowledge, timing, and balance necessary to complete a double play.

PROCEDURE

The coach hits balls both hard and slow to the shortstop in the following positions. (The balls thrown by the shortstop should be firm and chest high.)

A. *Balls Hit to the Left, Behind the Bag*. The shortstop attempts to get around the ball in a better position to make the throw to second base. The ball is taken from the glove and thrown as described in Drill No. 180-B for the second baseman. It is a backhand throw.

B. *Balls Hit to the Right*. The shortstop should attempt to get around the ball with his feet in position. The right foot should be forward of the left. This is done to open up the hips so that the second baseman can see the throw coming. The shortstop should make an overhand throw whenever possible. (Note Illustration No. 82.)

Illustration No. 82

C. *Balls Hit Directly at the Shortstop*. After moving in to field this ball, the shortstop should plant his feet parallel or his right foot slightly ahead of the left. He then throws the ball overhand to the second baseman.

D. *Balls Hit Near Second Base*. In this case, the shortstop should move over to field the ball and make an underhand throw while still moving forward toward second base. The toss should be firm and hard so that the ball does not hang in the air.

193. DOUBLE PLAY WITH THE SHORTSTOP AS THE MIDDLEMAN   by Woody Woodward

(Note Drill 180 and apply on this drill.)

PURPOSE

To acquaint the shortstop with all possible ways to receive throws and make the pivot to complete the double play.

PROCEDURE

The coach hits ground balls to the second baseman and other infielders, who throw to the shortstop; he receives the ball and makes the following plays:

A. *Pivot Steps:* (Note Illustration No. 83.) 1. Right foot drag: The shortstop runs toward the bag, and places his right foot just short of the bag before or after receiving the ball. He then steps with his left foot and drags his right foot across the bag for the out. After dragging his right foot across the bag, he plants it behind his left and throws off his right foot.

Illustration No. 83   Right Foot Drag

2. Right foot planted on the bag: If the shortstop has time, he can receive the ball, plant his right foot on the bag, and throw from that position. His forward follow-through carries him up the base line.

3. Left foot and pivot: (Note Illustration No. 84.) Moving across the bag, the shortstop hits it with his left foot, pivots to his right behind the left, and plants it to make the throw. His momentum should carry him toward right field, out of the way of the runner.

4. Tags bag with left foot and pivots right: The shortstop moves to the bag and takes the throw on the side nearer the mound. He tags the bag with his left foot and steps toward the mound with his right foot to complete the throw.

5. Receiving the ball behind the bag: (Note Illustration No. 85.) When a ball is hit to either the first or second baseman on the line, the shortstop assumes a position three to four feet behind the bag and lines up the throw. As he receives the ball, he takes a small crow hop to his right foot, stepping on the bag with his left as he throws. His momentum from the throw and a jump off the left leg carries him up and over the sliding runner. The ball is actually thrown before the jump is made. On throws to left of bag use Pivot 1, to the right of the bag, use Pivot 4.

B. *Receiving Throws from the Second Baseman*. The shortstop gets to the bag as quickly as possible, moving directly toward the ball, and tries to receive the ball chest high. Actually, time and practice will tell where he likes to receive the ball.

C. *Receiving Throws from the Pitcher*. The coach hits balls to the pitcher, who whirls and throws chest high to the shortstop. The shortstop should be straddling the bag, waiting for the throw just in back of the bag, or be on the third base side. He then makes the best pivot to complete the play.

D. *Receiving Throws from the Catcher*. This throw will result from either a bunt or a swinging bunt. The catcher throws chest high to the shortstop, and the play is completed in the same manner as Drill "C" above.

E. *Receiving Throws from the First Baseman*. (Described in Drill A-5 above).

F. *Timing the Double Play*. With a stopwatch, time the double play from the crack of the bat until the first baseman receives the ball. The elapsed time should be between 3.5 and 4.5 seconds.

194. OPTIONAL DOUBLE PLAY DRILL WITH RUNNERS ON FIRST AND SECOND BASE

PURPOSE

To teach the shortstop and other infielders to try for a different double play if the original play cannot be carried out.

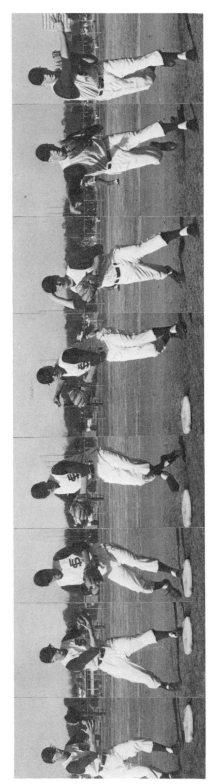

Illustration No. 84   Left Foot Pivot

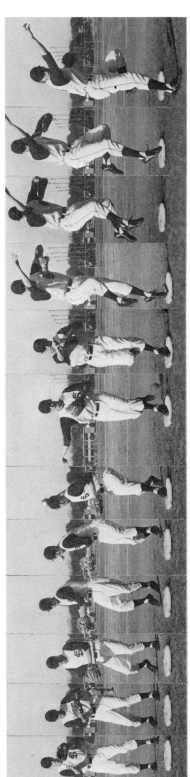

Illustration No. 85   Receiving the Ball Behind the Bag

PROCEDURE

Have the infield in the double play position. Place runners on first and second base, and hit a slow roller to one of the infielders. The infielder playing the ball throws to second for the first out. When it is obvious that the ball was hit so slowly that the second out cannot be made at first, the shortstop or second baseman covering second throws the ball to third in an attempt to catch the runner off the bag in case he has rounded third base. This throw should be made without hesitation, because looking first and then throwing would be too late. (Note Illustration No. 86.)

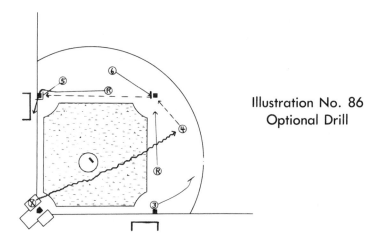

Illustration No. 86
Optional Drill

195. ALTERNATE DOUBLE PLAY

(Note Second Base Drill No. 183)

196. PICK-OFF DRILL

PURPOSE

To help the shortstop and other players master the pick-off play and to help them learn to keep the runner "honest." (Note other pick-off explanation Drills No. 47 and 122.)

PROCEDURE

Use the shortstop in position, pitcher on the mound, catcher behind the plate, and a runner on second base.

A. *Count System*. The pitcher receives the pick-off sign from the shortstop prior to getting on the rubber. He then sees the call of a pitch-out from the catcher. He now assumes a set stance and looks at the runner on second base.

As soon as the pitcher turns his head toward home, the shortstop breaks for second base. When the pitcher looks toward home, he starts counting "one-two-" and on "three" he whirls to his glove side and throws knee high to the shortstop covering second base.

B. *Another Count System*. After the pitcher gets his sign from the catcher, and is in his set stance, he does not look toward the shortstop, but continues to look toward the catcher and begins his stretch. When the ball meets the glove, chest high, the shortstop breaks for second base. The pitcher starts his count at the same time and again on "three" he throws to the shortstop at second base.

C. *Daylight System*. After the pitcher receives the signs, he assumes the set stance on the rubber, and looks back to the shortstop, who breaks for second base. When the pitcher sees daylight between the shortstop and the runner, he looks toward home, pivots toward his glove side, and throws to the shortstop at second base.

D. After the pitcher receives the signs, he assumes the set stance on the rubber, and looks back at the shortstop who holds his position until the pitcher looks at the catcher. The shortstop then breaks for second base. When the catcher sees that the shortstop has a good 1- or 2-step jump on the runner, he flips his glove down. The pitcher then pivots and throws to second base.

197. SPECIAL DRILL FOR FIELDING BALLS IN THE HOLE—SHORTSTOP'S RIGHT

PURPOSE

To teach the shortstop how to field balls and throw them when they are hit in the hole. This drill also helps to strengthen the shortstop's arm.

PROCEDURE

The shortstop is in a position directly in line with a ball hit in the hole. Place the shortstop on the edge of the infield grass. The coach rolls balls to him. The shortstop fields the ball, comes up with it, and throws to first base without taking a stride. His left shoulder is facing first base. His pivot foot is well behind his other foot. His legs are spread wide. In two weeks he should throw from the outfield grass.

The shortstop should work at this no more than 10 minutes for a period of three days; that is, 10 minutes per day. On the second day he should be moved back 10 feet behind where he worked the first day, and on the third day he should be moved back 10 feet farther. (Note Illustration No. 87.)

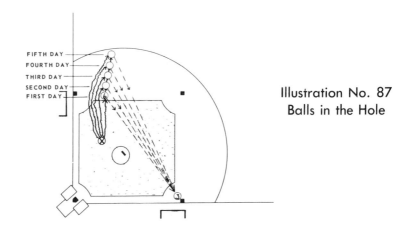

Illustration No. 87
Balls in the Hole

198. TEAMWORK WITH THIRD BASEMAN

PURPOSE

To teach the shortstop to work with the third baseman.

PROCEDURE

A. *Ground Ball Between Third Base and Shortstop*. With the shortstop and third baseman in fielding position, the coach hits ground balls between them at all speeds.

If the shortstop knows that he can field the ball and make the play to first base, he yells, "I got it; I got it!" Otherwise, the third baseman takes every ball.

B. *Runner on Second Base Only*. Have the runner on second base run to third at the crack of the bat. The coach should have hit the ball in the hole to the right of the shortstop, who fields the ball and throws the runner out at third.

C. *Relay of Pitch Called by the Catcher*. With the shortstop and the third baseman in position, the shortstop sees the pitch called by the catcher. By the use of a sign or voice the shortstop tells the third baseman which pitch is being thrown, especially if the pitch is a change-up and a right handed hitter is at bat. The coach should go through this drill until the players involved have mastered it and he is certain that the opposing team cannot read it.

199. TRAILER PLAY ON RELAYS

(Note Drills No. 44, 45, 186 and 170)

200. POP FLY DRILL

(Note Team Drill No. 42)

CHAPTER **11**

THIRD BASEMAN DRILLS

Since the third base position is the hot corner, the third baseman needs drills to help him develop fast reflexes. He needs sure, fast hands and an accurate arm. Although his throws need not all be hard, they may have to be made from any position. He must be able to get in front of the ball, knock it down if necessary, and throw the runner out.

The purpose of the following drills is to make a better third baseman out of any player with good hands.

201. CHECKLIST FOR PROPER EXECUTION

(Note Screening Candidates Drill No. 246)

202. IN-PLACE REACH AND FIELD DRILL

(Note First Baseman Drill No. 160)

203. FIELDING BUNTS

PURPOSE

To teach the third baseman how to field bunts of all types.

PROCEDURE

Place the following players in their defensive positions: Shortstop, third baseman, second baseman, first baseman, pitcher, and catcher. The coach assumes a position near home plate and rolls the ball to the third baseman, who throws the ball to the first or second baseman. The third baseman covers third for the force-out on throws from the other fielders. In fielding bunts, the third baseman must take a path to the ball which will give him good position for throwing.

A. *Fast Roll*. When the ball is rolling fast, the third baseman charges the ball, fields it with his glove, then makes his throw to the proper base. This bunt can sometimes be thrown to second base for an attempted double play or force-out.

B. *Slow Roll*. The third baseman charges the ball and picks it up with his bare hand by letting the ball roll into a cupped, relaxed hand. He then takes a firm throwing grip and throws it to first base only. (Note Illustration No. 88.)

Illustration No. 88

C. *Ball That Has Stopped Rolling*. Place several balls one foot apart half-way between home and third, perpendicular to the foul line, on the infield grass. The third baseman starts on the base path between second and third and charges the balls. He picks up all balls, one at a time, beginning with the one on the extreme left, and throws them to the first baseman. Generally a crow hop is used to throw the ball. (Note Illustration No. 89.) The pick-up and throw

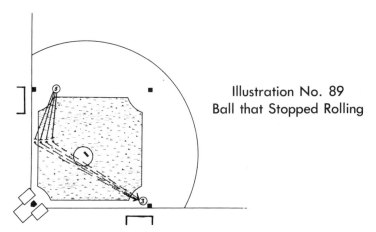

Illustration No. 89
Ball that Stopped Rolling

are made by pushing the ball into the grass with the thumb, index finger, and middle finger in a gripping position; the palm faces the ball as the hand goes down for the pick-up. Depending on practice, the ball can be picked up to the right of either foot. If it is picked up to the right of the right foot, it is thrown from there. If it is picked up to the right of the left foot, the ball is thrown as soon as the right foot hits the ground on the next stride. (Illustration No. 90.)

Illustration No. 90   Fielding It

D. *Bunt with a Runner on Second Base*. Both the pitcher and the third baseman break for the ball. When the pitcher and the third baseman see that the pitcher can field the ball, and the third baseman hears the pitcher yell, "I have it!" he breaks back for the bag to take the throw from the pitcher. He fields the ball in the manner of a first baseman stretching out for the throw. If the third baseman sees that the pitcher cannot get the ball, he continues his charge and makes the play to first base as described in the drill above. He should also yell, "I have it!" (Note Drill 156.) Third baseman yells. "Third," if he covers third.

204. THROWING FIELDED BUNTS

PURPOSE

To teach the third baseman the quickest or best throw to a base in a variety of ways.

PROCEDURE

Place all the infielders in their respective positions. You might include the outfielders in these drills. Roll balls that will stop, fast-rolling balls, and some that are slow to the third baseman.

A. *Throw to Home*. The throws home are usually made when the third baseman has charged the ball. Since this is the case, and because most of these throws have to be made quickly, the throw is made sidearm or underhand from the fielding position.

B. *Throw to First Base*. This throw is always made when the third baseman has charged the ball. The throw usually is made underhand or sidearm. The third baseman should get into fielding position with the left shoulder pointing diagonally toward first base before fielding the ball. Throws can be made with a crow hop or directly from the position of the feet when the ball is fielded. The overhand throw can be made if practiced.

C. *Throw to Second Base*. As the third baseman charges the ball, he works into position so that his chest faces first base and his left shoulder points diagonally toward second base. He fields the ball in his glove and throws overhand or three-quarters, chest high, to second base. This play should be made only on hard bunted balls.

205. FIELDING AND THROWING BATTED BALLS

PURPOSE

To teach the third baseman the necessary fundamentals to make all throws to all bases.

PROCEDURE

Place all infielders in position. The coach hits balls to the third baseman, who throws to the bases as follows:

A. *To First Base*. Balls are hit to the third baseman's left, right, and directly at him. Some are hit hard and some slowly. When he charges the slow ball, he usually has to make an underhand or sidearm throw. On balls hit to his left, he will make a three-quarter to a sidearm throw. And he will throw directly overhand on balls hit straight at him and to his right.

B. *To Second Base*. With the exception of the slowly hit ball, all other balls fielded should be thrown overhand to the second baseman.

C. *To Home*. All throws should be overhand when possible, the exception being the slowly hit ball.

D. *Relay Cut-Off Man with Runners in Scoring Position*. On balls hit to left field or to left center, the third baseman assumes a position on the infield grass between the mound and third base, lining up the throw from the outfield to the catcher. If the throw is not in line with the catcher, or the catcher yells, "Cut it!" the third baseman cuts it off and relays it either to the catcher or some other base. The pitcher also calls the base for the throw.

206. TEAMWORK WITH THE SHORTSTOP

A. *Ground Balls Between Shortstop and Third Baseman*. (Note Shortstop Drill No. 198-A.)

B. *With Runner on Second and a Ground Ball in the Hole to Right of Shortstop*. (Note Shortstop Drill No. 198-B.)

C. *Relay of Pitch Called for by Catcher*. (Shortstop Drill No. 198-C.)

207. RECEIVING THROWS ON BATTED BALLS

PURPOSE

To teach the third baseman how to cover third base and receive the ball for tags or force-outs.

PROCEDURE

Have fielders in position and roll or hit balls to the following:

A. *Catcher—for a tag play*. The third baseman straddles the bag and receives the throw from the catcher. He makes the tag as in Drill No. 178-E.

B. *Catcher—on a force-out*. The third baseman assumes a position on the side of the bag nearest to the catcher and tags the bag with the right foot. He should be ready for a possible throw to first base for a double play.

C. *Pitcher*. Assumes the same position as when receiving throws from the catcher.

D. *First Baseman*. The same as the above.

E. *Outfield*. The third baseman straddles the bag and faces the outfielder or the relay man making the throw.

F. *Shortstop*. (Drill No. 198-B.)

208. PICK-OFF PLAY

PURPOSE

To teach the third baseman how to hold the runner close to the base or to pick him off.

PROCEDURE

Put a runner on third base with the pitcher, catcher, and third baseman in position for pick-off plays, prearranged by a sign between pitcher and third baseman or catcher and third baseman.

A. *Pitcher*. 1. The pitcher uses the count system. In a windup stance, he gets the pitch sign from the catcher. The pitcher looks toward third, and when he looks toward home, the third baseman breaks for the bag and straddles it. The pitcher counts "one" and on "two" turns in a clockwise motion and throws knee high to third base.

2. The pitcher is in a set stance. He gets his sign, looks at third, to home, counts "one" and on "two" throws to third base. The third baseman breaks when the pitcher turns his head from third to home. The pitcher can deceive the runner to some extent by lifting his striding leg as if to deliver to the plate. As his head turns toward home and the leg comes up, he pivots toward third for the pick-off.

3. The pitcher backs off the rubber, fakes a step and throw to first base, then wheels and throws to third base.

B. *Catcher*. The catcher gives a pitchout sign to the pitcher and a pick-off sign to the third baseman. When the ball is 10 to 15 feet in front of home plate, the third baseman breaks for third. He stands on the infield side of the bag, but not straddling it. The catcher throws the ball about two or three feet on the infield side of the bag. This prevents his hitting the runner with the ball.

209. POP FLY DRILL

(Note Team Drill No. 42)

CHAPTER 12

OUTFIELD DRILLS

There is more to playing the outfield than catching a fly ball. If an outfielder misses a ball, the runner takes extra bases. However, if an infielder misses one, the runner may be held to a single by an aggressive outfielder, and there is a chance of a double play or a force-out. An outfielder must see how many plays he can get into on every ball hit. Nothing looks better than to see an outfielder backing up an over-throw or making a put-out in a rundown play. An outfielder is never a good outfielder until he can field ground balls, line drives and balls hit over his head, and make low hard throws.

Not only should the following drills improve an outfielder's skills, but they should also make him believe he is a large part of the game, and was not put in the outfield because he is the poorest player on the team.

210. CHECKLIST FOR PROPER EXECUTION

(Note Screening Candidates Drill No. 246)

211. TOUCH GRASS—RIGHT AND LEFT DRILL

(Note Drill No. 28 to work this drill.)

212. EQUILIBRIUM DRILL

(Note General Infield Drill No. 151 to work this drill.)

213. TOE-RUNNING DRILL   by Ron Oestrike

PURPOSE

A running drill for the entire squad, but the major purpose is to ''level off'' an outfielder's head when he is running after a fly ball.

PROCEDURE

We use ''three balls'' on the drill for each outfielder. We line the outfielders outside the right field foul line and call the term ''break.'' The outfielder will sprint to the right, catch a thrown ball and immediately break back to the left to catch the second thrown ball. He immediately breaks back to the right for the ''long throw.'' After catching the three balls he sprints to the coach and puts the balls in a bucket and returns to the foul line.

The coach has the opportunity to instruct the player to ''run on toes'' and not on his heels. The player picks a point about head high and concentrates on that point before looking for the thrown ball. Also the player is instructed to just turn his head to look for the ball and not turn his entire body. After running the drill several times you will be surprised in the results of ''Leveling the Head'' while running for a ball.

214. GROUND BALL DRILL

PURPOSE

To teach the outfielders how to block a ball and how to field various ground balls.

PROCEDURE

Outfielders should get around all balls, if it is at all possible, to get into position to throw the ball.

The coach hits ground balls to the outfielders telling them whether there is a play to make or not.

A. *With No Play*. The outfielder's job is to get the ball into second base, but above all to keep it from getting past him. When the coach hits the ball, the outfielder charges it until he gets 12 to 15 feet in front of the ball. If the ball takes a good hop and he can time it correctly, he fields the ball with two hands as an infielder, moving in and catching the ball, then crow hopping as he throws to second base. If the ball is rolling and not bouncing, the outfielder goes down on the knee of his throwing side, 15 feet in front of the ball. A right-handed outfielder goes down on his right knee, his left foot is parallel to his knee, and his right leg is extended out to his right, not directly behind him. A left-handed outfielder goes down on his left knee and the positions are reversed. However, both keep their shoulders perpendicular to the path of the ball. Then, using a crow hop, the outfielder fields the ball, comes up with it, and throws to second base. (Note Illustration No. 91.)

Illustration No. 91   Ground Ball—No Play

B. *With a Base Runner and a Play to Make.* The outfielder charges the ball hard until he is 12 to 15 feet in front of it; then he begins to take short choppy steps as a football player does when he is about to make a tackle. If the ball takes a true hop, he fields it with two hands, takes a crow hop and throws to the proper base. If the ball is not hopping, but rolling, the outfielder makes a one-hand glove pick-up of the ball, preferably on the glove side. It is fielded more easily on the outside of the foot. He then crow hops to make a good throw.

C. *Infield Work.* For ground ball work, the coach should put the outfielders in the infield and give them daily work in early season (and all season) practice.

215. FLY BALL PRACTICE

PURPOSE

To give outfielders practice on all types of fly balls.

PROCEDURE

The coach hits or throws fly balls to the outfielder without telling him where the ball is going to be hit or thrown.

A. *Position for Throwing.* As in the ground ball drill, the outfielder must get around the ball to be in position for throwing to the proper base.

B. *Line Drives.* For practice on the line drive, these balls should be hit very sharply and directly at the outfielder.

C. *Balls Hit Directly At and Over the Outfielder's Head.* Bring the outfielder in and hit lazy fly balls directly over his head. The right-hander pivots clockwise, to his right, and as he goes back, he runs in an arc to his right while looking at the ball. When he receives it, his glove hand will be facing the ball and he will be in good position to throw. The left-handed player breaks in the opposite direction. (Note Illustration No. 92.)

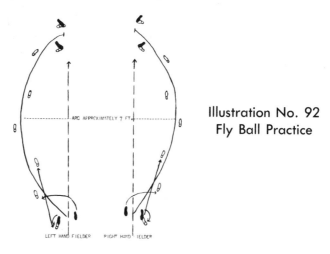

Illustration No. 92
Fly Ball Practice

D. *Balls Hit to the Fielder's Right.* Breaking to his right, the fielder goes back and around the ball as he gets in position to throw before making the catch.

E. *Balls Hit to the Fielder's Left.* The fielder breaks left and back while getting in position to throw.

F. *Short Fly Balls in Front of Fielder.* The fielder breaks in for the ball and decides either to catch or block it. For practice, do not let the fielder hold up on the ball, but make him come through on it. If the ball is low, he should catch it one-handed. If the ball cannot be caught, the outfielder keeps his arm down and out in front of his legs, glove perpendicular to the ground, fingers down, facing the ball. He remains in this position with neither a sweep nor a slap of the glove downward. His job is to keep the ball in front of him.

216. PLAYING THE BALL IN THE SUN

PURPOSE

To teach players to play the ball in the sun with or without sun glasses. (Note Illustration No. 93.)

Illustration No. 93

PROCEDURE

Put outfielders in position so that all fungoed balls will be directly in the sun for the fielders. The sun should be behind the hitter's back. Fungo balls will simulate actual hitting in a game situation. (Note Illustration No. 94.)

A. *Without Sun Glasses or if the Sun Is Directly Behind the Hitter.* Outfielders should attempt to play hitters to their strong side. As an example, a right fielder would play a left-handed pull hitter closer to the right field foul line than he normally would. While the pitch is being made and the batter is ready to hit, the outfielder shields his eyes from the sun with his glove. When the ball is hit, he attempts to keep his glove in this position as long as possible. He then attempts to get his body in position so that he is not looking directly into the sun when he catches the ball. (Note Illustration No. 93.)

B. *With Sun Glasses*. Keeping his glove in the position described above, the outfielder plays the hitter to his power side. Waiting until he knows exactly where the ball is, he then flips his glasses down and makes the catch. Flipping the glasses too early will cause the outfielder to lose the ball or misjudge it.

Playing in the sun and using the sun glasses requires extra practice.

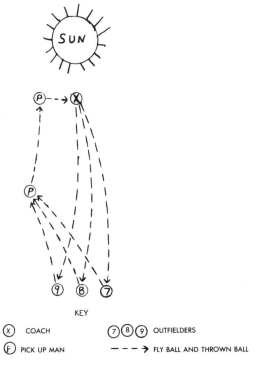

KEY

(X) COACH   (7)(8)(9) OUTFIELDERS

(F) PICK UP MAN   — — — → FLY BALL AND THROWN BALL

Illustration No. 94   Playing Ball in the Sun

217. CATCHING FLY BALLS AT THE FENCE

PURPOSE

To teach outfielders how to catch fly balls at or near the fence.

PROCEDURE

Place the outfielder 15 to 20 feet from the fence. Throw fly balls to the fence, so that the outfielder will have to run back to the fence and jump to catch the ball.

Have the outfielder approach the fence by getting to it as quickly as possible and feeling for it with his hand or glove while keeping his eye on the ball. After getting to the fence, the outfielder should turn his body sideways before jumping for the ball. Outfielders should not be permitted to back up to the fence before jumping, since this position often causes them to hit the fence with their buttocks, resulting in loss of balance and failure to catch the ball.

218. FENCE DRILLS

PURPOSE

To teach outfielders how to go to the fence and play a ball and to teach them how to play balls off the fence.

PROCEDURE

The coach hits or throws balls to the outfielders at or near the fence. He tries to give the outfielders all possible plays around the fence. A relay man should be placed to receive the throws.

A. *Balls Lying Against the Fence*. Place balls against the fence, and put the outfielders 25 to 30 feet away from the fence. Have the outfielders approach the ball from all angles and throw to a relay man. Right-handers should pick up the ball with their right foot on the right side of the ball, and left-handers should pick up the ball with their left foot on the left side of the ball without straddling it. The throw should begin directly from where the outfielder picks up the ball. As he picks it up, he should crow hop and throw to a relay man. (Note Illustrations No. 95 and 96.)

B. *Ball Rebounding from a Fence*. Hit balls against the fence at different angles for outfielders, who play the ball off the fence and throw to a relay man.

Right-
Hander   Left-
Hander

Illustration No. 95   Ball Lying Against the Fence

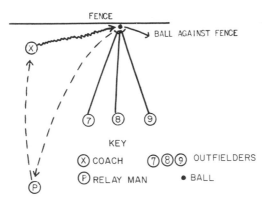

Illustration No. 96   Ball Lying Against the Fence

Illustration No. 97   Crashing the Fence

C. *Crashing the Fence*. The outfielder gets approximately 15 feet from the fence, and the coach throws balls so that they can be caught by the outfielder if he jumps high up against the fence. As the ball is thrown, the outfielder breaks to the fence as fast as possible and puts the foot and leg that are nearest the wall up against the fence, using them to take up the shock and to aid in climbing the wall. He should keep his eye on the ball as much as possible. He may take his eye off the ball just as he hits the fence. (Note Illustration No. 97.)

219. THROWING TO BASES

PURPOSE

To teach outfielders how to throw properly to bases.

PROCEDURE

Hit all types of balls to an outfielder, and have him throw to different bases. He should make a direct overhand throw that takes one long bounce to the base. The outfielder should use a crow hop to get something on the ball and for accuracy.

In order to get rid of the ball as quickly as possible, with maximum power in the throw, the outfielder should, if possible, time his catch so that the ball hits his glove just a fraction of a second before his pivot foot (foot on throwing side) hits the ground. He then crow hops to that foot and fires the ball. Naturally, he should be moving forward toward the ball and the base to which he is making the throw.

220. FAKING A THROW TO A BASE FOR A PICK-OFF

PURPOSE

To teach outfielders how to fake a throw to one base and catch a runner off another base. *Never attempt this from a deep position.*

PROCEDURE

Place defensive players in position and hit ground ball singles to the outfield. Put the runners on base and have them make big turns.

A. *Right Fielder*. The ball is hit to right field, between the first and second basemen. A runner goes to first base and makes a big turn. The catcher follows the runner and covers first base. The pitcher backs up the catcher, while the first and second basemen go out toward right field on ground balls in that area. The right fielder charges the ball, picks it up, and makes a motion toward second base. He immediately whirls and throws to the catcher covering first base.

B. *Center Fielder*. The ball is hit to center field. The runner rounds second base. Then the center fielder fakes a throw to third, but whirls and throws to second base. He can also fake to second and throw to first.

C. *Left Fielder*. Repeat as for center fielder.

221. HITTING THE CUT-OFF AND RELAY MEN   by Jim Phipps

PURPOSE

To teach outfielders how to make the throw for a perfect relay.

PROCEDURE

Place all outfielders and infielders in their proper positions. Hit to all positions in the outfield, and have outfielders make all plays where outfielders throw to the infield or relay man.

A. With a quick, snappy motion, the outfielders throw to the relay man, hitting him on the glove side, head high. The crow hop may not be necessary on the shorter throws. (Note Drills No. 44, 173-D and 189-E.)

B. Using the crow hop, the outfielder makes a hard overhand throw to the cut-off man. The ball is thrown so that it will take one long hop to the base and will hit the cut-off man's glove above his head. (Note Drill No. 44.)

C. Another method is to:

1. Line up all outfielders in one outfield position and fungo the ball toward centerfield.

2. Put relay throwers in a line around second base, taking turns receiving the ball from the outfielders and throwing the ball to the catcher.

3. The catcher gives the ball to the fungo hitter, who hits the next ball to the next outfielder who continues the relay outfield-infield throws.

The outfielder after the catch and throw moves to the area out of the fielding range of the other outfielders. When all outfielders have had their turn in the original starting position, the coach fungoes the ball to a different area of the outfield. The relay cut-off players line up the throws from the outfielders with the catcher as they would in a game.

This method of hitting the ball to all areas of the outfield gives the outfielders throwing and fielding experience similar to what they might get in a game.

222. BUNTING SITUATIONS—COVERING BASES

PURPOSE

To teach the outfielders duties other than catching ground and fly balls.

PROCEDURE

With the defensive team in position and nobody on base, set up all bunting situations.

A. *Right Fielder.* As soon as the bunter has committed himself to bunt, the right fielder breaks for a position to back up the throw. If the throw is to first base, he goes toward first, and if the throw is to second base, he goes toward second. His first steps, however, should be toward first base. His direction changes with the throw.

B. *Center Fielder.* The center fielder always breaks behind second base to back up all bunt situations.

C. *Left Fielder.* The left fielder backs up either second or third base, depending upon where the throw is made on the bunt. However, he usually breaks for third base, if there are runners on base, to be ready for a possible play at third.

223. BACK-UP PLAYS

PURPOSE

To teach the outfielder that he has a play to make in every situation.

PROCEDURE

With the defensive team in position, hit ground balls to the outfield.

A. *Backing Up Other Outfielders:*

1. Balls hit to right field are backed up by the center fielder.
2. Depending upon the position of the ball in center field, balls hit to this area are backed up by the right or the left fielder.
3. Balls hit to left field are backed up by the center fielder.
4. Back-up plays depend largely on who is closer to the outfielder at

the time he is receiving the ball. The other outfielder may be the relay man.

B. *Backing Up Bases:*

1. Right Fielder;

    a. The right fielder backs up first base on all throws except throws on balls hit to the right side of the infield. On these plays he backs up the infielders.

    b. The right fielder backs up all throws to second base from the left side of the infield.

2. Center Fielder;

    The center fielder backs up second base whenever there is a possible play at that base.

3. Left Fielder;

    a. The left fielder backs up second base on all plays to second base from the right side of the infield and, particularly, singles to right field.

    b. The left fielder backs up third base on all possible plays at third base, particularly on singles to right field with a runner on first, and on triples to right.

Outfielders can also get into run-down plays while backing up throws. They should back up the base near the area where the ball would go if it got past the infielder.

224. OUTFIELDER TEAMWORK DRILL

PURPOSE

To teach outfielders that they need help and should expect and give help to other outfielders.

PROCEDURE

Put the team in defensive positions, and place an imaginary runner or runners on base. Do not tell the outfielder catching the ball where the imaginary runner is located. The coach has this outfielder turn his back while he signals the other outfielders where the runner is stationed.

Signals. One finger for first base; two fingers for second base; three fingers for third base and the fist for no runner on base. The coach then tells all outfielders the number of outs and the score.

A. *Ground Balls.* The outfielder nearest the fielder catching the ball tells him where to throw it. He tells him this just before he catches the ball.

B. *Fly Balls*. Change the routine above and put an actual runner on third base. The outfielder nearest the fielder making the play tells him whether to throw home or to another base. In this case, imaginary runners are on other bases.

225. DUTY DRILLS—PRE-GAME

PURPOSE

To acquaint outfielders with the conditions under which they will play and the opposing team's strength and weaknesses.

A. *Opposing Team*. When the opposing team takes batting practice, look for their power and the direction the players hit most frequently. Look for speed, and watch their arms for throwing ability. Also look for injuries.

B. *Self-orientation*. The outfielders loosen up their arms by throwing to the bases during infield and outfield practice. While he is in the outfield shagging balls, the outfielder should study the length of the grass, hardness of the ground, position of the sun, the construction of the fence, and its effect upon the ball. Fungo hitters should hit all types of balls, some against the fence, and some near the fence. In a field where the ball may be played in the sun, some balls should be hit into the sun so that the outfielder can become oriented to it.

226. GAME SITUATION DRILL

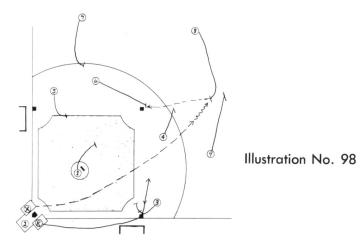

Illustration No. 98

PURPOSE

To let the outfielders experience as many game situations as possible. (Note Illustration No. 98.)

PROCEDURE

Place a complete defensive ball team on the field. Have extra men and pitchers take their turn at bat. The batter swings the bat, and at that time the coach hits a ball through the infield so that the outfielders make all the plays. To make it realistic, the hitters run the bases. All types of fly and ground balls should be hit, including singles and extra base hits. Suggested drills to go with this one are the following: No. 106, 145, 170, 173-D, 178-C, 189-E, 205-D, and 207.

CHAPTER 13

BASE-RUNNING DRILLS

Good base running will keep a ball club winning more than 50 percent of its games. A running club forces the opposition into making errors. A player who knows how to slide wants to slide, and will take the extra base. He will score from second and advance to third from first on most balls hit to center-field and right field. All players, including pitchers, need sliding and base-running drills.

Sliding directly at a bag is best when stealing. In stealing, most jumps are gotten on the pitcher, but occasionally a player can run on a catcher's poor arm or movements.

Since speed can be increased, running should be taught. Players must run in a relaxed manner, use high knee action, with elbows relaxed comforta-bly close to the body and bent approximately 90 degrees, and should be up on their toes. The toes should point directly ahead and should be placed in front of the nose. The body should lean forward. Exceptions to this body lean and foot placement are on the turns, when the body leans toward the middle of the diamond and forward. The left foot will naturally fall nearer to the inside of the diamond than the right foot.

The following drills on base running are designed to develop players into better base runners. It should be noted that coaches differ on how to make the turn at first base. Drill No. 233 will give your player the fastest turn.

227. CHECKLIST FOR PROPER EXECUTION

(Note Screening Candidates Drill No. 246)

228. BASE RUNNING—WITH A PURPOSE   by Jack Kaiser

PURPOSE

To condition the players and develop proper skills and mental alertness. Speed and agility are a must in developing a successful player and building a winning baseball team. They are vital to both the offensive and defensive phases of the game.

PROCEDURE

At St. John's we ran daily, as a matter of course, sometimes wind sprints, and at other times in drills—even on game days.

In teaching we used lectures, demonstration drills and game application. The player must understand what to do, and why, before the drills begin so he can apply his knowledge and have enthusiasm for the job.

We utilized a series of base-running drills that teach fundamental skills and condition the player physically and mentally at the same time. The following drills are used, of course, after the proper lecture and demonstration.

A. The player takes an imaginary swing or uses his bunt for base-hit technique at home plate, drops his bat properly and takes off for first base with his rear foot taking the first step. He heads directly for first base with a slight body lean forward (sprinter's position) arms pumping forward and back. When the 45-foot line is reached, he takes care to run outside the foul line and inside the restraining line (avoids throw coming from home plate area), and runs strongly *through* first base, touching the top and front of the base with either foot—not breaking stride, but finishing his sprint a short distance beyond the bag. Care is taken not to finish up *at* the bag with a long stride or lunge, thus losing time and risking possible injury (hamstring pull, heel bruise, ankle sprain). The runner, upon slowing down and stopping, turns back toward first base via foul territory (avoids tag out on turn toward second base).

B. As above, except finishes with a quick hook slide to the inside (diamond) side of first base, simulating that the first baseman has been pulled off the bag and into the base line by a poor throw. This is the *only* time a runner should slide into first base when coming from the plate.

C. As "A" above, until approximately 10 to 15 feet from the bag (simulating a ball hit to the outfield), the runner steps out into foul territory (3 to 5 feet) with his right foot preparing for a tight, well-controlled turn. After establishing this *angle* on first base, he proceeds to touch the inside, front corner of the bag with either foot while remaining in stride.

If the touch is made with the left foot, it is followed by turning the hips over and pointing the right foot directly at second base.

If the touch is to be made with the right foot, the above technique is carried out on the last stride (left) *before* the touch. This will prevent poor contact, and the resultant wide, time-consuming, "circle route" used by some runners. It would be helpful on the turn to lean in with the left shoulder and throw the right arm over to help balance and change of direction. The runner continues toward second base for about 20 feet (LF or CF) or 10 feet (RF) and puts the brakes on with good body control (tail down, knees bent, toes in) and retreats to first base while watching the throw in from the outfield. In case of a miscue, he is in proper position to react immediately, change direction, and take the extra base.

D. As in "C" above, except when runner is putting the brakes on, there is an outfield miscue, so he immediately accelerates on to second base. This is go-stop-go action.

E. As in "C" above, except after the touch at first base, the runner continues in full stride to second base, simulating an extra base hit.

In all these drills, it is emphasized that after the follow-through at the plate, and take-off, that the runner's attention should be *riveted* on first base, and he should expect encouragement and instructions from the first base coach. If the runner follows the flight of the ball for any period of time with his eyes, he will slow down and often lose the decision at first base in a bang-bang play.

F. As in "E" above, except runner continues in full stride from home to third base. Stop–go action *may* be incorporated after rounding second base, if the coach wishes to simulate an errant relay throw.

G. As in "F" above, except runner continues in full stride from home plate to home plate. Once again the coach *may* install a stop-and-go action after the runner rounds third base to simulate a wild throw at that point.

In the drills which conclude at second and third base and at home plate, the coach may wish to add a slide from time to time to simulate a close play. The coach should be alert to correct *in a positive way*, any incorrect or sloppy technique. It may be just as important to encourage aggressive, thoughtful, all-out, concentration and effort on the part of your players.

Both physical skill/aggressiveness and mental alertness/toughness will pull your team through many a tight spot.

Other drills which should be incorporated into your system, as you progress, are: leads (1st, 2nd and 3rd bases); steal (of 2nd, 3rd, and home); hit-and-run play; rundown; squeeze play (suicide, safety, double); double steals (1st and 2nd; 1st and 3rd series); advances off foul fly, passed ball or wild pitch and other similar situations; tag-up plays, sliding techniques and more. All involve skilled base-running techniques.

By covering the above in lectures, demonstration, drill and game application, you can be assured your players will be ready for any situation and, what's more, they will actually be anticipating them.

In amateur baseball circles, a coach is seldom lucky enough to field a "murderer's row" type of offensive lineup. Therefore, he must scratch out or steal runs at every opportunity. At St. John's, our huge field (400, 395, 438) precludes waiting for the long home run or big inning, so speed, agility and alertness are the difference in many one-run games. Be ready to run—with a purpose.

229. FULL TEAM BASE RUNNING   by Ron Fraser

PURPOSE

To simulate game-like defensive and base-running offensive situations.

PROCEDURE

Place a full nine-man defensive team on the field and a runner on all three bases. The pitchers try to make the batter hit the ball. (Everything down the middle and soft.) The defensive team is instructed to play every batted ball as if there was one out and a runner on first base only. They disregard all the other runners who are on base.

The runner on first base reacts to the batted ball which is thrown as in batting practice. He runs independently of the other runners. In other words, advances as he would if there were no runners on second or third base.

The runner on second also reacts to the batted ball and runs independently of the runner on third base or first base.

The runner at third base also reacts independently of the other runners.

Place coaches at first base and third base. They control the base running. There may be times when the third base coach will be bringing the first base runner into third base with a runner still on third base during this drill. You must remember each runner is running as if no other runners were on base.

When each base runner circles the bases, he can continue in the batting-base-running line at home plate or take a position on defense.

If a batter hits an extra base hit, runners are again placed on all bases to continue the drill.

Variations of the drill should include:

1. Runners on first and second base.

2. Runners on first and third base.

3. Bases-loaded situation.

4. Infield-in situations.

5. Two out, full-count situations.

6. Runner on first stealing a runner on the pitch.

7. Winning run on third base last inning (A) Top half of the inning—visitor at bat; (B) Bottom half of the inning—home team at bat.

230. ROUNDING BASES

PURPOSE

To keep runners from going too far out of the base paths while making turns at the bases.

PROCEDURE

When using Drills No. 233 and 241, have your players concentrate on their turns. The body should lean toward the infield while rounding bases. Being certain not to break his stride, the base runner should hit the base with either foot. Although some coaches teach that the runner must hit the base with his left foot, and some say the right foot, the important thing is that he hits the base without breaking stride.

A. *First Base*. 1. Have the player run straight for first base until he is 12 to 15 feet from the bag. At this time, he should cross his left foot over his right, making about a three-foot bend in his path before hitting the base.

2. Another method is for the runner to start to bend toward foul territory about halfway to first base, then turn in and touch the base with either foot.

B. *Second Base*. While rounding and coming from first base, the base runner should have enough bend in his path and lean of his body to make the turn at second. However,if he is coming directly from first base, he should turn as described for first base.

C. *Third Base*. When rounding and coming from second base, the base runner should have enough bend or arc in his path to make the turn without using the crossover step. The lead off second base should be taken on the outfield side of the base path instead of on the base line. His turn is similar to that made at first base.

231. WHAT TO TEACH A BASE RUNNER   by Gene Shell

PURPOSE

To make base running interesting and keep the players hustling on the base paths.

PROCEDURE

A. Base running from the plate to all bases. Line up all players in a single line at home plate. Each player takes a turn at bat, with or without a bat. They may also fake a bunt to teach breaking from the plate when bunting.

1. First trip from the plate—run straight through the bag. Teach proper technique for:

  (a) Getting out of the box.

  (b) Running down the line.

  (c) Running.

  (d) Touching the bag.

  (e) How to make the turn to return to first.

  (f) When to slide at first.

2. Next trip will be a single—Teach

  (a) Getting out of box.

  (b) Start your angle (10 feet down the line to an imaginary point 5 feet from first base). Make your turn as late as possible without losing speed.

  (c) Pick up sight of the ball halfway down the line.

  (d) Listen to your coach.

3. Next trip would be taking the extra base on a careless outfielder—

  (a) Take your turn by changing speeds at the bag.

  (b) Stutter-step—or just slow to 80 percent of your speed and go after you made the turn.

4. Next trip, two-base hits—Teach

  (a) Technique at first.

  (b) Proper turn

  (c) When, how and where to use the coach.

  (d) How to pick the ball up in different parts of the outfield.

5. Next try will be triples—Teach

  (a) Techniques at first.

  (b) Approach to second.

  (c) How to use the base coach at third and when to look for him.

  (d) When to pick up the flight of the ball.

  (e) How to approach third base or make the turn following the coaches signs.

B. Breaking from first base.

1. Form two lines to break for second base. This speeds up the activity. Teach proper techniques:

  (a) How to get a lead and return to the bag.

  (b) When to get a lead.

(c) Proper take-off.

(d) How to run when you go.

2. Types of steals.

(a) Straight steal.

(b) Delay.

(c) Walk to run.

3. Leads.

(a) Short lead.

(b) Long lead.

(c) One way lead.

4. Fake a break and use your imagination with intelligence. Study the pitcher for signs of delivery to first and home. Coach should put his own ideas into this.

C. Breaking from Second Base.

1. Form two lines from second base as you did at first base. Teach proper technique:

(a) Type of lead—

    (a) Short lead.

    (b) Long lead.

    (c) Walking lead.

(b) Who the runner is responsible for—

    (i) Pitcher.

    (ii) Catcher after pitch.

    (iii) Coach at third base watches shortstop and uses voice to help runner.

    (iv) Coach at first base watches second baseman and uses voice to help runner.

    (v) Runner, through corner of eye, watches second baseman. Listens for sound of feet of shortstop.

D. Breaking from Third Base.

1. Form two lines from third base as you did at other bases. Teach proper technique.

(a) Type of lead and return to base.

(b) Where to position yourself (outside base line, turf condition, etc.).

2. Suicide Squeeze.

(a) Walk (pitcher in his motion).

(b) Trot (pitcher coming to top of his motion).

(c) Run (when pitcher releases the ball).

3. Safety Squeeze.

(a) Take safe lead, move up the line with the pitch.

(b) Break for home on ball bunted on ground only.

4. Tagging on fly balls to outfield or line drives.

232. ALTERNATE SPEED BASE-RUNNING DRILL

PURPOSE

To develop players mentally and physically for base running.

PROCEDURE

As a closing drill for a day's work, this will give the necessary running for the day.

A. The team lines up at home plate. Each player stands in the batter's box, swings at an imaginary ball, drops the bat, and breaks for first base at full speed. He jogs to second base, runs full speed to third, and jogs home. Repeat five times.

B. The same start is used as in "A" above. The batter runs full speed to second base and jogs on around to the starting position. Repeat five times.

C. Use the same starting approach. The batter runs full speed to third base and jogs to the starting position. Repeat three times.

D. Using the same starting approach, the batter runs the bases full speed all the way. Repeat twice.

233. TIMED BASE-RUNNING PRACTICE   by Dick Siebert

PURPOSE

To make the players conscious of their speed and want to improve it. Twenty-six yards is the approximate distance a player must run when breaking for second base. We want our players to learn this distance well.

PROCEDURE

A. Have players run as in Drill No. 27 to loosen up their legs. When they are loose, get a stopwatch and time them running the bases in the following drill.

As a starting point for running, mark off four yards from first base toward second base and place a chalk line. The player's right foot must be on this mark to start the break toward second base, which is 26 yards away.

There should be two rows of runners starting with their right feet on the chalk line. There should be two timers, one for each runner. This speeds up the activity. There should be a pitcher on the mound and a catcher to catch his delivery.

The coach stands to the side at an angle where he can see the pitcher make his delivery and see the runners break for the timed running.

The pitcher takes his stretch as the runners get set on the chalk line to break for second. As the pitcher makes his first move to the plate, the runners go and the timers start their watches. If the player jumps or breaks before the pitcher makes a move, the coach blows a whistle. They then start again.

B. *Base Running for Time*. The speed of our base runners is timed with a stopwatch after players are in shape. Usually, this is the second week that they are out-of-doors. The watch should be started with the crack of the bat.

A good time for adult players to make first base is between 3.5 and 4.3 seconds. The best time recorded for a right-handed player is 3.3 seconds, and the best for a left-handed batter is 3.1 seconds.

The following are considered good times to the other bases: from home to second base in 8 seconds, to third in 12, and the complete circuit in 16 seconds.

The following directions should be used to increase the speed of runners on the base paths:

    a. Hit the bag with either foot, but never break stride.

    b. Curve out to your right slightly before reaching the bag.

    c. Use the bag as a pivot to avoid making wide turns.

    d. Lean in toward the infield as you hit the bags.

C. Clock the base runner during the game.

234. LEADS, RETURNS AND STEALS AT FIRST BASE
by Dave Keilitz

PURPOSE

This multi-purpose base-running drill is designed to improve on all aspects of base running at first base. Many items are worked on in the same drill—leads off first, returns to the bag on attempted pick-offs, secondary leads, and steals.

PROCEDURE

Use as many pitchers as you wish, each taking his turn at the mound. The pitcher works from the stretch, holding the runner at first. He may deliver the ball to the catcher at the plate or attempt to pick the man off first where the first baseman is holding the runner.

One runner leads directly off first toward second. A second, third and fourth runner do the same at the same time off the bases that have been set up down the first base line about 5 to 6 feet apart. (Note Illustration No. 99.) All four runners react to the pitcher's move.

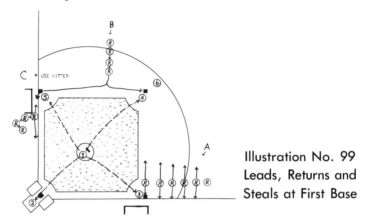

Illustration No. 99
Leads, Returns and
Steals at First Base

The coach will give the signs. If no steal is on, the runners work for a long "one-way" lead, experimenting on the length of it.

If the pitcher throws over to first, all four runners cross over hard and dive into their respective bases. If the runner makes it back safely, he tries to get a little more lead. If he is out, he shortens it up slightly. Each runner works for his maximum lead. If the pitcher throws home, each runner crosses over and takes his "secondary lead" working on squaring up as the ball gets to the plate. The catcher may throw to first occasionally so the runners can work on getting back safely from their secondary lead. This will give each runner an idea of how far he can go on his secondary lead.

When the coach gives the steal sign, the runners take their "two-way" lead, preparing themselves to go in either direction. When the pitcher starts his move to the plate, the runners break hard for their steal of second base. Then four more runners move into position. You can also incorporate the delayed steal in this drill.

Several things have been accomplished in this drill. You have worked on the length of the lead; the proper way to get back; proper techniques of the secondary lead, reading the pitchers; getting the jump; and developing the steal itself. It is advisable to have each runner work with a different pitcher every opportunity he gets. This helps the pitcher and the runner to learn how to study their opponent in game-like conditions.

235. BASE RUNNING AND CATCHING   by Jerry Kindall

PURPOSE

To pit the base runners against the catchers in stealing second base. After completing our conditioning and exercise program at the start of every practice, we start this competition.

PROCEDURE

A. Measure and mark off two lanes of 90 feet some 10 or 20 feet back off the base line from first base to second base. Mark a line 12 feet out from the base to indicate a "safe" lead and another line 15 feet out to indicate an aggressive base-stealing lead.

B. Have two loose bases from which the pair of runners take their lead out to the 12-foot line (right foot on the 12-foot line).

C. Have the runners paired off according to speed (the fastest runners together to challenge one another).

D. Have catchers in full gear with a hitter at the plate ready to swing and miss at the pitched ball to simulate game situations.

E. A right-handed pitcher on the mound who is warmed up and ready to throw game speed.

F. Two coaches at second base with stopwatches. A recorder at second base to write down the times.

G. A coach at home plate with a stopwatch to time and record glove-to-glove times (pitch hits catcher's glove and throw to second baseman's glove).

H. A large screen behind second base to protect the runners from wild throws by the catcher. Also to protect the timers.

The procedure is this: the two runners take their 12-foot lead as the right-handed pitcher stretches and comes to a set. If the pitcher attempts a pick-off, the runners must get back to first base or a penalty mark is assessed them by the recorder. Once the pitcher makes his move to the plate, the runners pivot on the balls of their feet, cross left foot over right, and sprint toward second base in an attempted steal. We make it mandatory that our runners take two strides and then look to the plate to see if the ball has been hit, missed, passed ball or wild pitch. If they fail to look a penalty mark is assessed. The runners sprint across the line at second base. No sliding is allowed. The timers start the watches at the pitcher's first move and stop the watches as the runner crosses the line.

The runners each run a second time each day in the other lane to accommodate any human error on the watches.

One coach works with and times the catchers while the remaining coach(es) work with the runners. This is not a good drill for the pitchers because, to maintain consistency and keep the variables to a minimum, the pitcher should be consistent in his stretch and set.

We run from a 12-foot lead for at least one week and get ten times on each runner. The next week we run from a 15-foot lead to emphasize the significant difference in time (approximately 2/10 of a second). (Note Illustration No. 100.)

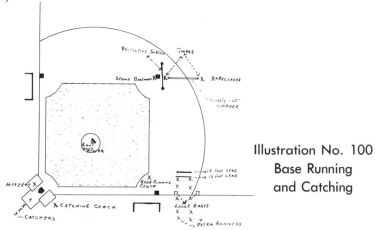

Illustration No. 100
Base Running
and Catching

236. LEAD-OFF-BASE DRILL

PURPOSE

To teach players how to get a better lead off all bases.

PROCEDURE

Each player is taken individually and put on base. The pitcher goes through the same motions he would use in a game. If the runner takes too much lead, he picks him off. To insure a better start, rock or shuffle on the balls of the feet. (Note Illustration No. 99.)

A. *Lead Off First Base*. Teach the lead-off as in Drills No. 231 and 234. However, a walking lead may be more desirable for some players. The player starts walking slowly with short steps as the pitcher gets set, and when he throws to the catcher, the runner takes off for second base. His return, however, may have to be a head-first dive.

B. *Lead Off Second Base*. The runner lines up about six feet behind the base line between second and third base and takes a lead that normally would not cause him to get picked off. As the pitcher is looking back at him, the runner takes short, choppy steps while moving toward the pitcher, but at an angle toward third base. By the time the pitch is made, he is almost on the base line with a good lead, if he is going to steal. If he is not going to steal, he does not move up to the base line, but remains behind it to get a better angle for rounding third base. Getting back to second base can be executed by a head-first dive or by a feet-first slide. (Note Drill No. 231-C.)

C. *Lead Off Third Base.* The runner normally takes three good-sized steps for the lead. On the pitch, he moves toward home, stopping when the ball goes past the batter and returning to third base. Give the runner practice by having the batter hit the ball. If it is a ground ball, the runner breaks for home. If it is a fly ball, he tags up and tries to score. This is a very important phase of the drill. Runners should be cautioned not to move so fast and far toward home that they will be returning to third base when the ball is hit. (Note Drill No. 231-D.) Runner takes lead in foul territory, and returns in fair territory.

237. SLIDING DRILLS—INDOORS

PURPOSE

To learn how to slide during inclement weather. Some teams cannot get outside until a few days before their first game. In this case, sliding should be taught indoors.

PROCEDURE

Use the same approach and sliding techniques as Drill No. 238. The only exception is the equipment used. For the approach, use a rubber mat, or a gymnastic mat, on the gymnasium floor. For the protection of the body, use pads for the elbows and knees, several pairs of sweat pants, sweat socks on the hands, and stockings on the feet. The best slide can be made by placing a heavy duty plastic sheet on top of a gym mat. Spray silicone on the plastic and some on the pants of the slider. Hold the plastic in place and you get a beautiful slide.

238. SLIDING DRILLS—OUTDOORS

PURPOSE

To help all players develop skills in the basic slides to the extent that they execute them well, safely, and with confidence and enthusiasm.

Basically, sliding is needed to get that extra base, not for the purpose of stealing. These drills should help all players, including pitchers, learn to slide instead of jumping at the bag, a cause of numerous injuries.

PROCEDURE

Lay a bag loose, not tied down, on a spot well-covered with grass. Be sure that the ground is not bumpy, and that it does not contain rocks, glass, or other dangerous matter.

Instruct your players to put on old sweat pants over their practice pants. Be sure that they pull off their shoes and run in their stocking feet. Have beginners go through the motion of sliding on the side of their choice at a slow speed. As they improve, the coach can call for more speed. The coach should supervise all practice.

A. *Straight-in Slide*. Most beginners want to do this slide, although it is one of the most dangerous since there is little relaxation in the slider as he hits the bag. The first attempt by a beginner may be this slide, although it is not recommended.

The slide is executed by the player half-sliding, half-jumping at the bag with legs extended straight in front of the slider.

B. *Hook Slide*. This slide can be made to either side, which should be determined by the position of the fielder and where he moves.

The factors below can serve as a checklist for the coach as he watches players practice the hook slide. (Note Illustration No. 101.)

1. Extended foot leaves ground first. It is relaxed and slightly bent.
2. Hooking foot is the take-off foot. It is relaxed and bent.
3. The feet are pushed out in front of the body which goes into nearly a prone position. The soles of the feet never touch the grass or dirt, only the sides of the feet touch.
4. The body is not at right angles to the bag, but angled at about 45 degrees.
5. The slide is on the hip of the extended foot.
6. Hooking foot contacts the bag. This is done with the instep of the inside foot.
7. The body and extended foot are carried away from the bag.

C. *Bent Leg Slide*. If there is a need to get up in a hurry, the player may slide into the bag with a bent leg. The momentum of the body and push of the bent leg against the bag will bounce him to his feet. This slide can be made on either side. (Note Illustration No. 102.)

1. The extended leg leaves the ground first. However, both feet leave at nearly the same time.
2. The foot of the bent leg comes under the knee of the extended leg.
3. The body is perpendicular to the base.
4. The slide is on the bent leg and hip, mostly on the outside of the calf.

Illustration No. 101   Hook Slide

Illustration No. 102   Bent Leg Slide

5. The bent leg slides into the bag for the push-up.

6. The extended foot goes to the rear of the bag or beyond, and the slider comes up, but remains on the bag.

D. *Bent Leg-and-Go Slide*. Although this slide can be executed on either side, the bent left leg is preferable. (Note Illustration No. 103.)

Illustration No. 103   Bent Leg-and-Go Slide

1. The right leg leaves the ground first.

2. The foot of the bent leg comes under the knee of the right leg.

3. The body is perpendicular to the base and almost in a sit-up position.

4. The slide is on the calf of the left leg and left hip.

5. The left leg starts the push-up before arriving at the base.

6. The right leg hits the bag for extra push-up.

7. The left leg push-up and the right leg hitting the bag spin the slider so that he is facing the next base with momentum in that direction.

239. DELAYED STEAL DRILLS

PURPOSE

To throw opponents off balance and to keep your team alert for such steals.

PROCEDURE

Place the infield, pitcher, and catcher in position. Also, place runners on first and third bases.

A. *Walk-Off.* When the pitcher becomes set, the first-base runner takes a normal lead. He starts walking when the ball is delivered by the pitcher. When the runner sees or hears the ball hit the catcher's glove, he takes three more walking steps, counting one, two, three and breaking at full speed for second base at the count of three.

B. *Forced Balk* by Russ Frazier. When the pitcher takes the sign on the rubber and does not look at the first-base runner, the base runner breaks for second when the pitcher starts any motion with his hands to go into his set stance. This usually happens when his hands are near his thighs, after he gets his sign.

In the above drills, if the runner on first is caught stealing, he should get in a run-down and stay in it as long as possible in order to give the runner on third an opportunity to attempt to score.

The runner on third takes such a lead that, if a play is made on him, he will have to dive back to third base to be safe. On the walk-off play, he holds until the catcher throws to second, then breaks for home.

On the forced balk, he holds until the pitcher throws the ball to second. The success of the play depends upon perfect timing and full speed by the runner on first base.

240. GETTING OUT OF A RUNDOWN

PURPOSE

To throw opponents off balance and to keep your team alert for such steals.

PROCEDURE

When using infield run down Drill No. 153, players should attempt to

(1) run into a fielder in the base line without the ball; or (2) get a player with the ball chasing them at full speed, stop quickly and fall flat on the ground causing the player with the ball to stumble over or miss the base runner, thus giving the base runner a chance to advance to the next base; or (3) attempt to get hit by the ball.

241. BASE COACH DRILL

PURPOSE

To teach the base coaches how to handle base runners and to teach the base runners how to look for and listen to the base coaches' signals. (Note Illustration No. 104.)

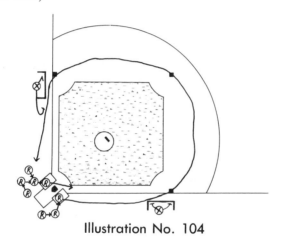

Illustration No. 104

PROCEDURE

Line up all ball players at home plate. At the slap of the coach's hands, the first runner breaks for first base. Only the first-base coach knows where the imaginary ball has been hit. Based upon where the ball has been hit, the first-base coach tells the runner what to do—beat it out, make his turn, go for second base, or make his turn and go for two with a slide.

When the runner goes for second, prior to hitting the base, he must look at the third-base coach, who is signaling him whether to hold up or go on to third. When the runner comes into third, the coach will tell him to slide, hold up, make his turn, or go on home. The third-base coach must listen to the instructions of the first-base coach so as not to bring a runner into third who was told to slide. (Note Illustration No. 105.) Figure No. 1 is third-base coach, hold-up sign. Figure No. 2, slide. Figure No. 3, score. Figure No. 4, hold up and get back on base. Figure No. 5, make your turn, hold and wait for a possible error.

Illustration No. 105   Base Coach Drill

242. HOW TO GIVE SIGNS

PURPOSE

To acquaint the players and coaches with the signs and to make them simple. Signs should never be so complicated that they confuse your own players. There are many signs that are good. Below we give you some basic signs from which to work.

PROCEDURE

A. *By the Coach*. The basic signs a coach needs for offense are the hit, bunt, take and steal. From here we go into the signs for suicide bunt, hit and run (unless the coach allows his players to put on their own sign), fake bunt and steal, delayed steal, walk-off steal or some other pet running or hitting tactic a coach may have.

Take the above offensive plays and do something that tells the batter or runner what you want him to do. For example, touch a different part of your body or clothing for each situation.

It is never wise to just make one move for the sign. Always touch different things, at least three or four. For example, if your bunt sign is touching your face with your right hand, tell your players the sign will be on the first, second or third thing you touch. Let's say it is the second sign you give. Your sequence or series of signs could be, touch your cap, face, shirt, belt, pants. The sign would be to bunt because the second sign you gave was touching your face with your right hand. All the other signs were decoys.

If you want to change your mind or you're not sure the batter or runner got the sign, you must have a rub-off sign to wipe all signs off and start over. This could be simply dusting yourself off with both hands. If one hand is the sign, using two hands is nothing. For example, two hands to the face or left hand to the face means nothing, only one hand, the right hand, to the face puts the sign on.

If you believe a team is getting your signs you can change the sign from the second sign to the first, third or fourth as the sign to use. You can also use a key sign which means the sign will not go on until you give a key sign. Let's use the key sign of touching the left arm with the right hand and then go to the sign: using the above sign, right hand to the face for the bunt, you might give the bunt sign like this: touch the cap, pants, left arm, face, pants, cap. The key was left arm, face. Now we come back and touch cap, face, pants, left arm. The batter would be hitting and not bunting.

When a batter goes to bat, he should always be hitting and continue to do so until the coach gives him some other sign. He continues to hit on every pitch until another sign is given. A hitter should not be hitting when he has three balls and no strikes. This is an automatic take sign unless the coach gives him a hit sign.

It is important to instruct your players to keep looking until you have gone through your signs. A tip-off on the sign is a player who looks away from the coach as soon as he sees the sign. Players on the opposing bench are instructed to look for this. Two players are assigned to look for signs. One looks at the coach and repeats everything he does. The other player watches the player and says, "He's looking, looking, looking, now he turned away." The question answered was what did the coach do when the batter looked away from him. Often this is the key to what the coach wants the runner or batter to do.

Giving signs to runners is done in the same manner as described above. If possible, it is good for the batter to know what the runner or runners are going to do. For example, if he knows they are stealing he can help them out by swinging late and missing the ball if he can afford to take a strike, or he can hit behind the runner or runners if he wants to.

B. *By the Batter.* 1. Hit-and-Run—Sometimes the coach allows the batter to give the hit-and-run sign instead of giving it to both the players himself. If this is the case, the batter must give the sign to the runner and the runner must answer it.

The batter must do something that he does not do naturally at the plate and the runner must answer, doing something that he does not do naturally.

When the batter knows the runner is looking at him, he might tap the plate with the bat, holding it in the left hand only. The runner touches his nose with his left hand. The hit-and-run is now on. If the runner does not touch his nose with his left hand the play would not be on. The hitter would now hit naturally.

2. Suicide Squeeze—This, like the hit-and-run sign must be given and answered by both the runner and hitter.

Normally, the coach gives the sign to the runner and the batter at the same time. The runner and batter must look at each other and give their signs. They could be as described above for the hit-and-run or some other sign of the coach's choice.

C. *Signs to Give*. Obviously, there are many signs to give, but, as stated earlier, don't make them complicated.

Signs can be given with hands, feet, or position in the coaching box.

Signs can be given by the coach in the coaching box or from the bench to the coaches in the coaching boxes or directly to the players.

CHAPTER **14**

PRE-GAME PRACTICE

Pre-game practice must be carried out with real enthusiasm. By scaring the other team in practice, some games are won. A catcher, for instance, by showing his arm, can keep the opposition from stealing. Outfielders, with strong throws, will discourage them from tagging up and advancing on fly balls or scoring from second on a single.

The umpires should be advised to report to the field one-half hour before game time. This allows time for delays in transportation and prevents a late start. GAMES MUST START ON TIME!

243. PRE-GAME BATTING PRACTICE

PURPOSE

To give each team an equal amount of organized batting practice.

PROCEDURE

Make a time schedule, starting with the time of the game, and work backward from game time. In the schedule allow enough time for: visiting team batting—30 minutes; home team batting—30 minutes; visiting team infield and outfield practice—10 minutes; home team infield and outfield practice—10 minutes; groundskeeping—10 minutes. During batting practice, someone should hit fungos to the infielders and outfielders. Caution should be used in hitting to the infielders. Do not hit fungos at the same time pitched balls are hit. Hit fungos between pitches.

All extra men should take three swings at the beginning of batting practice. Following them, the starting lineup should start a round of one bunt and four swings each. If time permits, let them continue one bunt and four swings on a second round. If a few minutes are left, do some hit-and-run practice by giving each batter one pitch only.

For faster batting practice use a pitcher who can throw perfect strikes and a catcher.

Below is a sample time schedule of pre-game practice for a 3:30 game. Since the visitors are normally free earlier than the home team, the visitors should take their hitting practice first. However, if they have a late arrival time they should notify the home team coach, and his team can reverse the order of hitting and fielding practice.

2:00—Visiting team batting

2:30—Home team batting

3:00—Visiting team infield and outfield practice

3:10—Home team infield and outfield practice

3:20—Groundskeeper prepares the field for the game

3:25—Umpires and coaches discuss ground rules. Home team coach presents his lineup card to plate umpire first, then the visiting team coach presents his lineup card

3:30—Game time

244. INFIELD-OUTFIELD PRACTICE

PURPOSE

To have an organized pre-game practice for infielders and outfielders.

PROCEDURE

While the home team is taking batting practice, the visiting team, which has finished its batting practice, starts warming up on the side. This is ten minutes before they take the field, which is 30 minutes before game time. As soon as the home team completes batting practice, the visitors charge to their positions. The coach, with four balls, assumes a position near the mound and hits to the outfielders, who make several throws to the following bases: The left fielder throws to second base and home; the center fielder and the right fielder throw to third and home. A fungo hitter then hits to the outfield for fly ball practice. This hitting should be done from a position just outside the foul lines beyond first and third bases. From these positions there is no danger to infielders, who are taking infield practice as the coach hits balls to them.

While the visiting team is taking infield practice the home team is loosening up for their practice, which is taken in the same manner. The home team practice stops ten minutes before game time, and the groundskeeper uses this time in preparing the field for the game.

245. PITCHER WARM-UP

PURPOSE

To give the starting pitcher ample time to get ready for the game.

A. *Home Team*. Twenty minutes before game time have the pitcher do some type of loosening up exercise. Ten to 15 minutes before game time, depending upon the weather and the individual, the pitcher should begin to throw. Starting easily, he should gradually increase his speed until he feels loose. Then he should throw his curve and fast ball. Once he feels loose enough, he should work up a sweat, gauging his time so that he will not be warm too long before game time. He will need a few minutes' rest prior to going out on the mound—long enough to wipe off the sweat and get a drink of water. Never rest longer than five minutes.

B. *Visiting Team*. This should be the same as above, except that the pitcher should begin warming up five minutes later, since his team will bat first. This gives him at least five minutes extra in which to warm up. If he gets loose at the same time as the home pitcher, he may have to sit around in the dugout while his team hits. He could cool off too much to be effective in the first inning. He, too, needs a little time on the bench prior to going out on the mound. It is not advisable to rest more than five minutes. If he gets loose and it is a long inning, he should return to the bullpen for a little more throwing.

CHAPTER **15**

SCREENING CANDIDATES

All coaches have new players report to them for practice. Often there are too many to include with the regular players. So a special screening or tryout day is assigned for these players. With this checklist, new candidates can be checked for their ability to make the team. The checklist can also be used for players on the team. We have a coach's checklist covering all positions. He can check the progress of each player from spring training through the entire season. If a player has trouble it would be wise to use the checklist to help spot and correct the trouble.

246. CHECKLIST FOR PROPER EXECUTION

Grade: A—Excellent   Player's Progress:
        B—Good   (1) Beginning of Season
        C—Fair   (2) Middle of Season
        D—Poor   (3) End of Season

BATTING

(1)	(2)	(3)	
—	—	—	1. Knows strike zone
—	—	—	2. Strides correctly
—	—	—	3. Hitches, yet hits well
—	—	—	4. Swings level

BATTING

(1)	(2)	(3)	
—	—	—	5. Has proper hip action
—	—	—	6. Rolls wrists on swing
—	—	—	7. Has good follow-through
—	—	—	8. Never guesses
—	—	—	9. Steps toward pitch
—	—	—	10. Keeps elbows away from body
—	—	—	11. Can hit curve
—	—	—	12. Can hit change of speeds
—	—	—	13. Can hit fast ball
—	—	—	14. Can hit behind runner or opposite field
—	—	—	15. Not afraid of pitched ball
—	—	—	16. Bends knees slightly prior to pitch
—	—	—	17. Starts swing at proper time
—	—	—	18. Has proper grip on bat
—	—	—	19. Is relaxed at plate
—	—	—	20. Weight on balls of feet
—	—	—	21. Keeps both eyes level and on the ball
—	—	—	22. Takes signs easily

BUNTING

(1)	(2)	(3)	
—	—	—	1. Bat parallel with ground
—	—	—	2. Angle of bat is good
—	—	—	3. Bunts from front end of batter's box
—	—	—	4. Can bunt toward first
—	—	—	5. Can bunt toward third
—	—	—	6. Always bunts strikes
—	—	—	7. Commits himself to bunt at proper time
—	—	—	8. Carries bat shoulder high
—	—	—	9. Weight on balls of feet
—	—	—	10. Pivots to bunt correctly
—	—	—	11. Bends knees
—	—	—	12. Relaxes arms and grip
—	—	—	13. Gets on top of ball

PITCHING

(1)	(2)	(3)	
—	—	—	1. Control
—	—	—	2. Holds fingers on ball properly
—	—	—	3. Curve
—	—	—	4. Fast ball

PITCHING

(1)	(2)	(3)	
—	—	—	5. Change-up
—	—	—	6. (a) Rotation of ball on fast ball
—	—	—	(b) Rotation of ball on curve ball
—	—	—	7. Conceals pitches
—	—	—	8. Stands on mound or rubber correctly
—	—	—	9. Follows through, bends back
—	—	—	10. Striding foot lands properly
—	—	—	11. Pivot foot pivots correctly on rubber
—	—	—	12. Keeps eye on target
—	—	—	13. First base pick-off
—	—	—	14. Second base pick-off
—	—	—	15. Third base pick-off
—	—	—	16. Holds runners close to bag
—	—	—	17. Throws to second on double play ball
—	—	—	18. Checks position of teammates before delivery
—	—	—	19. Backs up bases
—	—	—	20. Covers first
—	—	—	21. Fields position on batted ball
—	—	—	22. Fielding bunts
—	—	—	23. Keeps eye on wind

CATCHING

(1)	(2)	(3)	
—	—	—	1. Shifts well
—	—	—	2. Gets rid of ball quickly
—	—	—	3. No lost motion in steps of throw
—	—	—	4. Throws well on double steal
—	—	—	5. Can catch pop flies
—	—	—	6. Picks up bunts with ease
—	—	—	7. Uses one hand only when necessary
—	—	—	8. Blocks home plate well, tags properly
—	—	—	9. Blocks pitches well
—	—	—	10. Removes and throws mask properly
—	—	—	11. Relaxes whole body when catching ball
—	—	—	12. Hides signs—can switch signs
—	—	—	13. Is good field general
—	—	—	14. Weight on balls of feet
—	—	—	15. Hands and arms are relaxed
—	—	—	16. Calls pitches well
—	—	—	17. Uses voice
—	—	—	18. Checks defense before pitch
—	—	—	19. Backs up play
—	—	—	20. Keeps eye on wind

INFIELD

(1)	(2)	(3)	
—	—	—	1. Anticipates what to do with ball
—	—	—	2. Feet spread properly
—	—	—	3. Bends knees, keeps tail low
—	—	—	4. Weight on balls of feet
—	—	—	5. Uses crossover step when breaking to sides
—	—	—	6. Fields ball out in front of body
—	—	—	7. Fields ball on side only when necessary
—	—	—	8. Relaxed wrists in fielding ball
—	—	—	9. Straightens up to throw only when necessary
—	—	—	10. Gets rid of ball quickly
—	—	—	11. Uses crow hop or throws well without step
—	—	—	12. No hitch before throwing
—	—	—	13. Charges ball, does not let ball play him
—	—	—	14. Can make double play steps
—	—	—	15. Tags runner correctly
—	—	—	16. Can move to right and left well
—	—	—	17. Makes run down play correctly
—	—	—	18. Uses voice to help teammates
—	—	—	19. Makes relays and cut-offs properly
—	—	—	20. Backs up plays
—	—	—	21. Keeps eye on the wind

OUTFIELD

(1)	(2)	(3)	
—	—	—	1. Gets jump on ball
—	—	—	2. Plays ground balls well
—	—	—	3. Gets in position to throw
—	—	—	4. Knows how to get set to throw
—	—	—	5. Throws low
—	—	—	6. Throws to proper bases
—	—	—	7. Anticipates running speed of base runners
—	—	—	8. Backs up bases and other fielders
—	—	—	9. Runs on toes
—	—	—	10. Uses voice to help teammates
—	—	—	11. Plays the fence well
—	—	—	12. Knows how to play sunny field
—	—	—	13. Hits cut-off and relay man consistently
—	—	—	14. Keeps eye on wind

BASE RUNNING

	(1)	(2)	(3)	
	—	—	—	1. Runs on toes and is relaxed
	—	—	—	2. Has high knee action
	—	—	—	3. Body leans forward when running
	—	—	—	4. Body leans in toward infield when making turn
	—	—	—	5. When running straight line, feet are placed directly in front of nose
	—	—	—	6. Elbows comfortably near body, bent nearly 90 degrees, uses pump action with arms
	—	—	—	7. Uses crossover step to break to bases
	—	—	—	8. Rounds bases well
	—	—	—	9. Takes enough lead
	—	—	—	10. Is daring on base paths
	—	—	—	11. Slides correctly
	—	—	—	12. Slides all different ways
	—	—	—	13. Knows how to break up double play
	—	—	—	14. Uses good judgment
	—	—	—	15. Runs with head up
	—	—	—	16. Checks position of defense before each pitch
	—	—	—	17. Watches wind
	—	—	—	18. Looks at coach before rounding bases
	—	—	—	19. Knows number of outs
	—	—	—	20. Watches preceding runners on base hits and stolen bases

247. RUNNING PERFORMANCE—TIME

(Use Drills No. 233 A and B, Timed Running Practice)

248. THROWING PERFORMANCE

PURPOSE

To check the throwing abilities of players.

PROCEDURES

A. *Outfielders and Infielders*. 1. Accuracy: After proper warm-up, at a distance of 150 feet, have players throw three times at a base. Use a fielder to back up the base.

2. Distance: When the players' arms are completely loose, have them throw twice for distance.

B. *Pitchers*. Have pitchers throw to a catcher, who checks their fast ball, curve ball, and control. Count the number of strikes each pitcher throws.

C. *Radar Speed Gun*. If you have access to a radar speed gun (used by most police departments), borrow it for the tryout session. It can be used for players other than pitchers to check the velocity of their throws. (Note velocity of age brackets in Drill No. 128.) The Jugs Speed Gun is used by the author.

249. BATTING PERFORMANCE

PURPOSE

To give the coach an opportunity to determine who can hit and who cannot.

PROCEDURE

Let each batter bunt three balls down the third base line and three down the first base line. After he attempts the bunts, have him take four swings at balls thrown at medium speed and straight, then four swings at curve balls.

As an added skill test, have him hit several balls to the opposite field.

250. FIELDING PERFORMANCE IN POSITION

PURPOSE

To give the coach an opportunity to learn how well candidates can play a position.

PROCEDURE

Put players in the position they think they can play best and hit balls to them, giving them all possible plays that are likely to happen in that position. Use Multiple Infield Drill No. 154.

A. *Infield*. (Drill No. 147 can be used for screening a large group.)

1. Hit infielders all types of ground balls and high fly balls.

2. Hit all types of ground balls and have infielders make the different situation throws from that position.

B. *Outfield*. 1. Field ground balls in outfield grass and make plays from their normal outfield position.

2. Hit outfielders all types of fly balls.

3. Hit them all types of fly balls and have them make the different situation throws from that position.

C. *Pitchers*. 1. Use Pitcher's Fielding Skill Drill No. 102.
2. Use Spot Control Pitching Drill No. 96.

D. *Catchers*. 1. Use Drill No. 235, Base Running and Catching.
2. Use Drill No. 135, Steps for Throwing.
3. Use Drill No. 136, Ball in Dirt.

CHAPTER 16

TEACHING AIDS

This could be one of the most important chapters of the book from a standpoint of helping the coach develop the individual player. All of these teaching aids have been used, and some are being used successfully by many coaches. They have been created or designed to correct a weakness or to improve a player's ability. Since most coaches are either the groundskeepers or the supervisors of the playing field, we have added a few ground tools designed by George Toma, the groundskeeper of the Kansas City Royals. These tools are simple to make and are the basic tools needed to maintain a good field.

Batting Aids

251. BATTING TEE

(Note Drill No. 76 and see Illustration No. 25)

252. WHIFFLE BALL

The whiffle ball is slightly smaller than a baseball, made of plastic, hollow, with holes in one side only. Although ideal for indoor batting practice, it should not be thrown by pitchers. It can be used without damage to anything and can be hit with a full, powerful swing. Excellent for curve ball practice, the whiffle ball should be thrown at a distance of about 45 feet from the batter.

253. CORK BALL

Many major league baseball players have used or played with a cork ball. Made exactly like a baseball, the cork ball is slightly smaller than a tennis ball, but larger than a golf ball. It looks like a miniature baseball.

Ideal for outdoor batting practice, it makes the batter keep his eye on the ball. It should not be thrown by pitchers. The cork ball can be fielded just as a baseball is fielded and is very lively. Although it has a tendency to sail when pitched, it can be thrown the regulation pitching distance.

254. BOTTLE CAP AND BROOMSTICK

Old bottle caps thrown and hit with a broomstick have developed the hitting eyes of many major players in their youth. When thrown, a bottle cap does numerous tricks. In order to hit the cap, a player must keep his eye on it. It is thrown from a distance of about 30 to 45 feet from the batter. A half of a rubber ball also works well for this drill.

255. SPONGE RUBBER PRACTICE GOLF BALLS

Many golfers use a soft sponge rubber ball for practice swings. They do not go far and can be used for batting practice to make the hitter keep his eye on the ball. Since they are light and are thrown from a distance of about 45 feet, pitchers should not throw them. Bat boys make the best pitchers for these balls. The ball cannot hurt anyone it may hit, and bat boys enjoy striking out the varsity players.

256. PLASTIC GOLF BALLS

Use as described in Drill No. 255 above.

257. STUFFED STOCKING

(Note Drill No. 69)

258. BALL TOSS FUNGO BATTING

(Note Drill No. 64)

259. INSTRUCTIONAL BUNTING BAT

(Note Drill No. 83)

260. BALL ON SWINGING ROPE

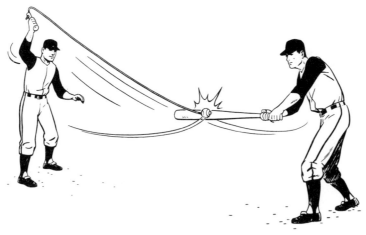

Illustration No. 106

Bore a ¼-inch hole through a ball, and pull a good strong nylon rope through the hole with a fish-stringer. Tie a large knot in the end of the rope. At the other end of the rope, which is about 10 to 12 feet long, tie a portion of a bat handle. This is done by boring a ¼-inch hole ½-inch from the end of the portion of the bat away from the handle end, inserting the rope through the hole, and tying it.

A player puts the bat handle in his hand and swings it around his head. At the perimeter of the circle made by the ball, a player attempts to hit the ball with a bat. A left-handed swinger and a right-handed swinger can get at opposite sides of the circle and attempt to hit the ball back and forth. This is good training for the eye and excellent practice for learning to hit the curve ball if the ball is swung in a steady circle. (Note Illustration No. 106.)

261. HITTING TIRE

By hitting a tire with a bat, a player can develop the drive in his swing.

The tire should be placed in front of the plate area so that it is in the position where the bat should meet the ball. The tire can be suspended on a rope, braced against a wall, or built on a frame at strike-zone height. (Note Drill No. 22.)

262. LEAD BAT

Many coaches drill a hole lengthwise in the head end of a bat and fill it with lead. It usually is a ⅝- to ¾-inch hole six to eight inches deep. Near the end of the bat, a nail or steel pin is driven through the wood and lead to hold the lead in place. To keep the bat from chipping, and as an added precaution to keep the lead in place, tape the bat end thoroughly. The lead could slip out when the bat is swung viciously.

This bat is normally used for pre-swing exercise before the player goes to bat. It tends to make the bat to be used feel lighter. A player can develop powerful and faster wrists for hitting by working with such a bat during the winter months, and the bat can be used during the season. It should be swung 50 to 100 times every day. The real function of the bat is to force the arms away from the body when the hitter is swinging.

263. FIFTY-OUNCE BAT

This is a regular bat made of the heaviest wood a bat company can use. It has a medium-sized handle, is 35 inches long, and weighs approximately 50 ounces. Worth Sports Company makes this bat in wood or metal.

The bat is used for swinging as in Drill No. 65 and is ideal for the Ball Toss Fungo Drill No. 64. Suitable for pepper games, it can also be used for slow-pitch batting practice. The bat teaches players how to swing while keeping their arms away from their body.

264. MULTIPLE BATTING CAGE

As compared with the usual batting cage, which allows only one hitter and one pitcher to work, this batting cage is constructed so that many hitters and pitchers can work at the same time. (Note how it is used in Illustration No. 107.) Each batter is in his own stall and has his own pitcher outside the stall to throw to him. Only space and money dictate the number of stalls that can be built. It is recommended that a coach start with at least three stalls. Should he have a typical two-man cage, he can make a five-stall cage of it. Providing a team maximum batting practice, the five-stall cage produces live batting practice in one day equal to five days of regular practice.

Pitchers also get maximum work, plus the help they get in control development. Standing 48 feet away from the hole on the outside of the cage, pitchers must first throw the ball through the hole before it gets to the batter, who stands 12 feet behind the hole, in the stall. The hole in the net is three feet wide by four feet high, and the bottom of the hole is two feet off the ground. (Note Illustration No. 107.)

Illustration No. 107   Multiple Batting Cage

265. BALLS STRIPED WITH DIFFERENT COLORS

Take four baseballs and paint a one-inch stripe of a standard, but different color around each ball.

During batting practice, when a hitter comes to the plate, give the pitcher the colored balls. Without showing it to the hitter, the pitcher throws one of the balls. The batter swings at it, but misses, then tells the catcher the color of the ball. If he calls three out of three colors correctly, he can hit four regular balls for practice. If he does not call them correctly, he loses his turn to hit.

This will make the hitter watch the ball while swinging the bat.

Throwing Aids

266. STRING TARGET

(Note Drill No. 97)

267. TAPED MAT TARGET

Hang a mat on the gym wall, and tape a strike zone target on it as suggested with the string target (Drill No. 97). If the wall is constructed of concrete or other material which is sturdy enough to withstand the blow of a thrown baseball, tape can be applied directly to the wall, or paint can be used.

268. MIRROR FOR PITCHING PRACTICE

Illustration No. 108

Many pitchers give something away in their movements, permitting numerous hitters to read them and tell what they are going to throw before they throw it. In order for the pitcher to see what the batter sees, we have developed a mirror* with which he can see his pre-pitch movements and delivery. The pitcher throws the ball at the mirror, which absorbs the blow and rebounds the ball to the pitcher.

The mirror can also be useful to other players. It can be helpful to the outfielder in showing him what he is doing on his throws; it can help teach a catcher how to make the correct throw to second base, and batters can study their swings by watching their movements in the mirror. (Illustration No. 108.)

269. EYE PATCH DRILL

If a pitcher is having poor control, he probably is taking his focus eye off the catcher or target. Every person has a focus or dominant eye. It can be found by pointing at an object as if the finger were a gun, aiming with both eyes open. Close first one eye, then the other. One eye will be aiming at the target, and the other will be off the target. The eye on the target is the focus eye. By putting an eye patch over the non-focus eye, the focus eye does the job for pitcher. Have him throw easily like this for a short time, and then have him throw hard for several times. Do this daily until he learns to hold his focus eye on the target and his control gets better.

270. YO-YO PITCHING DRILL

It is possible to develop a curve ball by using a good yo-yo. If a pitcher has a very poor curve ball and the coach cannot teach him the mechanics of a curve, he can improve through using a yo-yo. Put the pitcher on the rubber, and have him assume the wind-up stance with the yo-yo in his hand. He takes his wind-up and follows through slowly with his delivery. As he comes through with his arm and hand, they follow the same path taken when throwing a ball. When the hand gets about at his head, he bends and shortens his arm. His palm is facing his face, and the yo-yo is held by the thumb, middle, and index fingers, so that it will roll off the side of the index finger, down toward his feet. This is an exaggerated way of spinning a ball for a curve. The yo-yo should go straight downward and spin at the end of the string. The pitcher should jerk it up and start all over again. After this action has been mastered, he should assume a set stance and go through the motion with his arm and hand. Soon, he should have a much better curve ball.

---

*Since the construction of this mirror is too elaborate for the scope of this book, the author has promised to answer personally any queries concerning it. He may be contacted c/o Department of Athletics, Michigan State University, East Lansing, Michigan 48824.

271. METAL BALL OR MEDI BALL

Some players have made a mold of a regulation baseball and used it for molding a heavy metal ball. The ball is used during the off-season for the Pillow Throw Drill No. 273, and also for general wrist development. However, the ball is not used for making actual throws, since this could injure the arm. For throwing, a ball can be made slightly heavier than a regulation ball. (Note Drill No. 16.)

272. WEIGHTED BASEBALLS

(Note Drill No. 14, Overload: For the Fast Ball)

273. PILLOW THROW DRILL

During the winter months or off-season, players can aid in the development of the wrist snap by throwing or snapping a ball into a pillow at close range. Three to four feet from the pillow is a good range for the throw.

274. ROPE FOR SNAP THROW

(Note Drill No. 113 and Illustration No. 47)

275. BATON WEIGHT WIND-UP

Bore a quarter-inch hole through the center of a round piece of wood which is 12 inches long and 1½ inches in diameter. Pass a strong cord through the hole and tie it. At the other end of the cord, which is three feet long, tie a weight of 10 to 20 pounds.

Hold the wooden handle, or baton, by both hands; lift it up and away from the chest, begin to move the hands and wrists so that the cord winds around the wood. Then, reverse the motion of the weight so that the cord unwinds. This drill will develop the wrists and forearms. (Illustration No. 109.)

276. ROPE-PULL ARM STRENGTHENER

(Note Drill No. 5 and Illustration No. 1)

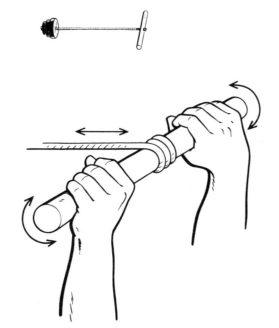

Illustration No. 109   Baton Weight Wind-Up

277. SPEED GUN TO CHECK VELOCITY

(Note Drill No. 128)

General Aids

278. STUFFED GLOVES

Take an old catching glove and stuff it so that it has no pocket. The material used should be something that will not form a pocket, such as a product called "absorblo," or a very firm piece of foam rubber.

Have fielders practice fielding with the glove. Whereas the good fielder gives with the ball when fielding it, the poor fielder kicks many balls out of the glove. Since many balls are missed while using this glove, fielders will get practice in scrambling for the ball to throw the runner out. Fielders will learn to use two hands on the ball.

It is an excellent glove for teaching the catcher to use two hands, and is excellent for use in double play practice.

279. THIRTY-GALLON OIL DRUM

Take an empty thirty-gallon oil drum and roll it at the shortstop and second baseman as they are turning over the double play. Put stones inside of the can to make more noise.

The coach gets on his knee approximately 15 feet from second base in the base path toward first base. When the starting player receives the ball off the bat, the coach rolls the barrel at the bag. The barrel should be near the bag as the player is turning over the double play. (Note Illustration No. 110.)

Illustration No. 110

280. "DIAMOND GRIT"

This is a calcined clay, sand-like in appearance, used to condition a wet field. With very little effort by the groundskeeper, "Diamond Grit," when raked into wet dirt, puts any field or spot on the field in excellent playing shape. The area can be soupy, but with the application of this grit it is ready for play within a few minutes.

281. SPRAY DRAG

Most coaches have very little time or manpower with which to get a field ready for the game after practice. A machine can be made which will spray and drag an infield in less than five minutes, and it needs only two men pushing and a third man helping. Between a set of two pairs of wheels we suspended a 40-foot triangular TV antenna and stretched three sprinkler-type hoses through the antenna. Proper couplings produced an ideal sprinkling system 40 feet long. Approximately five feet in front of the front wheels we placed a brace on each set of wheels to hold a double length of one-inch hose stretched between the pairs of wheels for dragging. For pushing purposes, we put lawn mower-type handles on each set of wheels. The front wheels of each set of wheels are swiveled, and the back wheels are stationary.

The drag can be pushed or pulled back and forth to give the field a good conditioning. The three sprinkler-type hoses water the field and the double-length hose drags the field.

282. SPIKE DRAG

Every field needs a daily raking and working of the topsoil in the skinned area. An ideal tool can be made by building a drag 36 inches square. The following materials are needed: 3 two-by-fours, each 3 feet long, 3 one-by-fours, each 3 feet long, 2 one-by-twos, each 3 feet long; approximately 130 spikes five inches long, and some rope with which to pull the drag.

Directions:

1. Bore holes slightly smaller than the spikes, two rows in each two-by-four, one inch from the edges and one inch apart. No hole is directly behind or beside another.
2. Drive the spikes through the holes, and nail the one-by-fours on top of the heads of the spikes.
3. On the ends of the two-by-fours, nail the one-by-twos. The first two-by-four is at one end; the second one is in the middle, and the third one is at the other end. This results in a three-foot-by-three-foot spike drag.
4. At the ends of a two-by-four (that is, at the corners of the drag), attach a rope for pulling. Then, the spike side will cut the dirt, and by reversing the drag, the flat side of the one-by-fours can be used for floating or leveling the dirt.

283. BOARD FLOAT

Every infield needs a good float to level the skinned area of the field. This can be made by shiplapping three 2″ by 12″ planks eight feet long. Tie a rope for pulling on the ends of the plank that is ued for the bottom to start shiplapping. The planks overlap approximately four inches on each other.

284. FIRST BASE PROTECTION SCREEN

When he is covering the base for infielders fielding ground balls between pitches, during batting practice, the first baseman needs protection from
batted balls.

A screen for this purpose should be approximately seven feet high and
five feet wide. It can be made of a framework of ¾" pipe or two-by-fours, and
is held up by two free-swinging legs. It is covered with heavy chicken wire.

285. PITCHER PROTECTION SCREEN

Some coaches like to protect the batting practice pitcher from the batted
ball. However, the screen is used mostly for non-pitchers such as the coach and
fielders. The screen is made of a framework of either ¾" pipe or two-by-fours,
covered by fine chicken wire. It is four feet high and five feet wide, and is held
upright by two free-swinging legs.

286. RUBBER BASES FOR INDOORS

Cut bases of actual regulation dimensions out of rubber floor runners.
They can be painted white and will not slip when used indoors. On road trips a
rubber home plate can be carried along for use in the bullpen where one is not
provided.

287. INDOOR PITCHING MOUND

With a few pieces of scrap wood and two plywood sheets of ¾", 4' by
8', an indoor pitching mound frame can be constructed. To complete the
mound, one will also need some thin strips of foam rubber and a sufficient
amount of "Laykold," "Grasstex," or similar asphalt-like material, used in
the construction of all-weather tracks and tennis courts, to cover the frame two
inches thick.

Directions:

1. Cut lengthwise two ¾" plywood four-by-eights.
   a. Cut one piece in half, making two pieces, each two feet
      wide.
   b. Cut the other large piece of plywood into two pieces, one
      three feet wide and the other one foot wide.
2. Butt the three-foot piece and one of the two-foot pieces lengthwise

side by side. You now have a five-foot-by-eight-foot board, which serves as the sloping area from the rubber toward home. (Note Illustration No. 111, Isometric View.)

3. The other two-foot piece is cut five feet long, making the flat area at the rubber where the pitcher stands while in his windup stance. (Note Illustration No. 111, Plan View.)

4. To get height for the mound, use two 2″ by 10″ by five-foot pieces of board under the two-foot-by-five-foot pieces in instruction 3. (Note Illustration No. 111, Side View on page 278.)

5. Across the front edge, toward the catcher, nail on the bottom a 2″ by 4″ by five-foot plank. This makes the slope from the rubber to the front of the mound.

6. Three partitions or braces must go crosswise under the long eight-by-five-foot board at two-foot intervals. These braces are one, 2″ by 5½″ by five feet; one, 2″ by 7″ by five feet, and one, 2″ by 8½″ by five feet. (Note Illustration No. 111, Side View.) It must be braced on the sides from front to back, preferably with ¾″ plywood. The one-foot strip which was cut off in instruction 1-b and the piece left from instruction 3 can be used, plus a scrap piece to complete the job. For the finished construction, see Illustration No. 111, Isometric View.

7. At the center of the two-foot-by-five-foot board (instruction 3), is

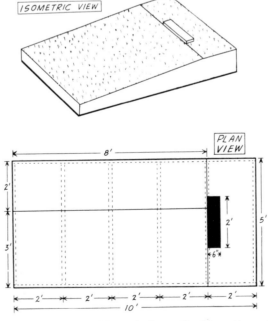

Illustration No. 111   Indoor Pitching Mound

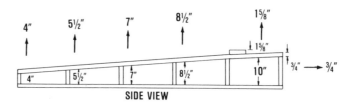

SIDE VIEW

placed a 2″ by 6″ by two-foot board for the pitching rubber. It is placed on the edges where the two boards meet and the slope begins. (Note Illustration No. 111, either Isometric or Plan View.)

8. Cover the board mound the thickness of the pitching rubber (two inches) with an asphalt-like material, and taper this covering to zero inches at the edges of the mound. The best covering materials are those mentioned earlier, or other similar products.

9. For protection of the gym floor and to prevent slipping, glue a covering of foam rubber to the bottom edges of the frame, and lay a tarpaulin under it so that the tarp extends well out from under the frame. This will catch any material which might come off the mound.

10. Pitchers will use shoes with golf spikes, or they will use gym shoes. Track spikes ⅛″ long would be ideal.

CHAPTER 17

ORGANIZATION FOR ONE DIAMOND OR PRACTICE AREA

It is of prime importance for a baseball coach to keep his players busy every minute of a practice session in order to impress upon them that they have to work before they can become a winning team. It is necessary to have a set pattern for practice so the players will know what they are supposed to be doing every minute. The coach should be alert to take weather and other last-minute developments into consideration.

The coach must think in terms of the player and how to get the most out of him. When a player comes on the field, the first thing he wants to do is either throw or bat a ball, and he should be permitted to start his practice this way after he has done some loosening up exercises. Since these are the most important fundamentals of the game, they should be done first in practice.

288. LOOSENING-UP PERIOD: 15 MINUTES

As soon as they come onto the field, the outfielders and infielders should begin organized pepper games. Pitchers and catchers should begin working together. They should all be doing some type of loosening-up, running, throwing or calisthenics. Suggested Drills: 1, 3, 6, 7, 8, 9, 11, 13, 15, 16, 25, 26, 27, 28, 29, 32, 34, 35, 37 and 40.

289. BATTING PRACTICE: 60 MINUTES

Here is where a coach can get the most out of a practice. While the batters are taking their licks (no more than two on deck at a time), the extra pitchers and catchers should be assigned to infield and outfield fungoing. At first this practice may appear chaotic, but if it is properly arranged, the player who is hitting the fungos to the infield will learn to time his hits so they are made between pitches to the plate.

Meanwhile, the infielders are learning to field the ball off the bat at the plate, in addition to the fungos. It sharpens their wits and keeps them busy all the time.

Infielders, outfielders and catchers should alternate daily as to who hits first. Pitchers may be included in this practice by giving them the first ten minutes, providing the designated hitter is not used. Base running drills can and should be added to this practice.

After each player hits his last ball, he gradually works his way from base to base practicing different base running possibilities. Suggested Drills to aid batting practice: 63, 75, 79, 80, 81, 82, 84, 87, 88, 89, 91 and 92.

290. FIELDING IN POSITION: 10 MINUTES

After batting practice the coaches, managers and pitchers who hit good fungos should be assigned a position in the infield where they can hit the ball in rapid succession for about 10 minutes. During this time every fielder will receive individual attention from the coach, who can point out his fielding weaknesses and work with him to correct them.

While this part of the practice is going on, fungo hitters are assigned to hitting to the outfielders. The catchers are working along the sidelines on pop flies, blocking the ball, shifting to either side to handle wild pitches and working on bunts. Suggested Drills: 41, 54, 146, 149 and 154.

291. FUNDAMENTALS OF PLAY: 20 MINUTES

After fielding practice, everyone should be called and instructed to work on the general fundamentals of the game such as sliding, base running, actual bunt situations, pick-offs, cut-off plays, rundown plays, the defense and offense of the delayed and double steals, and handling of pop-ups by the infield and outfield. Considerable time should be spent on pop-ups. All the players should learn to distinguish each other's voices and know who should be the one to make the catch. The value of Drill 42 cannot be underestimated. Many games are lost because of a mix-up on a seemingly easy pop fly.

292. OUTFIELD-INFIELD PRACTICE: 10 MINUTES

The regular infield practice, with the outfielders making their throws to the bases and infielders throwing around the horn, should be started.

The outfielders should throw in from the outfield first. The left fielder throws three or more throws to second base and the same to home. He can fake some throws to third and throw to second. The center fielder makes his throws to third and home, faking to third and throwing to second. The right fielder throws to third and home, faking to second and throwing to first. The first baseman cuts off the throws to home from the right fielder and the center fielder. The third baseman cuts off the throws to home from the left fielder. The shortstop cuts off the throws to third base from the center fielder and right fielder.

The outfielders can either run after throwing or continue fielding fly balls. The infielders now take over with all the enthusiasm they can put forth. The coach should have a routine way of hitting infield and a routine way of throwing the ball around. Use this same system prior to all games. It keeps a team from looking lost on the field. Suggested Drills: 157 and 178.

293. RUNNING: 5 MINUTES

The five-minute running is used for the infielders. The outfielders will have run about 10 minutes. The catchers run according to what work they have in infield practice. The pitchers have a 15-minute running session. This running session must be made as enjoyable as possible. No player likes to run just for the sake of running; he usually thinks of running as a pill he has to take with every practice. Suggested Drills: 10, 25, 27, 213.

294. ALTERNATE PRACTICE SESSIONS

Once the team is in shape to play, the above practice session should be used on alternate days (Monday, Wednesday, and Friday). Games or scrimmages should be held on Tuesday, Thursday, and Saturday. In case of rain, the coach should decide which is needed most, games or practice.

Suggested Drills for game practice: 48, 49, 50, 51, 52, 53 and 58.

* * * * * * *

"LET US DO IT SOME MORE"

Through the whole muddy spring, all the whole baseball season,
The tough coach drilled the team, as it seemed, without reason.
They would throw, they would catch, they would slide, they would run,
It was mighty hard work, and it wasn't much fun.
They would practice a play till their muscles were sore,
And the coach would just say, "Let us do it some more."
They all thought it was foolish to practice so much
On a play that would only be used in a clutch.
And why in the name of the hottest of places
Were they drilled day by day in just running the bases?
They would grumble and say, "Let us play a real game,
And we surely will use all those plays just the same."
But the coach kept on drilling each intricate play
For long hour after hour and for day after day.
Then at last the awaited and longed for hour came
When they took to the field for the championship game.
Then the shortstop soon started a quick double play
Just the way they had practiced it day after day.
And a runner at first dared a little too much,
And he found in surprise he had gotten in Dutch.
Then a hit was lashed out into left center field
Which the runner decided two bases would yield.
But the ball was there first in the baseman's left mitt,
Just exactly the way they had long practiced it.
When at bat they pulled off a quick cute double steal,
And, oh, boy, how it made the whole cheering team feel!
In the ninth with the score tied up tight, one to one,
Then they bunted and squeezed home the game's winning run.
Then the team stormed the coach with a yell and a roar,
"Let us go out tomorrow and drill a lot more."

Raymond F. Bellamy
Professor Emeritus
Florida State University

Index

A

Abdomen reducer, 24
"Absorblo," 273
Aids to teaching, general, 273-278 (see also "Teaching aids")
Ankle weights, exercise with, 39
Appling, Luke, 94
Arm and back stretch exercise, 44-45
Arm strengthener, 52-53
    for catcher's form, 156-157

B

Ball on swinging rope as teaching aid, 267
Ball toss fungo batting, 87-88
Bare hand drill for pitchers, 125-126
Base running drills, 234-254
    alternate speed base-running drill, 241
    base coach drill, 251-252
    and catching, 244-245
    checklist for proper execution, 234
    full team, 237
    lead-off base drill, 245-246
    leads, returns and steals at first base, 242-243
    with purpose, 235-237
    rounding bases, 238
    run down, getting out of, 250-251
    signs, how to give, 252-254
        by batter, 253
        by coach, 252-253
        signs to give, 254
    sliding drills indoors, 246
        outdoors, 246-250
    steal drills, delayed, 250
    timed practice, 241-242
    what to teach, 238-241
Base throwing for outfielders, 228
Bat swinging exercises for conditioning, 39-43
    figure eight, 41-42
    hanging target swing and stuffed stocking, 40-41
    isometric bat drill, 42-43
    "Power Swing," use of, 39
    tire hitting, 43
    weighted bat swing, 40
Bat throwing drill, 91-92
Baton weight wind-up as teaching aid, 272
Batting aids, 265-269 (see also "Teaching aids")
Batting drills, 86-96
    ball toss fungo batting, 87-88
    bat throwing drill, 91-92
    batting tee, 92-93
    breaking from home, 92
    checklist for proper execution of bat grip, 86-87

Batting drills *(cont.)*
    dry swing team batting, 89-90
    figure eight, 90
    hanging target swing and stuffed stocking, 90
    hip rotation drill, 91
    isometric bat drill, 91
    mirror swing, 90
    pepper games, 93
    place hitting and hit-and-run drill, 94-95
    poor hitting, improving, 94
    practice drills, 96
    shadow drill, 90-91
    soft toss from side drill, 88-89
    swing strengthener, 89
    team batting practice, 95-96
Batting practice period, 280
Batting tee, 92-93
Bent leg slide, 247-249
Board float as teaching aid, 275
Body position for bunting, 98-100
    pivot in tracks, 99-100
    square around, 99
Body position for catcher, 146-148
Bottle cap and broomstick as teaching aids, 266
Break for and cover first base drill, 178-179
Breaking from home drill, 92
Bunt defense, 62
Bunting drills, 74, 97-110
    angle of bat, 100-102
    for base hit:
        first base area, 104-105
        third base area, 106-107
    bat for all bunting drills, 97-98
    checklist, 97
    fake bunt and hit, 108
    fake bunt and steal, 109
    feet and body, position of, 98-100
        pivot in tracks, 99-100
        square around, 99
    sacrifice bunting to proper infield area, 102-103
    squeeze bunt, 108
    strings to denote perfect bunting area, 103-104
    wet grounds—bunting time, 109-110
Bunting situations:
    for outfielders, 230
    for shortstop, 205
Bunts:
    catcher's fielding of, 158-160
    defensing with first and second occupied, 172-173
    fielding of by first baseman, 182
    fielding of by pitcher, 120-121
    fielding by second baseman, 188
    fielding by third baseman, 214-217
        throwing, 217